THE METROPOLITAN FRONTIER

THE MODERN AMERICAN WEST

Gerald D. Nash, editor

Carl Abbott

The Metropolitan Frontier: Cities in the Modern American West

THE METROPOLITAN FRONTIER

Cities in the Modern American West

—

—

—

CARL ABBOTT

The University of Arizona Press / Tucson & London

The University of Arizona Press
Copyright © 1993
The Arizona Board of Regents
All rights reserved
♾ This book is printed on acid-free, archival-quality paper.
Manufactured in the United States of America

98 97 96 95 94 93   6 5 4 3 2 1

Library of Congress Cataloging-in-Publication Data
Abbott, Carl.
    The Metropolitan frontier : cities in the modern American
West / Carl Abbott.
        p.   cm. — (The Modern American West)
    Includes bibliographical references and index.
    ISBN 0-8165-1129-2 (hard : alk. paper)
    1. West (U.S.)—History—1848–1950. 2. West (U.S.)—
History—1951–. 3. Cities and towns—West (U.S.)—
History—20th century. I. Title.   II. Series.
F595.A24   1993
978'.033—dc20   93-11035
                                              CIP

British Cataloguing-in-Publication Data
A catalogue record of this book is available from the British
Library.

CONTENTS

FIGURES

TABLES

INTRODUCTION

Perched on the corner of my desk is a book of matches that has survived the five moves and forty years since a family vacation from Tennessee to Idaho and back. The picture on the cover is a silhouette of the Wyoming cowboy atop a bucking horse, but the text carries a different message: "Casper, Hub of Wyoming. Gateway to the Last Frontier. The Acknowledged Convention and Industrial City of Wyoming." Inside the cover is a map on which all roads lead to Casper—from Sheridan, Sundance, Green River, Thermopolis, Lusk, and Cheyenne. We're invited to write for information to the Casper Chamber of Commerce. The matchbook itself was manufactured in Denver.

The producers of the matchbook unintentionally summarized the most important contradiction embodied in the modern American West, for the nation's most open and empty region is also its most heavily urbanized. As early as the 1840s and 1850s, visionaries and town boosters had forecast a "West of great cities." They could point to impressive accomplishments by the 1880s and 1890s, when the Western itineraries of travelers like James Bryce and Rudyard Kipling took them from one city to the next—from Bismarck to Seattle, from San Francisco to Denver. William Thayer's inventory of *Marvels of the New West* in 1887 included the "populous and wealthy cities that have grown into power and beauty as if by magic."[1]

Except in the oil patches of Texas, Oklahoma, and southern California, Western urbanization slowed during the regional economic depression of the 1920s and 1930s. Mobilization for World War II was the central event that introduced a new era of sustained city-building that has now lasted for fifty years. Thayer's *Marvels* predicted that Western cities would eventually surpass those of the East in enterprise and economic power. A century later, Los Angeles, Phoenix, Dallas, and the region's other great cities may not quite represent what Thayer called a "growth and consummation without a parallel in human history," but they have certainly reshaped the American nation and mediated new relationships with the broader world.[2]

The book that follows is my effort to place this last half-century of Western experience in its urban context. My underlying arguments are two. First, it is Western cities that organize the region's vast spaces and connect them to the even larger sphere of the world economy. Second, urban growth since 1940 has constituted a distinct era in which Western cities have become national and even international pacesetters.

> Wide, no limit, the whole
> state an airport, a continent
> marbles could roll across . . .

Most Americans would agree with the opening of William Stafford's poem "Texas."[3] We think of the western half of our country most often in terms of its size. It is big, open, high, wide, and handsome. It is a land of expansive margins and elbow room, bright air, big skies, and great winds. Writers who try to capture the essence of the region have cast upward for their titles—*The Big Sky, Storm, Sky Determines, In This House of Sky*. California poet Robinson Jeffers built an entire career by writing about the "great cloud mountains" and "gales of piercing light" where the Pacific Ocean meets the land. Extremes of climate structure the daily routines of the Great Plains with droughts, blizzards, downpours, and tornadoes.

On closer look, however, we find that the nation's emptiest region is also its most urbanized. Americans have entered, developed, and organized the Western landscape through their cities. By 1990, 80 percent of Westerners lived in metropolitan areas ranging in size from Enid, Oklahoma (with 60,000 people), Casper, Wyoming (66,000), and Grand Forks, North Dakota (71,000), to the Los Angeles-Anaheim-Riverside complex, with its 14,532,000 people. Roughly half of the rest lived in smaller towns and cities of 2,500 or more, leaving only one Westerner in ten for the "real West" of farms, ranches, lonely desert gas stations, and railroad hamlets clustered around the gray columns of grain elevators.

The development of this concentrated pattern of settlement in Western cities matches the classic definition of urbanization as a dual process that involves the creation of new points of population concentration and the growth of existing points. As urbanization proceeds, the proportion of the total population living in cities increases, and the proportion living in the small towns and countryside decreases. Between 1815 and 1930, urbanization transformed the entire United States from a collection of rural societies to a metropolitan nation. In the last half-century, this two-pronged process has continued most clearly and completely in the West.

Established metropolitan areas have grown far faster than the national average. Taken together, the half dozen largest metropolitan areas in the West in 1940 grew by 380 percent over the next fifty years. The six largest in the East grew by only 64 percent. In addition, Westerners have continued to fill in their hierarchy of urban centers. Cities like Albuquerque and Anchorage have made the transition from small city to metropolis since World War II. It takes a vigorous act of will to remember that Phoenix in 1940 was the same size as present-day Yakima, Washington (186,000), or that Colorado Springs in 1940 was the same size as contemporary Grand Island, Nebraska (36,000). Dozens of smaller regional cities have grown to official metropolitan status—from Anchorage and Bremerton to Visalia, Yuba City, and Yuma.

Although they hold nearly all the region's population and economic power, Western cities have also been distinguished by a special relationship with wide open spaces. Key industries such as defense, aerospace, and leisure have flourished in the West because of the elbow room available in the region's metropolitan areas. Save perhaps in coastal California, the accessibility of physical space has prevented the emergence of the intensely urban culture found in eastern North America or Europe. Western city people prefer to construct widely spread and open cityscapes. They presume that direct and immediate contact with the outdoors is their due. The classic fish story about the city dweller redeemed from doubt or despondency by the discipline of angling is alive and well in novels about Portlanders, Missoulans, and San Franciscans.[4]

The contrast and interaction between city and region has also given social and economic structure to the continental spaces themselves. Now as much as ever, cities facilitate the survival or further development of the traditional resource frontier. Ranchers, miners, and loggers come to town to buy, sell, borrow, lobby, consult a doctor, and go to school. City dwellers spread into the country to build new types of low-density cities. What one observer calls the "reopening" of the Western frontier turns economically depressed farm and mining towns into thriving tourist zones. Indeed, Western cities have been the engines of a widespread and often stressful economic transition that has left few Westerners engaged in primary produc-

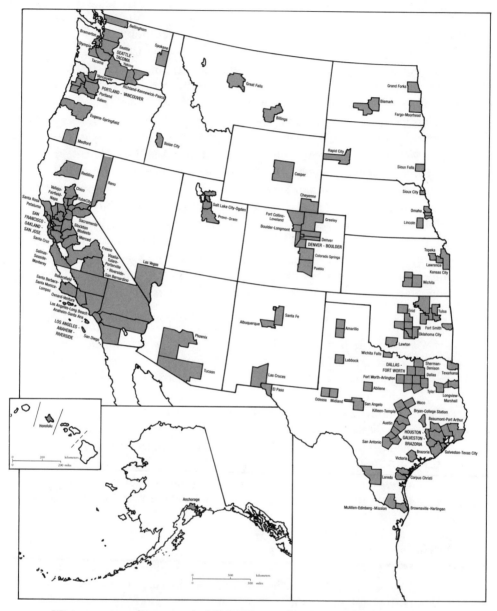

Western metropolitan areas in 1990. Western cities have arrayed themselves in north–south corridors defined by the margins of the Great Plains, the foothills of the Rocky Mountains, the Pacific lowlands, and the Pacific coast. (Map redrawn from U.S. Department of Commerce, *1990 Census of Population; General Population Characteristics: United States* [Washington: USGPO, 1992], 4:4)

tion. At the regional takeoff point in 1940, 28 percent of Western workers made their living directly from the land. The proportion was down to 6 percent by 1980, when fewer than 1.7 million workers out of 28 million were employed in agriculture, forestry, fisheries, and mining.

Cities do more than tie together the open spaces and isolated individuals of the American West. They also link the continental space into national and international systems for the exchange of people, products, and ideas. As the contact points with the global economy, cities have made the American West a major participant in the ongoing restructuring of the world system.

The second half of the twentieth century has brought a new turn in the process of world urbanization. New technologies of production, transportation, and communication have restructured the relative positions of the industrial core and the developing nations. The massive decentralization of production and consumption has been apparent at all levels. Suburbs have outpaced cities; "sunbelts" in North America and Europe have outpaced manufacturing belts; and newly industrialized nations have challenged the United States and Europe. Global statistics show the rebalancing of the world urban system. Between 1920 and 1940, the industrial nations of Europe, North America, and Oceania added 88 million people to their cities while the rest of the world added only 77 million. Between 1960 and 1980, in contrast, the developed nations added 178 million city dwellers while the developing nations added 415 million. Tokyo, Seoul, Djakarta, Singapore, Cairo, São Paulo, and Mexico City now rival New York, Chicago, London, Paris, and Amsterdam.

The explosive urbanization of the American West since 1940 has been part of this global rebalancing. Houston, Dallas, and Denver are key points in the system of international energy exchange. Seattle, Portland, San Francisco, San Jose, Los Angeles, and Honolulu are part of the industrializing Pacific Rim. San Antonio, El Paso, Tucson, and San Diego are daily witnesses to the social upheaval of Latin America.

Even settlements that were deliberately located in the very center of Western space to gain the benefits of isolation have been firmly tied into wide-reaching networks. In a region that likes to think itself the home of rugged individualists, cities are the centers for the administration of regional and national networks of consumption and control—electric power supply, supermarket chains, U.S. Forest Service planning, and federal reserve banking, for example. When he was living in the heart of the empty West in Moab, Utah, in the 1950s, Edward Abbey noticed that "in the accelerating process of urbanization, the Mormons of Utah are already discovering their interdependence with the rest of the nation and the world."[5] The federal government built Los Alamos on its magnificent New Mexican mesa to maximize the security and isolation of its atomic researchers, but Los Alamos housed an international set of scientists from the start. Modern utopias like Rajneeshpuram and mining towns reborn as ski heavens have all marketed their special services to national and international clienteles.

The painful transformation of the regional myth is encapsulated in the contrast between the novels of Ken Kesey and Thomas Pynchon. *Sometimes a Great Notion* (1964) is Kesey's impassioned story of a fiercely (even pathologically) independent family of loggers on the southern Oregon coast. The urban West appears only by implication in the form of a despised labor organizer from California. The novel is usually read as a tribute to the vanishing American pioneer. Thomas Pynchon's frantic and fantastic *Vineland* (1990) fictionalizes the same territory, in this case the environs of Eureka, California, but places its timber workers, union activists, and hippies in a world that stretches easily and instantly to San Francisco, Los Angeles, Las Vegas, Tokyo, and Washington. Like it or not, Pynchon's Vinelanders are firmly connected to the rationalized bureaucratic society that radiates from the office towers of the contemporary city. The redwood country may still bear some superficial resemblance to a nineteenth-century frontier, but Pynchon knows that it is a full participant in the new worlds of the 1990s.

The tensions among rural space, urban space, and global space in the American West imply a related balancing between past and present. The contemporary role of Western cities as global gateways revisits the first era of European city-making. The Western states are dotted with cities and towns left by the high tide of European expansion between 1609 (when Pedro de Peralta founded Santa Fe) and the 1830s (when the British began to relinquish the Western fur trade). Los Angeles, Monterey, Santa Fe, San Antonio, and other Spanish towns anchored the northern frontier of a Spanish empire that touched five continents. Vancouver and Spokane in the future state of Washington were British fur-trading posts before they became the nuclei for new cities in the growing United States. Finally, Russians founded a permanent European settlement at Sitka in 1804, the same year that Meriwether Lewis and William Clark began to work their way slowly up the Missouri River.

From the 1840s through the 1930s, cities in the Western territories and states were byproducts of the urban-industrial revolution that was transforming the Atlantic world. The global transition from a rural to an urban society began around the margins of the North Sea in the eighteenth century, spread eastward through Europe and westward to North America in the nineteenth century, and reached Asia and Latin America in the twentieth. By the early 1900s, the great manufacturing and commercial cities of northern and western Europe and northeastern North America had become the core of a world economic system. The cities of Asia, Latin America, and the southern and western United States served the core as initial processors of raw materials, entrepôts for trade, and centers of the political and financial control of their hinterlands.

In the American West, the "imperial century" spanned two distinct periods of urban development. The 1840s through the 1880s constituted an era of urban foundations and often booming growth. English-speaking Americans rushed to create new cities along the Pacific Coast and the interior lowlands, at access points to the Rocky Mountains, and at the margins of the Great Plains. Sacramento, Salt Lake City, and Portland appeared in the later 1840s. Seattle, Dallas, Fort Worth, Denver, Omaha, and Topeka date to the 1850s. The extension of the railroad system after the Civil War allowed townsite speculators to fill in the gaps between the earlier cities with communities like Cheyenne, Tacoma, Colorado Springs, Bismarck, and Fresno. By the 1870s the level of urbanization in the West had passed that of the East. The census of 1880 recorded that 30 percent of the population of the Rocky Mountain and Pacific states lived in urban places compared to 28 percent of all other Americans. During the next decade, the always-quotable James Bryce visited Portland and Tacoma, Seattle and San Francisco, Bismarck and Walla Walla. He found in these communities "the most American part of America," a West of "passionate eagerness" where "men seem to live for the future rather than the present." Charles Dudley Warner in 1888 reported from the Twin Cities on the "joyousness of conquest and achievement" and the "marvelous building up of new societies" as railroad towns sprang up across the northern plains.[6]

The transition from the era of the Western urban frontier to a half-century of consolidation came with the depression of the 1890s. Whether we use the census West, with its thirteen states, or the "historians' West," which adds the Great Plains states to those in the Rockies and on the Pacific Coast, the region held its narrow margin of 1 to 3 percentage points in level of urbanization over the rest of the United States from 1890 to 1940. In the opinion of local leaders, the dominant concern was to demonstrate the maturity of their communities. To use Gunther Barth's terms, they were eager to prove that their "instant cities" had become "regular cities" full of settled and respectable Americans.[7]

Residents of Denver, for example, boasted by the turn of the century that they had negotiated the transition from small town to large city. Despite the depression of the 1890s, the local economy had diversified, public services had improved, and socially distinct neighborhoods had become firmly established. The census of 1900 reported for the first time that women outnumbered men in Denver, and citizens of both sexes could choose among scores of literary groups, fraternal organizations, charitable associations, churches, and clubs. Visitors could find little to complain about and little except the setting to differentiate Denver from Eastern cities. San Franciscans matched Denverites by planning and building a new civic center along the most modern lines. Western cities staged a series of international expositions to demonstrate their parity with those of the settled East—Omaha in 1898, Portland in 1905, Seattle in 1909, and San Francisco and San Diego in 1915.

Social and political maturity, however, masked economic and cultural quiescence in the cities of the northern and central West. Denver and Seattle businessmen sent their sons to Yale and Princeton. They took their orders from New York, Philadelphia, and Chicago and passed the word down the line to Cripple Creek or Juneau. The decline of mining and the onset of an agricultural depression in the 1920s curtailed prospects for further growth. As a result, many Western cities that had hummed with energy and excitement one and two generations earlier now offered some of the nation's blandest environments. Journalists characterized Portland as a "spinster city." San Antonio earned a reputation as the "stodgy mother-in-law of the army." Denver struck even its friends as "a city prematurely grey."

In the nineteenth and early twentieth centuries, Western cities had helped to "civilize" the West by recreating the social institutions and reestablishing the values of longer-settled portions of the country. Since the 1940s, however, Western cities have quit playing catch up. The World War II changed the growth curve for every Western subregion, reversing decline or stagnation in much of the West and accelerating growth in a few favored areas. The war and its aftermath mark the takeoff when Western cities as a group changed from followers to trendsetters. In one sense, Western cities have been national leaders because of their simple size and rate of growth. The total metropolitan population in the Western states surged from 11.8 million in 1940 to 28.7 million in 1960, 50.9 million in 1980, and 63 million in 1990. Los Angeles–Anaheim formed the nation's second largest urban complex by 1980, the Bay Area conurbation ranked fourth, Dallas–Fort Worth ninth, and Houston-Galveston tenth. During the 1980s, nineteen of the nation's thirty-nine biggest metro areas (with populations of a

Table 1. Metropolitan Growth in the West Compared to the Other
Regions of the United States

	1940	1960	1980	1990
Metropolitan population (in thousands)				
West	11,791	28,723	50,912	62,956
Other U.S.	57,746	84,095	118,519	130,052
Metropolitan population as proportion of total U.S. population				
West	8.9%	16.0%	22.5%	25.3%
Other U.S.	43.8%	46.9%	52.3%	52.3%
Metropolitan population as proportion of region's population				
West	42.8%	64.0%	77.5%	80.4%
Other U.S.	55.2%	62.5%	73.7%	76.3%
Number of metropolitan areas[a]				
West	33	60	95	101
Other U.S.	107	142	217	231
Proportion of all metropolitan areas				
West	24%	28%	31%	30%
Other U.S.	76%	72%	69%	70%

[a] In 1940 Metropolitan Districts, in 1990, Metropolitan Statistical Areas and Primary Metropolitan Statistical Areas.

million or more) grew faster than the country as a whole (11 percent or more for the decade). Twelve of these boom cities were located in the West, with an aggregate population increase of 8.4 million residents for the decade. One out of every four Americans now lives in a Western metropolitan area, up from one out of eleven in 1940 (tables 1 and 2).

These impressive statistics are the product of a single long cycle of economic growth whose effects were concentrated in the Southwest and West. The current wave of economic development began to gather in the late 1930s. It surged through the 1940s and 1950s to crest in the 1970s, before slowly receding through the 1980s. The idea of long waves or fifty-year cycles in the global economy (discussed in more detail at the end of chapter 1) is based on underlying characteristics of innovation in the capitalist system, which is driven by periods of "creative destruction," in which new industries shoulder aside older industries and open opportunities for new regions to come to the fore. As an explanatory concept for the history of the

Table 2. Largest Metropolitan Areas in the West, 1940 and 1990

Population (In thousands)			
1940[a]		1990[b]	
Los Angeles	2,905	Los Angeles	14,532
San Francisco-Oakland	1,429	San Francisco-Oakland-San Jose	6,253
Houston	510	Dallas-Fort Worth	3,885
Seattle	453	Houston	3,771
Portland	406	Seattle	2,559
Denver	384	San Diego	2,498
Dallas	376	Phoenix	2,122
San Antonio	319	Denver	1,848
Omaha	288	Sacramento	1,481
San Diego	256	Portland	1,478
Oklahoma City	221	San Antonio	1,302
Fort Worth	208	Salt Lake City	1,072
Salt Lake City	204	Oklahoma City	964
Tulsa	189	Honolulu	838
Sacramento	159	Austin	748
Tacoma	156	Tulsa	728
Spokane	141	Tucson	636
Beaumont	138	Las Vegas	631
San Jose	129	Omaha	622
Wichita	127	Fresno	615
Phoenix	121	El Paso	586
El Paso	116	Bakersfield	520
Austin	106	Albuquerque	493
Fresno	97	Wichita	483
Lincoln	88	Stockton	456

[a] Metropolitan Districts
[b] Metropolitan Statistical Areas or Consolidated Metropolitan Statistical Areas

American West, the long-wave theory describes the context within which Western cities have experienced and responded to the conflicting demands of the continental resource frontier and global networks. In more concrete terms, it links the experiences of Casper in 1950 and San Jose in 1991.

Western cities have also been pacesetters that have made full use of the new technologies of production and consumption. As Americans have struggled to understand the nation's urban character in the years since World War II, the boom cities of the West have provided some of the most compelling symbols of the new urban reality. They have defined new directions for American economic growth that we have tried to capture with coinages like "Silicon Valley" and "Sunbelt." When the editors of *Fortune* magazine wanted to study an "exploding metropolis" in 1957, they flew to San Jose. In the 1950s and 1960s, Los Angeles was a frequent example of the "ultimate city" where New Yorkers could ponder the future of American civilization. By the 1970s, a procession of journalists had decided instead that Houston was the latest word in American cities. Western city dwellers have used automobiles, airplanes, and telephones to introduce and epitomize new forms and patterns of urban settlement. The California suburb has emerged as a typical community comparable to the New England village of the eighteenth century and the Midwestern town of the nineteenth.

The structure of this book assumes the fundamental importance of the long wave of economic growth. Within the half century from 1940 to 1990, the argument moves from economic change to social and political response. The first two chapters examine the impact of World War II on urban industries and populations and the resulting politics of growth and city making. The next three chapters take up the same topics of economic and demographic change and political response for the increasingly complex decades from 1950 to 1990. The final chapters examine the impacts of Western cities on their local environments, on the Western regional character, and on the national imagination and identity. Although economic development, politics, social adjustment, and cultural revaluation move at separate and complex rhythms, it is apparent that the 1960s were pivotal years in one arena after another.

The analysis attempts to integrate the recent urban experience of all nineteen Western states, ranging for evidence from Honolulu to Houston and from to Fargo to Fairbanks. Because of their importance as centers of economic change and cultural expression, it gives special attention to the big four of greater Los Angeles, the San Francisco Bay area, Dallas–Fort Worth, and Houston. Equally important are the middle-sized and smaller cities that have been incorporated into the urban system of the West, whether as members of a hierarchy of regional centers like Oklahoma City and Amarillo or as special-function communities like Austin (government) and Las Vegas (recreation).

Any working definition of a historically complex region is obviously arbitrary. I have drawn "the West" broadly rather than narrowly, including all of the Great Plains and Pacific states. Nevertheless, the boundaries could arguably be bigger still. As I will describe in chapter 4, many U.S. cities have twins immediately across the Mexican border and mirror images somewhat more distant across the border with Canada. For many purposes, it might be more meaningful to tell the story of western North America rather than the western United States. The eastern boundary of the West is likewise troublesome for urban specialists, as it is for many other historians. Houston, for example, is historically Southern in many characteristics but enthusiastically Western as a contemporary city. The metropolitan areas of Fargo, Sioux Falls, and Omaha straddle my east–west boundary but rate as Western here because of the location of their principal cities. In contrast, Minneapolis–St. Paul and Kansas City are located in "Eastern" states. Because their merchants and bankers have traditionally served hinterlands that stretch westward into the plains, however, they will make occasional appearances in discussions of the economic geography of the West.

The central goals of this book are to recognize and describe common patterns in Western urban development and to stimulate further investigation of suggested regularities and patterns. Compared to the eastern half of the United States, Western cities have had the physical and institutional space to allow the full development and expression of new urban trends. Elbow room has provided the opportunity to create entirely new communities and to realize extreme patterns of dispersal and decentralization. In the negative, these tendencies have allowed Westerners to act out the American taste for social segregation by eroding public space with fortified buildings and guarded subdivisions in the name of safety and status. In the positive, institutional "space" or flexibility has allowed Western cities to adapt rapidly to new trends. Ironically, the narrow, resource-linked regional economy of the early twentieth century allowed quick and effective response to the new directions of the Sunbelt and the "postindustrial" era. The absence of entrenched political machines and ethnic-group politics opened the way for professionalized government in central cities and self-directed suburbs. As environments open to growth and change, Western cities remain national pacesetters for good and for bad. In short, I do not join the popular critique in which Western cities are tested against an idealized New York or Paris. In the second half of the twentieth century, Western cities have most often expressed the American democratic tradition of open communities designed to accommodate new industries, new immigrants, and new ideas.

PART 1   GROWTH AND POLITICS IN THE WARTIME GENERATION

1

WAR AND THE WESTWARD TILT, 1940–1950

Between February 18, 1939, and September 29, 1940, San Francisco staged the nation's "other" world's fair. The New York World's Fair, erected over an ash dump in the far reaches of Queens County, attracted national attention with its gleaming white Trylon and Perisphere and its General Motors Futurama. Opening two months ahead of New York, however, the Golden Gate International Exposition offered a unique site on an artificial island in San Francisco Bay beneath the newly opened San Francisco–Oakland Bay Bridge.

Its 17 million visitors received an art deco introduction to the Pacific Ocean as an American lake. The official style was Pacific Basin, an amalgam of Mayan, Incan, Cambodian, Malayan, and Thai elements laid on with Hollywood exuberance and painted in pastel greens, blues, pinks, and yellows. Two high Towers of the East cast salmon and gold reflections on the Lake of All Nations. An eighty-foot statue called *Pacifica* loomed over the Fountain of Western Waters, representing the cultures of the Pacific basin. The modern lines of the Pacific House, the theme building for the fair, sheltered a relief map of the bottom of the Pacific Ocean and six large murals by Miguel Covarrubais on themes in Pacific culture.

Visitors who watched Pan American Airlines' China Clipper take off from Yerba Buena Cove outside the Hall of Air Transportation could see the Golden Gate International Exposition as part of the American dream of a peaceful imperialism that incorporated Asia into the world of American commerce. It reprised the themes of Portland's Lewis and Clark Exposition of 1905, Seattle's Alaska-Yukon-Pacific Exposition of 1909, and San Diego's

Panama-California Exposition of 1915–16. San Francisco's own Panama Pacific International Exposition of 1915 had looked westward, with transplanted villages of Samoans, Hawaiians, Maoris, Japanese, and Filipinos and a five-acre working model of the Panama Canal.

At the same time, the Golden Gate exposition unknowingly anticipated a very different relationship with the Pacific Rim. In 1941 the Navy purchased the 400-acre Treasure Island site for a training and patrol station, adding to San Francisco's huge complex of naval bases and support facilities. Over the next five years, the San Francisco–Oakland metropolitan area would find room for more than half a million war workers who moved there from out of state. It would receive $3.99 billion in war contracts, $364 million in federally funded industrial facilities, and $452 million in new military base facilities. Hundreds of warships and cargo vessels slid down the ways at General Engineering and Drydock in San Francisco, Western Pipe and Steel in South San Francisco, Bethlehem Shipbuilding in South Alameda, Moore Drydock in Oakland, Todd-Kaiser in Richmond, and Marinship in Sausalito. The area's manufacturing jobs grew from 100,000 to nearly 300,000. By May 1944 the Bay Area accounted for 26 percent of all ships delivered in the United States. Vallejo and adjacent areas tripled in population. Richmond's job total jumped from 15,000 to 130,000. Workers at Mare Island had to commute as far as fifty miles on rationed gasoline, while Richmond imported old elevated railcars from New York for a new line into Oakland. San Francisco itself became a giant dormitory housing war workers, servicemen between assignments, and their dependents.

World War II stands as an important turning point in the growth of the region and its cities, launching the entire West into a half-century of headlong urbanization. During the war itself, the federal government would spend $4.4 billion to build and expand Western military bases. The Defense Plant Corporation, the Reconstruction Finance Corporation, and the Maritime Commission put another $4.1 billion into industrial plants for the war effort. War supply contracts would total $27.8 billion for combat equipment and $5.8 billion for other supplies. The war revitalized graying cities that had stagnated with the agricultural and mining depressions of the 1920s and 1930s. It transformed small communities into booming cities and built entirely new towns on desert mesas and sagebrush flats. The mobilization of Western resources and the drafting of Western *places* into the war effort gave the region a jump on the long economic upswing of the 1940s, 1950s, and 1960s. The West ended six years of mobilization and war with a vastly expanded regional market, a new industrial infrastructure, and a new base of workers and wealth. It also found itself changed as a cultural region—

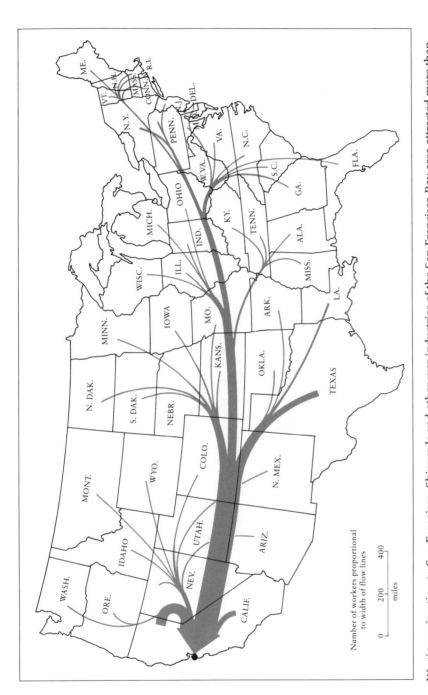

Wartime migration to San Francisco. Shipyards and other war industries of the San Francisco Bay area attracted more than half a million workers from all parts of the United States. Heavy wartime migration from Texas helped to tie California into the Southwest. (Adapted from the President's Committee for Congested Production Areas, *Final Report* [1944], 32)

Number of workers proportional to width of flow lines

0   200   400
    miles

Southernized in population, introduced to national problems of race relations, and placed at the center of American relations with the world.

At the same time, neither the war nor the directions that it established were surprises. Although the scale and pace of mobilization in 1941 and 1942 were unanticipated, most Western cities had already tried to enlist in the metropolitan-military complex. Wartime booms were built on foundations put together over one or even two decades of determined preparation.

Throughout the 1930s the federal government had poured money into the Western states to create a new economic infrastructure. Nevada, Montana, Wyoming, Arizona, and ten other Western states had led the nation in federal grants and loans per capita between 1933 and 1939. Federal funds helped to build U.S. 30, U.S. 66, and the other all-weather highways that connected Western cities to the Middle West and East. The Civil Aeronautics Act of 1938 had established a federal aid program for airport construction that had special importance for the widely spaced cities of the West. Great dams rose to block Western rivers—Fort Peck on the Missouri, Hoover on the Colorado, Shasta on the Sacramento, and Bonneville and Grand Coulee on the Columbia. Easily transmitted over long distances, hydroelectric power facilitated the industrial growth of cities from Spokane to Los Angeles to Austin.

Cities like San Antonio, San Diego, and San Francisco had already been pursuing a conscious military marketing strategy for two decades before the attack on Pearl Harbor. As early as World War I, the San Antonio Chamber of Commerce had embraced military aviation as the winning card in the city's rivalry with Dallas and Houston. Kelly Field and Brooks Air Base had been established during the war, and Randolph Air Base in the 1920s. All were vigorously defended throughout the Depression decade by San Antonio congressmen and business leaders. Aggressive business organizations in Salt Lake City helped to persuade the War Department that Utah was the appropriate site for the new Hill Air Base in the mid-thirties. A few years later, Ogden business leaders countered farmer protests about the loss of agricultural land to smooth the way for the Clearfield Naval Supply Depot.

San Diego was a big winner when the navy transferred half its fleet from the Atlantic to the Pacific between 1919 and 1921. Through the next two decades, the Army and Navy Committee of the San Diego Chamber of Commerce looked to the navy as the guarantor of economic stability. The San Diego naval strategy worked by increments as the city sought to be the site for one proposed facility and then another. Abetted by active and retired naval officers, San Diego went all-out to meet the changing needs of the navy. It canceled a new bridge at the navy's request, provided thousands of waterfront acres, furnished water at cut rates, constructed recreation facilities for sailors, ran new railroad spurs, dredged its harbor, and eagerly danced to every new tune the navy called. In return it gained a naval training station, a destroyer base, a supply depot, a naval hospital, and a new naval district headquarters.

During the same interwar years, the cities along San Francisco Bay had stumbled over each other in their eagerness to make the Bay Area the "American Singapore." Even though designation as the home base of the Pacific Fleet promised up to $100 million in immediate construction contracts, Vallejo's congressman, Charles Curry, blocked the navy's choice of Alameda because he feared it would undermine the Mare Island Navy Yard. Since most navy planners had long since decided in favor of San Francisco and Oakland over San Diego or Los Angeles–Long Beach, the service circumvented local rivalries by building its home base piecemeal and spreading components among all the key cities in the Bay Area. San Francisco Mayor Angelo Rossi and the San Francisco *Chronicle* helped to organize a Bay Cities Naval Affairs Committee to back the navy and keep the pressure on Washington for naval rearmament. As Roger Lotchin has pointed out, San Francisco area promoters knew full well that "a main home base required planes to defend it, repair shops to mend its ships and planes, depots to supply it, and marine detachments to patrol it. These necessitated laboratories to improve the planes, reserve outfits to supplement the regulars, bridges and roads to connect the whole complex, and shore batteries to defend the lot."[1] Vallejo kept Mare Island, San Francisco got a shipyard at Hunters Point, Sunnyvale got a dirigible base and research laboratory, Alameda got an air station, and Oakland got a supply depot.

The armed peace of 1940 and Franklin Roosevelt's interventionist stance against Nazi Germany triggered even more focused competition for defense dollars. The Dallas Chamber of Commerce and its Citizens Council (which spoke for the city's movers and shakers) campaigned in Washington offices and corporate headquarters for a naval reserve aviation squadron base and a North American Aviation Company plant. By 1943, employment in the federally financed plant would top 40,000, and the Chamber of Commerce could happily proclaim that Dallas was "the War Capital of the Southwest." Fort Worth secured Tarrant Field and a Consolidated Vultee Aircraft (Convair) plant, with the previously unthinkable support of arch-rival Dallas. In both cases, civic boosters made good use of their political connections. The Defense Plant Corporation, which built the North American and Convair facilities, included a board member from Dallas and operated under the

Reconstruction Finance Corporation, directed by Houston banker and booster Jesse Jones. In the Convair campaign, *Fort Worth Star-Telegram* publisher Amon Carter—"Mr. Fort Worth" from the 1920s to his death in 1955—chatted directly with Franklin Roosevelt on behalf of his city.

Other cities followed the same script. The Oklahoma City Chamber of Commerce led the campaign that brought Tinker Air Base. Denver's campaign was orchestrated by city parks director George Cranmer, who showcased the Rocky Mountains to visiting congressmen and joined forces with the Union Pacific Railroad to secure an ammunition plant. Phoenix organized a Municipal Aviation Commission and a Chamber of Commerce aviation committee to work for a "huge air program in the sun."[2] Senator Carl Hayden helped to secure Phoenix Military Airport (Luke Field) in January 1941 on land purchased and donated by the city. Other training bases soon followed in Arizona at Glendale, Chandler, and Mesa.

The federal recruitment of Western states and cities into the war effort was based less on preexisting industrial capacity than on the *regional* resources of location and elbow room for military bases, shipyards, and airfields and of electric power for the production of primary metals. Though they were the home of 20.4 percent of the nation's population in 1940, the Western states accounted for only 10.7 percent of value added by manufacturing. As the ratios in table 3 indicate, the Western states built nearly twice as much combat equipment as would have been the case if the supply contracts had been allocated in proportion to existing industrial capacity. They received four times their proportionate share of federally funded war plants. Judged on the basis of the region's share of national population in 1940, the West also received more than its share of new military base facilities.

In turn, the bulk of the defense spending went to the West's major cities. Its thirty-two officially designated metropolitan areas received 85 percent of Western war contracts, absorbed 58 percent of federally funded industrial facilities, and accounted for 38 percent of new military facilities. The figures increase to 88 percent, 69 percent, and 41 percent if the immediately adjacent but officially nonmetropolitan communities of San Bernardino, Vancouver, Bremerton, and Provo are included. Eight metro areas received more than $1 billion in war contracts, four received between $500 and 999 million, and six more received at least $100 million (table 4). The relative impact of war production was greatest in thirteen metropolitan areas where the *increase* in manufacturing jobs from 1940 to 1943 was more than 20 percent of the total employment in 1940: Seattle, Tacoma, Portland, San Francisco, Los Angeles, San Diego, Fort Worth, Dallas, Houston, Tulsa, Wichita, Denver, and Salt Lake City.

Table 3. Federal Wartime Spending in Seventeen Western States
         Compared to U.S. Total

	Western States	Percent of U.S. Total
Population in 1940	26,024,000	20.4%
Value added by manufactures, 1940	$2.6 billion	10.7
Federal wartime spending, June 1940 to June 1945		
Industrial war facility projects	$4.1 billion	40.4
Military facility projects	$4.4 billion	25.9
Combat equipment contracts	$27.8 billion	20.5
Other war supply contracts	$5.8 billion	12.9

SOURCE *County Data Book: 1947* (Washington, D.C.: USGPO, 1947).

NOTE War facilities are all projects of $25,000 or more reported to the War Production Board. They include projects financed by the Defense Plant Corporation, the Reconstruction Finance Corporation, the Maritime Commission, the Army, and the Navy, but they exclude housing projects.

Planners for the U.S. Army Air Corps decided in 1940 that future training bases should be located in the southern third of the country. "Wherever you can grow cotton you can grow aviators," said one officer. General Davenport Johnson put it more carefully when he wrote a Northern senator that "with the exception of some areas on the Pacific coast, in general, it can be stated that the difficulty of continuous flying training is in direct proportion to the distance north of approximately the 37th parallel."[3] The Air Force's "sunshine belt" received most of the new training bases, auxiliary fields, and supply depots from May 1940 (when the *blitzkrieg* in France and the Low Countries shocked the army into doubling its goal of trained pilots) until 1944 (when air space near Southwestern cities became dangerously congested). In fact, nearly every Western city south of the forty-first parallel saw new or expanded bases—Lowry Air Base at Denver, Peterson Air Field near Colorado Springs, Kearns Army Air Base southwest of Salt Lake City, Davis-Monthan Air base in Tucson, Biggs Field in El Paso, and Kirtland Field in Albuquerque.

In the Western war boom, the cities that reaped the greatest economic benefit were those that could build on existing industries. Seattle, for example, was already home to the Boeing Company and to a naval shipyard in

Table 4. Defense Facilities and Contracts in Western Metropolitan Areas,
June 1940 to June 1945 (In Millions of Dollars)

	Combat Equipment	Other Contracts	Industrial Facilities	Military Facilities
Amarillo	48	3	38	13
Austin	—ᵃ	11	15	7
Beaumont	239	697	144	2
Corpus Christi	1	124	23	66
Dallas	718	76	44	14
Denver	237	73	159	39
El Paso	1	7	3	33
Ft. Worth	1,037	21	65	27
Fresno	55	3	1	8
Galveston	26	163	73	30
Houston	752	678	350	36
Lincoln	30	4	5	18
Los Angeles	8,383	1,207	404	183
Oklahoma City	468	21	51	36
Omaha	37	31	15	1
Phoenix	67	23	47	26
Portland	1,608	129	89	8
Pueblo	8	17	6	30
Sacramento	7	4	2	46
Salt Lake City	76	20	53	16
San Antonio	36	27	—	79
San Diego	2,009	25	52	215
San Francisco	3,213	778	364	453
San Jose	258	31	42	13
Seattle	2,088	204	121	77
Spokane	4	19	74	53
Stockton	88	12	10	58
Tacoma	550	40	19	39
Topeka	—	2	10	24
Tulsa	574	146	40	0
Waco	46	45	31	15
Wichita	1,323	22	40	4

SOURCE *County Data Book: 1947* (Washington, D.C.: USGPO, 1947).

ᵃ Indicates a value of less than $500,000.

nearby Bremerton. As the war contracts rolled in, Boeing factories in Seattle, Everett, and Renton rolled out thousands of B-17s and B-29s. Todd-Pacific and a score of other shipyards launched destroyers, patrol boats, and minesweepers. The Puget Sound Navy Shipyard worked overtime. Extra ferries purchased from San Francisco after the opening of the Bay Bridge carried 5,000 commuters daily from Seattle to Bremerton. "Seattle, 1942, is definitely a boom town," commented *Business Week* in May 1942. "The crowds are there and the air is vibrant."[4] A decade later, in the midst of the new war in Korea, Seattle's economy would be as strong as ever, with the naval shipyard and Boeing holding on to most of their expansion.

The defense boom also transformed the aircraft industry in Los Angeles. In 1939 it was a business of skilled craftsmen with about 20,000 total jobs. In 1943 it was an assembly-line operation with 243,000 workers in Los Angeles County alone. To the future benefit of the Los Angeles economy, most of the growth came from the expansion of local companies such as Douglas, Hughes, North American, and Lockheed, who shared information on engineering and tooling and supported the growth of a network of suppliers. UCLA created a new engineering program designed to meet the technical needs of the aircraft manufacturers. In combination, the base of management and engineering expertise, trained workers, and satellite companies put Los Angeles in a position to hold the bulk of remaining military aircraft contracts during the demobilization of 1946–49 and to grab the lion's share of rearmament dollars in the 1950s.

The wartime and postwar expansion of Houston's petrochemical industry also built on one of that city's basic industries. Jesse Jones of the Reconstruction Finance Corporation played an important role in channeling federal funds into new chemical plants and refineries; the federal government also constructed two pipelines—the Big Inch and Little Inch—to move East Texas gas and petroleum products to the Northeast on a route that, unlike the Atlantic shipping routes, was safe from German submarines. Federal contracts then put the new plants into operation. The Humble Oil and Refining Company and Shell Oil produced aviation fuel and toluene for explosives. General Tire, Goodyear, and Sinclair Oil produced butadiene and transformed it into Buna-S rubber, the synthetic substitute that replaced the natural Malayan rubber lost to the Japanese. Investment in the Houston chemical industry totaled $600 million during the war and $300 million immediately afterward. Houston's Harris County led the United States in the value of industrial construction for 1945–48 and emerged as the focus of a great complex of petrochemical plants and pipelines stretching from Freeport to Port Arthur.

The success of Houston's chemical industry, which grew directly from the city's petroleum business, contrasted sharply with the mixed results of attempts to expand magnesium and aluminum production in the West. Anticipating shortages of nonferrous metals, the federal government's Bonneville Power Administration sold energy from the new Columbia River dams to subsidize aluminum plants in Spokane and Longview in Washington, and Portland in Oregon. Plants to process magnesium ore appeared outside Austin and Las Vegas. The latter plant benefitted not only from the availability of electricity from Boulder Dam but also from the influence of Senator Pat McCarran, who took full credit for winning over President Roosevelt and bringing industrialization to the desert. The Defense Plant Corporation shut the plant down in November 1944 because of excess capacity, sending its 15,000 workers to search for other jobs. The aluminum industry, however, would remain an important contributor to postwar growth in the West.

Coastal cities like Seattle and Houston could also be contrasted with an interior city like Denver, where the direct impact of industrial expansion was more modest. The federal government built the sprawling Denver Ordnance Plant on the western edge of the city in 1941 and the Rocky Mountain Arsenal in 1942. Twenty thousand workers at Denver Ordnance produced ammunition under the management of the Remington Arms Company, and another fourteen thousand workers at the arsenal produced military chemicals. The Kaiser Company also employed a thousand workers to finish rough-cast artillery shells. The Rocky Mountain Arsenal remained after the war, but the buildings of the ordnance plant were turned into office space for federal employees. Gates Rubber, the city's largest manufacturer, enjoyed abundant contracts, but metal fabricating firms benefited less in the long run. Prefabricated subchasers whose sections traveled by railroad to Vallejo meant immediate business but were scarcely a growth industry. It would be Korea and the cold war that firmly enlisted Colorado in the defense economy in the 1950s.

New industries meant new workers. In nearly every Western city, floods of inmigrants crowded available housing and stressed public services. In the first year of mobilization it was possible to pick out individual cities where the impact of growth was most obvious. Between April 1940 and October 1941, San Diego recorded the highest U.S. population growth rate with 27 percent and Wichita the second highest with 20 percent. Close behind were Long Beach, Corpus Christi, and Wichita Falls. The largest absolute increases in population during the same months were 40,000 in Seattle, 50,000 in Washington, D.C., and 150,000 in Los Angeles.

By 1943 the federal executive department was listing all five of the major metropolitan areas of the Pacific Coast as "congested war production areas." Although the enrollment of millions of men and women in the armed forces actually cut the nation's civilian population by 4 million between 1940 and November 1943, 28 of the West's 32 metropolitan districts gained civilian residents. The figures for metro areas in the eastern half of the country were 53 gainers and 52 losers. San Diego and Wichita were still the fastest growing, followed by Corpus Christi, Beaumont, Tacoma, Portland, and San Francisco–Oakland. Only Topeka, Omaha, Lincoln, and Austin showed civilian population decreases (the last two presumably because of the impact of the draft on university enrollment).

To many journalists San Diego epitomized the city at war. The House Committee on National Defense Migration (the Tolan Committee) made the city its first stop on a tour of war centers. Reporters for *Life, Business Week, Fortune,* and the *Saturday Evening Post* all wrote about its jammed schools, overpacked hotels, dusk-to-dawn nightlife, and other problems of "the rip-roaringest Coast boom town." The Chamber of Commerce told the Tolan Committee that San Diego had absorbed 55,000 immigrants in the past year, and continued growth of its aircraft industry and naval complex promised equal numbers the following year. As housing specialist Catherine Bauer described it, San Diego in 1939 "was still a Utopian haven for tourists and retired people, with a few sailors for local color. By 1940, airplane workers were already crowding into auto courts and make-shift trailer parks. In 1941 the Tolan Committee found it a seething boom town, with housing as the core of every problem and controversy."[5]

The boom nearly overwhelmed city officials. Operating on their own high-pressure schedules, federal agencies located new defense plants and emergency housing on isolated sites that forced extra service costs and created painful traffic problems. At the start of 1942, only half of the city's new families had separate permanent housing. The others crowded into trailers and hotels or doubled up with other families. San Diego's city manager complained that "this sudden growth . . . has meant a disorganization of practically all municipal services. Our plans were laid for orderly growth. Suddenly we find ourselves with a disordered growth, and we have to step up the tempo of every community function."[6]

Honolulu was another city that found itself in extraordinary circumstances. Servicemen who arrived with picture-postcard expectations found an overcrowded city that offered a pan-Pacific population of Anglos, Chinese, Japanese, Hawaiians, and Filipinos. As they maintained the Pacific Fleet or waited to ship out to MacArthur's island-hopping war, many of them found Honolulu little more than Coney Island with hula girls or "Amarillo with a beach." The city's old Anglo elite of merchants and agriculturalists supported the USO and worked to welcome officers and other socially acceptable servicemen. Many of the GIs, however, found their way to Honolulu's Chinatown and its Hotel Street—"a rush of reeking fish markets, overflowing tattoo parlors, dinging pinball games, sing-songing concessionaires and pushing, shouting, elbowing men in uniform and out."[7] Hotel Street was also where long lines of men waited for a few minutes in one of the fifteen regulated brothels that operated with the approval of Honolulu's military government. The several hundred women who owned and worked in the city's sex business were among the best-paid women war workers.

More typical was the wartime transformation of Portland, pitched headfirst into prosperity by shipbuilding, aluminum reduction plants, and lend-lease shipping to the Soviet Union (whose neutrality in the Pacific gave its ships safe passage past Japan to Vladivostok). New workers arrived in a steady stream during 1941, adding 30,000 to the city's population. They came in a flood in 1942 and 1943 as shipyard employment climbed to 115,000. Portland's "Virginia City atmosphere" was a mixed blessing for a community that had avoided basic change for a generation. The sudden increase in industrial jobs in a single quadrant of the city doubled the city's public transit ridership. In a city with a disproportionate population over forty-five, the arrival of young families nearly doubled the number of children under ten, placing new demands on the limited park and school systems. Fast money was as much a problem as fast growth. The average shipyard wage was twice the figure for other local industries, splitting Portland between newcomers with dollars in their pockets and old-timers nursing a sense of grievance. Every third face in line at a movie theater or department store belonged to a stranger who had arrived since 1940. Mayor Earl Riley patriotically shut down the red-light district near Union Station and pushed gambling into the back alleys—perhaps a futile effort when half of the newcomers were unmarried and half were under thirty.

The war also changed Portland by opening up regular wage-earning jobs to women, who made up 27 percent of the shipyard labor force at peak employment. The shipyards turned first to women who were already in the labor force in occupations from retail clerk to farm worker. The recruiting program turned to unemployed women in late 1943 with a block-by-block

Workers at the Portland shipyards. Women in the West Coast yards filled clerical positions, served as helpers for production workers, and occasionally found training and jobs as skilled workers. (Courtesy of the Oregon Historical Society; neg. no. 24146)

canvas, but it is likely that many of the "housewives" who signed up were women who now needed to work to support families because of absent spouses or would have been working except for the Depression. As one of the workers recalled nearly forty years later, she and a friend went to the shipyards because "we both had to work, we both had children, so we became welders, and if I might say so, damn good ones." The most common jobs were as clerical workers and general helpers, but the acute shortage of welders opened up more than 5,000 journeyman positions, including half the welders in one of the Kaiser shipyards. A few women also crossed over into occupations like electrician and crane operator. Women who achieved journeyman status tended to find shipbuilding far more interesting than waiting on tables or doing assembly-line work in clothing factories. "There's something about a ship," remembered Lorena Ellis, "even when it's being built, that has a fascination to it."[8]

Employment patterns in the Bay Area, where 30,000 women constituted about 20 percent of the total shipyard labor force, showed the special problems of minority women. They faced formal resistance from the Boiler-makers Union, which assigned both women and blacks to powerless auxili-ary organizations despite company and government pressure. The clerical and service positions in administrative offices that many women filled were largely closed to African-American women. So were production-line jobs. Beatrice Marshall, for example, was trained by the National Youth Admin-istration as a machinist and was sent from Indiana to Portland at federal expense only to find that the shipyards refused to consider her application despite their dearth of skilled workers. In 1944 and 1945 black women were able to make some advances by taking advantage of a new openness in hiring to move from domestic service to industrial jobs.

Many African-American men found even more limited opportunities for skilled work. The aircraft companies of greater Los Angeles were par-ticularly insistent on whites-only hiring. The black writer Chester Himes, who moved to California at the start of the war, remembered that his mechanical skills contributed little to the war effort. Out of the twenty-three jobs he held over the course of three years, only two required any skills— one as an apprentice shipfitter in Richmond and the other as a shipwright's helper in San Pedro. "Otherwise," he later wrote, "I was employed as a laborer, shoveling gravel and sand for the California Rock Company, mov-ing two-ton rolls of towel paper for the California Towel-Saver Company, laboring in the warehouse of the Hughes Aircraft Company."[9]

Because of their Caucasians-only policy in hiring, the aircraft companies found themselves even more dependent on women than did the shipyards. Women constituted 40 percent of the workers in California aircraft plants and nearly half in Dallas. The companies developed new power tools and production techniques to accommodate the smaller average size of their female workers, increasing efficiency for everyone on the production lines. At the same time, however, problems of day care and inadequate shopping facilities in wartime housing projects compounded the problems of women who tried both to work and to carry the continuing burden of family management.

Women workers' "double day" problem brought experiments with sup-port services. A number of defense plants followed the advice of the Women's Bureau of the U.S. Department of Labor and hired counselors to assist their female workers with advice and assistance in finding child-care facilities, making medical appointments, and otherwise coping with daily routines. The Kaiser shipyards went further by establishing their own day-care program to reduce absenteeism and turnover. Each of Kaiser's two child-care centers in Portland provided a ring of well-lighted classrooms around a central play area. They were open around the clock for women on swing and night shifts. They paid good wages, had medical personnel on staff, and offered take-home meals that mothers could pick up along with their children. The Kaiser child-care centers in Portland and Oakland also raised the standards for the more numerous community-based day-care providers.

If the number of newcomers was a break from the past, their sources were the same as for previous urban migrants. War industries reached all across the United States for their workers but drew most heavily from traditional migration pools—the northern tier of states for Northwestern cities, the Midwest and Mid-South for Southwestern cities. San Diego and Los Angeles drew their average out-of-state worker from a distance of more than a thousand miles. A survey by Portland's Kaiser shipyards found that more than 5,000 workers came from Idaho, more than 4,000 from Montana, more than 3,000 from blustery North Dakota, and more than 2,000 from South Dakota, Nebraska, Iowa, Minnesota, and Illinois—the states most easily reached by Portland's Union Pacific and Northern Pacific rail connections. The 3,000 New Yorkers and 1,000 Alabamians, in contrast, reflected special recruiting drives and chartered railroad cars. The Kaiser shipyard in Richmond took its largest number of non-Western recruits from Minneapolis, Memphis, Little Rock, St. Louis, and Chattanooga.

As every American knew, the Depression years had already sent thousands of Okies and Arkies (and Missourians and Texans) westward to California fields and factories. Now, new jobs drew thousands of these same migrants from small San Joaquin Valley towns like Arvin and Weedpatch to Oakland and Los Angeles. The states of the earlier exodus also continued to furnish 25 to 30 percent of new out-of-state workers in the war cities. Malvern, Arkansas, moved en masse to Los Angeles for shipyard jobs in a textbook example of serial migration, triggered when Raymond and Wendall Wall found jobs and wrote home of earning wages of eighty-eight cents an hour. Hundreds of Malvernites followed them to the Wilmington, San Pedro, and Long Beach shipyards. There were enough to stage community picnics and old-home get-togethers.

The terms Arkie and Okie continued to serve as general-purpose pejoratives for any new migrants from the American midlands who crowded the old-timers on the bus or in the movie lines. A Portlander complained in the newspaper that "when the people of Portland make it clear that an Arkie or an Okie is the most undesirable person on earth and when plant officials allow supervisors to openly discriminate against them and when the churches and schools openly brand them as undesirable, is it hard to see why they go elsewhere?"[10] Like other war workers, "Defense Okies" and "Aviation Okies" concentrated in the most crowded neighborhoods near the war plants. War housing projects were often branded "Okievilles." Observers at the Moore Drydock in Oakland or the Kaiser shipyards in Richmond encountered Okie jokes and anti-Okie graffiti. The abundance of jobs in 1942 and 1943, however, made the reaction far less virulent than the hostility that had greeted earlier migrants in the state's farming counties.

A brief back-migration to the Mississippi Valley after V-J Day turned out to be mainly for vacations and visits. Arkies and their neighbors were filtering back to the coast by the winter of 1946, reinforcing an Oklahoma-California cultural axis that, over the next generation, found its most obvious expression in evangelical religion and country music. As James Gregory has written, a spin of the radio dial in the southern San Joaquin Valley "brings in a few Spanish-language broadcasts, some rock and roll of various vintages, a bit of news and listener talk programming, but mostly the dial belongs to country music and religious stations . . . the twin keys to the dynamic influence of Southwesterners in California."[11] Bakersfield emerged in the 1960s as a second Nashville. Evangelical and Pentecostal churches redefined the religious character of California. In concert with black and Mexican migrants during and after the war, they tied California more closely to the culture of southern North America than at any time since the 1840s.

The situation of Hispanics paralleled that of the Arkies. As largely a rural labor force in the 1910s and 1920s, Mexican-Americans made their way to Western cities, with their social support networks and possibilities for occasional employment, when farm and railroad jobs disappeared during the Depression. Denver's Hispanic population had doubled during the 1930s. Nevertheless, the most important destination was Los Angeles, where the outcome of ethnic tension was violence rather than just name-calling. New migrations in the early 1940s doubled the size of the Mexican community in Los Angeles to an estimated 400,000 people. The city was also a destination and distribution point for the 100,000 temporary Mexican workers who assisted the U.S. war effort under the bracero program.

Conflict focused on young second-generation Mexican-Americans who adopted distinctive haircuts and clothing styles. The "chucos" (as they called themselves) or "zoot suiters" (as they were called by the press and the police) were simply acting out their ambivalent position in American society, but they were seen as a continuing affront by soldiers and sailors stationed in Los Angeles. A low-intensity riot began on June 3, 1943, and continued for nearly a week as groups of enlisted men roamed downtown and nearby neighborhoods and beat up zoot suiters, with blacks and Filipinos as incidental targets. The military finally placed the downtown off-limits after hundreds had been assaulted.

Along with Okies and Mexican-Americans, black migrants from the lower Mississippi Valley helped to Southernize the Far West. Few blacks moved into Rocky Mountain or Pacific Coast states until 1943, when federal officials finally began to put pressure on contractors and unions for open hiring. The migration of blacks peaked in 1945, two years after the peak of white migration. Though they were largely ignored by labor recruiters other than Kaiser, the newcomers set in motion a chain migration that would continue into the 1970s. Bastrop, Louisiana, for example, furnished a large number of black workers for the Moore shipyards in Oakland, and a local Baptist church coordinated a steady migration from Shreveport to the Bay Area in general. By war's end, African-Americans constituted a tenth of the migrants to Arizona and the coastal states. Seattle's African-American population grew from 3,000 in 1940 to 16,000 in 1945. Portland's grew from 2,000 to 15,000, the San Francisco–Oakland area from 20,000 to 65,000, and greater Los Angeles from 75,000 to 160,000. As Mike Davis has pointed out, African-American musicians from Texas, Oklahoma, and Louisiana would make postwar Los Angeles and its Central Avenue clubs a center for an emerging rhythm-and-blues sound that blended jazz with Southwestern blues in a black equivalent of the country music that had accompanied the migration of white Southerners.

African-Americans found unequal services and limited housing choices. Los Angeles kept its police and fire departments segregated and made fewer than 4,000 units of war housing available to blacks. In San Francisco, blacks clustered in housing projects around the Hunter's Point shipyard. In the East Bay cities of Oakland, Berkeley, and Richmond, public housing projects created what Marilynn Johnson has called a "federal corridor" along the undesirable land between San Pablo Boulevard and the bay. Richmond housing officials put black residents along the shoreline near the shipyards and used white-occupied public housing as a buffer for the established white community. Oakland segregated previously integrated housing projects out of fear of trouble from white Southerners.

The pattern of segregation would strengthen in the postwar years. Many of Oakland's and Richmond's black war workers decided to stay, often returning from short visits home with more friends and family members.

California offered better job possibilities and greater freedom than Arkansas, but less than 1 percent of new private housing units were open to black buyers. As a consequence, blacks piled up in public housing and war projects as whites were able to move out. In turn, the eventual demolition of most wartime projects in the 1950s forced their residents into old African-American neighborhoods that were already overcrowded and underserved. The segregated social geography that haunted the 1960s was the product of conscious decisions in the 1940s.

Farther east, the wartime growth of the black population in Dallas confirmed and strengthened preexisting segregation. Residents of South Dallas responded to black expansion into white neighborhoods with at least thirteen bombings between 1940 and 1942. The city council tried to enact racial segregation by ordinance before being warned off by the courts. At the end of the war, with virtually all wartime and veterans' housing reserved for whites, 26,000 black households had to squeeze into 10,500 houses and apartments, two-thirds of them substandard and distributed among nine neighborhoods, each surrounded by hostile whites. As private-home builders ignored the African-American market and more bombs exploded in 1950 and 1951, the Dallas establishment finally swallowed its pride and built 1,500 units of public housing on the Trinity River bottomlands in West Dallas for African-Americans and 500 units for Mexican-Americans.

Wartime migrations also put minority groups into direct competition. Chinese-Americans in cities like Portland and Los Angeles took advantage of the internment of Japanese-Americans as an opportunity to buy up Japanese businesses and properties at cut rates. Black newcomers to San Francisco found themselves shunted into housing in the Western Addition, which had been forcibly emptied of Japanese-Americans. Denver's black and Hispanic populations both doubled during the 1940s. Already established in a number of service trades, blacks were able to take advantage of the quotas for black employment that many local war industries set to protect their federal contracts. Government offices and military facilities that were established in the forties also began to employ blacks at a rate higher than their share of the state's population. In contrast, Mexican-American Denverites, many of whom were recent arrivals from farming towns along the Platte and Arkansas rivers, found themselves at the bottom of the ladder in the 1940s. As they spread northeast and southwest of the downtown area, civic leaders began to make official gestures in the direction of harmony. In 1947 Mayor Quigg Newton followed the recommendations of a wartime conference on the needs of Spanish-speaking Coloradans by appointing a Committee on Human Relations. Social-service agencies flooded concerned citizens with reports on the social and economic status of Denver's minorities. Their findings were consistent: Although blacks fared better than Spanish-speaking residents on all statistical indicators, discrimination against both minorities was standard operating procedure in every area of daily life—housing, jobs, health care, education, and law enforcement.

In significant measure, the chaos of mobilization in 1941 and 1942 gave way to systematic community building in 1943. In a number of coastal cities, comprehensively planned communities for war workers began to replace shoehorned housing and improvised services. In the arid interior, entirely new industries required new cities on sagebrush and creosote flats and mesas. At the same time that the new communities looked to the future, they reflected the past twenty-five years of sporadic federal involvement in community planning.

The most famous of the federal new towns is Los Alamos, built on a 7,300-foot plateau backed by the Jemez Mountains and facing the Sangre de Cristo Mountains across the valley of the Rio Grande. General Leslie R. Groves and J. Robert Oppenheimer picked the site in 1943 for its combination of isolation and accessibility to the transportation center of Albuquerque. Oppenheimer's initial expectation of bringing together two or three dozen scientists was soon replaced by the realities of a community that housed 6,500 by 1945 and 15,000 by the 1960s. During and immediately after the war, Los Alamos was a closed town—owned, managed, and guarded first by the army and then by the Atomic Energy Commission. The AEC opened up Los Alamos 1957 but allowed only limited private ownership of houses and commercial properties until the 1960s.

The canyons that cut the mesa top allowed the builders of Los Alamos to define residential clusters with looping roads in approved planning style. In the first years, apartments were assigned on the basis of family size, with rents set at a percentage of family income. Oppenheimer and the chief military representatives occupied the handful of log and stone houses left over from the boys' school that had previously occupied the mesa. Their homes were known as Bathtub Row, Laura Fermi explained in her memoir, because "they were provided with bathtubs, while Army-built apartments were provided with mere showers."[12] In the tight world of the atomic engineers, scientists (that is, male scientists) whose spouses were willing to take on the necessary clerical work were especially attractive recruits. In turn, the Los Alamos housing office carefully allocated the household help bused in from the surrounding Hispanic villages and pueblos. For its mostly young residents caught up in the effort to engineer a major new weapon, Los Alamos was sometimes "the Magic Mountain" and sometimes "Shangri-La." Twenty years later, it had evolved into a sprawling elite suburb that happened to be separated from its parent city of Santa Fe by thirty-five miles of open landscape.

At the other end of the social scale was Henderson, Nevada, built fifteen miles southeast of Las Vegas to house workers for Basic Magnesium, Inc. Despite complaints from Las Vegas boosters that BMI personnel could squeeze into the existing city, the Defense Plant Corporation required the company to erect worker housing that met U.S. Public Health Service standards. That meant a real community with streets, sewers, stores, and recreational spaces instead of a work camp of temporary houses and dormitories. Work on both the BMI plant and what was first known as the Basic Townsite began September 1941. The Basic Townsite was completed in increments over the next two years (and renamed Henderson in 1944 to honor a former Nevada senator and chair of the Reconstruction Finance Corporation). When BMI hired black workers from Arkansas and Mississippi, it also added the separate and segregated Carver Park with its own elementary school and athletic fields. In what was essentially a federally funded company town, union officials served as community advocates to a cost-conscious Defense Housing Corporation. Despite the merciless sun, dusty prospects, and decline of population to 5,000 in 1950, the town incorporated in 1953 and evolved into a blue-collar suburb of Las Vegas.

Construction of the massive Hanford Engineer Works in Washington state on 620 square miles of dry benchland along the Columbia River actually called forth two cities—a temporary analog of Henderson and a less elegant version of Los Alamos. Built in 1943 and 1944 to produce plutonium from uranium 238 with the help of Columbia River hydroelectric power, the Hanford facility displaced about 1,500 people. Farmers with irrigated acreage were allowed to harvest their 1943 crops of asparagus, mint, and berries before vacating, but residents in the minuscule towns of Hanford and Richland had just thirty days to pack up and clear out.

Construction of the massive plutonium factory replaced the prewar town of Hanford and its hundred residents with a "tar paper metropolis." Construction workers came in largest numbers from elsewhere in Washington and also from California, Missouri, Texas, Arkansas, Illinois, and Minnesota. Hanford at its peak housed 51,000 men. They described it, according to their mood, as a carnival (with music played over the public-address system), as a concentration camp (with barracks and guarded fences), and as a gigantic bus station (where you wouldn't want to leave your luggage unattended). It contained 1,177 buildings and eight mess halls, a hospital, and a trailer camp. There were 7.5 men for every woman or child. The settlement was completely dismantled by 1948. Most of the workers had long since left, pursued by the "termination winds" that drove great clouds of dust and caused mass turnover in the work force.

Richland was a very different community. As planned and built—and as managed first by DuPont and then by General Electric, the corporate operators of the Hanford plant—Richland was intended for a permanent staff of engineers and technicians. Like Henderson, it was a company town with no privately owned homes, no city government, and no property taxes until it was sold off by congressional mandate in the 1950s. Like the best contemporary suburbs, it was built with neighborhoods clustering around shopping centers, curving streets, and communal play areas on the interior of blocks. Many of the first houses were "the last word in prefabs," built according to standard models with letter designations and filled with identical furnishings. Street names memorialized military men like G. W. Goethals and Alfred Thayer Mahan. Since employment at the Hanford works was a condition for renting, Richland had no poor, no elderly, no unemployment, and virtually no crime. Low rent and good services tied technically skilled workers to the isolated location. It was, as Paul Loeb has written, "the atomic age equivalent of a homey small town" as it grew from 15,000 to 22,000 residents in the years immediately after the war.[13]

While DuPont and the Department of the Army were experimenting with a prototype for the San Fernando Valley, the shipyard divisions of the Kaiser and Bechtel companies were building new communities for the new worker citizens of Portland and San Francisco. Both Vanport and Marin City were improvised responses to the housing emergency of 1942 that tried to provide comprehensive social facilities and services to reduce worker turnover. By definition, however, they were socially segregated communities whose newcomers, out-of-staters, and blue collar workers remained isolated from the larger metro area. In the short run in Vanport and in the long run in Marin City, they also failed to provide an effective alternative to racial segregation. Vanport was a surprise to everyone except Edgar Kaiser and the U.S. Maritime Commission. Meeting behind closed doors in August 1942, Kaiser signed a contract to use federal funds to erect a massive housing project of 6,000 units (soon raised to 10,000) on a square mile of Columbia River floodplain just north of Portland. Within three days, bulldozers were scraping out the foundations for 700 identical apartment buildings. The first of 40,000 residents moved in on December 12. Portland's new Housing Authority, which took on the management of Vanport, found itself creating

its own ad hoc city government, with a fire department, a recreation department, and an independent school district that provided extensive day care
as well as classroom instruction.

Vanport received national attention as the country's largest war housing
project, a "miracle city" that was "one of the marvels of the war effort." In
many ways, however, the Kaiser Company was more interested in social
innovation than was the Housing Authority. In part to hold women in his
work force, Edgar Kaiser provided day-care facilities and experimented
with precooked meals that employees could take home after work. He also
pressured the Housing Authority to boost morale by building a sense of
community responsibility and providing Vanporters with "health, recreation, education, and the opportunity to express their cultural desires." In
practice, however, the Housing Authority was swamped simply by the need
to provide a minimum of social services. Members of its social-work staff set
up tenant councils, but the managers refused to cede to them any but the
most limited advisory functions. The Housing Authority was equally cautious about supporting a community newspaper that might articulate griev-
ances. In fact, there was little in Vanport's crackerbox design or social
context to persuade residents that it was anything more than an auto camp
multiplied a hundred times over.

Both the Housing Authority and the city council were also uncomfort-
able with the city's new African-Americans. Mayor Earl Riley believed that
the arrival of black workers threatened Portland's "regular way of life."
Housing officials were careful to group blacks into clearly delimited buildings in Vanport and other projects. Vanport schools were integrated but
not its hospital, and the Multnomah County sheriff tried to enforce informal segregation of Vanport's recreation facilities on the grounds that
mixed use led to violence. Several members of the Housing Authority board
would have supported him if federal regulations had not intervened. By V-J
Day, Vanport possessed a largely segregated population of 6,000 African-
Americans whose presence alone was enough to give the community a bad
name in the rest of the city. After the war, Vanport grew increasingly
segregated until a Columbia River flood destroyed the community in 1948,
forcing its black residents into the established black neighborhood of Al-
bina.

The outcome of social activism in Marin City was essentially the same.
The Bechtel Company's Marinship operation in Sausalito doubled the
town's population over the course of 1942 and turned a small community
into a town that never slept. As a partial solution to the local housing crisis,
Marinship executives designed and built Marin City during the summer of

Vanport, Oregon. Rising from a sea of mud in 1942 and 1943, Vanport housed more than 40,000 war workers and family members in several hundred identical apartment buildings. Within just three years of V-J Day, it would be only a memory. (Courtesy of the Oregon Historical Society; neg. no. 56002)

1942 on a hill overlooking the bay and shipyard. With well-built houses, a full commercial center, and an innovative elementary school whose classrooms opened onto walkways and courtyards, Marin City got high marks for planning, design, and management from visiting officials such as Congressman George Bates.[14] Project manager Milen Dempster, a former Socialist candidate for governor, made sure that housing units were available without regard to race. When the community survived the war as Marin County's major public housing project, however, new blacks replaced whites and confirmed a color line no different from Portland's. Model communities, it turned out, were no better able to handle the issue of race relations than were very ordinary communities like Richmond and Oakland.

It was obvious to every observer that the wartime decade shifted the American center of gravity westward. As Carey McWilliams told the readers of *Harper's Magazine* in 1949, the Pacific War and its aftermath were "tipping the scales of the nation's interest and wealth and population to the West."[15] The Western states and territories attracted an estimated 7 million new residents between 1940 and 1945 and an official population increase of 8.3 million for the decade—a surge of 31 percent.

Less publicized was the urban character of the westward tilt. Before recruiting from the farms of the South and the city streets of the Northeast, the West's shipyards, aircraft plants, and military suppliers had hired the underemployed miners and struggling farmers of the mountain and plains states. Arkies and Okies who had made their first move from the lower Mississippi Valley to the farms of central California made their second move to the lucrative jobs of Los Angeles and Oakland. The increase in the West's urban population alone during the 1940s was 8,245,000–virtually identical to the region's total population increase of 8,302,000. In effect, every new Westerner was a city dweller. The wartime boom pushed eight Western states over the 50 percent mark for urban population. California, Washington, Utah, and Colorado, which had already passed 50 percent, showed a rural-to-urban shift of at least ten percentage points. Only the northern interior states of Idaho, Montana, Nebraska, and the Dakotas remained predominantly rural.

Albuquerque, which posted a metropolitan growth of 110 percent, topped the list of all American boom cities for the decade. Lubbock followed with 95 percent growth and San Diego with 92 percent. Six of the West's metropolitan areas grew by 75 percent or more, compared with only one in the eastern half of the country. Twelve other Western metro areas grew by at least 50 percent, compared with four in the East.

The economic mobilization and demographic transformation of the war years gave the West a jump on the rest of the United States for the second half of the century. In retrospect, the war was less important as a break with the Western past than as an introduction to its future. It laid the groundwork for Western cities to play a leading role in the nation's fourth long cycle of industrial growth. The reference is to the phenomenon that economists sometimes call Kondratieff waves—long cycles in the capitalist economy first identified by Nikolai Kondratieff and given theoretical interpretation by Josef Schumpeter. Since the late eighteenth century, the world has experienced four "long waves" of economic expansion and consolidation. Each has lasted approximately fifty years, and each has been associated with the technical and market exploitation of a cluster of new products and processing technologies. The first cycle centered on steam engines, power looms, and large-scale iron production between the 1780s and 1840s—what textbooks once called the Industrial Revolution. The second was driven by the interrelated steel, railroad, and steamship industries from the 1840s through the 1880s. The third involved the development of uses for electricity and manufactured chemicals, with new products ranging from electric lighting to automobiles that used refined petroleum.

The onset of a new wave reduces the importance of old advantages and opens the way for "sunrise industries" and "sunrise regions." The United States used its position as a sunrise region in the second wave to declare its economic independence of Europe. Germany used the third wave to push past Britain as the leading European power. The states of the Northeast and Midwest used the same wave of industrialization to consolidate their industrial dominance over the South and West. Similarly, an outstanding example of the regional impact of a sunrise industry can be seen in the rise of the auto industry in Detroit, with its network of affiliated companies and suppliers in Akron, Toledo, Dayton, South Bend, and elsewhere in the Great Lakes states.

The beginning of the fourth Kondratieff cycle is dated by various experts between 1938 and 1947, and its end will presumably come in the 1990s. In the United States, the growth forces of this long wave have been identified especially with the cities of the West. It has involved the mass marketing of earlier innovations, such as automobiles, consumer appliances, and petrochemicals, and the exploitation of a new innovation cluster in electronics, telecommunications, and aerospace. This is the cluster of industries, of course, in which the war gave Western cities their head start.

A related effect of the war concerns the age of Western urban populations. The wartime migration rate was highest for men and women in their early twenties, who would remain productive members of the labor force into the 1980s. The median age of Americans in 1950 was fourteen months older than it was in 1940. Four plains states and the retirement destination of Arizona aged more rapidly than the rest of the country, while the mountain states and Texas aged more slowly, and the Pacific states actually grew younger. This lowering of the median age on the Pacific Coast between 1940 and 1950 meant there were more potential entrepreneurs there and more people in their prime productive years.

At the same time, population growth and high wages during the war years vastly expanded the regional market. As a result, personal income increased relative to the national average in fifteen of seventeen Western states between 1940 and 1950. Businesses could respond to the customer base by offering local products in place of imports from the East, generating new profits and providing capital for reinvestment. In turn, the presence of more locally supplied goods and services made it cheaper and easier to start new businesses.

The impact of World War II can be summed up with a look at the community of Westchester in Los Angeles County. Over the course of three wartime years, large-scale builders covered five square miles of rolling vegetable fields near the Los Angles Municipal Airport with 3,230 housing units. The Marlow-Burns company sold its development as "Homes at Wholesale," including "double bungalows" and two-bedroom houses for under $4,000. Buyers were restricted to defense workers. As Greg Hise has argued, Westchester was one of many industrial bedroom communities that accelerated the decentralization of Western cities by bringing workers to outlying aircraft factories—to North American Aviation in the case of Westchester, but also to Lockheed in the case of North Hollywood, and to Douglas Aircraft in the cases of Midwest City outside Oklahoma City and Westside Village near Santa Monica.

As sketched by Carey McWilliams four years after the war's end, Westchester was still an inadvertent development. Despite its having a theoretical master plan, simultaneous construction by several large home-builders had given Westchester a hodgepodge of houses and streets characterized by a "jumble of unrelated numberings and sharp, criss-crossing turns."[16] Public services were simply borrowed from more established municipalities. At the same time, Westchester was an emerging community. Its skilled workers, craftsmen, and white-collar workers were bound together by their dependence on the aircraft industry. Its racially homogeneous population consisted of adults in their early thirties and children ready for the first grade. The extraordinary pace of its development was itself the impetus for

War boom housing in Los Angeles. This Associated Press photo from the early 1950s carried the caption: "They met housing needs then. These small, unpretentious homes in a Los Angeles suburb were built just after the war when thousands of home-hungry people needed places to live. Similarity in design and small rooms were not detriments to sales." (From the Hearst Newspaper Collection, courtesy of Department of Special Collections, University of Southern California Library)

community building. As of 1949, the people of the wartime migration were staying put, finding work in booming postwar Los Angeles, worrying about inadequate schools, and preparing to tame the metropolitan frontier of the last half of the twentieth century.

2

THE POLITICS OF GROWTH

It took a wartime migrant to remind Denverites how to make money. Elwood Brooks was a Kansas banker who moved to Denver at the height of the war to revive the seriously ailing Central Savings Bank and Trust Company. As his son later recalled, he found a downtown business establishment that shunned new people and new ideas: "They had a nice deal here in Denver. It was a quiet little city and they didn't want any growth at all."[1] The "big six" banks followed the example of Gerald Hughes of the First National Bank, who hated to have more than 20 percent of his institution's capital out in loans (compared with a national standard of more than 50 percent).

Like Gerald Hughes, Denver's old-line business leaders of the 1940s were crusty, contented, and unembarrassed by charges of complacency. As conservators of family fortunes established by parents or grandparents, men like Hughes, John Evans, and Claude Boettcher held interlocking investments in banks, utilities, railroads, and real estate. A procession of journalists who surveyed the city immediately after World War II came to the same conclusion: mobilization for war had shaken neither the leadership nor their desire to preserve clean streets, clean air, and a safe 5 percent. John Gunther called Denver "immobile . . . Olympian, impassive, and inert . . . the most self-sufficient, isolated, self-contained, and complacent city in the world." Denverites Charles Graham and Robert Perkin were even less tactful: "Denver, citadel of these inheritors of wealth without vision, has been described as 'the city of dead pioneers.' "[2]

Elwood Brooks, of course, was a live pioneer. A fiftyish man with gold-rimmed glasses, he began to do the unusual. He advertised the Central Bank and Trust; he opened its doors at hours that working people could use; he used his Kansas touch to attract the deposits of small-town banks. At the same time that the big bankers were forcing Gates Rubber to find its financing in New York and telling Henry Kaiser to pack up and leave town after V-J Day, Brooks was responding to returning veterans with home mortgages and previously unheard of automobile loans. Apart from his profit-and-loss statements, his main encouragement came from Palmer Hoyt, a new editor who arrived in 1946 to turn around the *Denver Post*.

Old Denver clung to its old ways into the 1950s. When New York real estate developer William Zeckendorf tried to buy the old courthouse square, other real estate owners did everything they could to block him. As Brooks described the contest of wills a decade later, "the old birds sat out there and chewed tobacco and told stories. Some of the property owners nearby took surveys to show that Zeckendorf's hotel and his big four-basement garage would cause their walls to slant. Zeckendorf was kept in the courts for four years before he could take title to the property."[3] As other new buildings joined the New Yorker's new department store and Hilton Hotel in the middle fifties, however, the Chamber of Commerce and the U.S. National Bank began to produce booster literature that no one would have imagined in the 1940s. New voices began to argue that Denver should emulate Pittsburgh with a dynamic program of downtown redevelopment. Even members of the old crowd finally conceded that making money from a booming city was not as painful as they had feared.

Denver is not the only Western city where World War II rearranged power and politics as well as people. The majority of Western cities were status quo communities in 1941. As in the placid capital of the Rocky Mountain Empire, economic power lay in the hands of absentee owners or satisfied members of the second generation. City hall cliques and personal political organizations ran caretaker governments. There were strong sentiments to hold on to a good thing, for industrial growth might bring immigrants, labor agitators, and air pollution to spoil the view of the Rockies or the Cascades.

Seattle, for example, met its postwar readjustment with the dull, inactive administration of Mayor William Devin (1942–52). The wide-open city of an earlier generation grew complacent after 1945 as downtown real estate and business interests feared rapid growth and refused loans to outside entrepreneurs. Instead, the members of the Seattle establishment preferred to cut their deal with Teamsters Union leader Dave Beck, who delivered good wages to his members by guaranteeing to keep his workers on the job.

As described by historian Constance McLaughlin Green in 1957, Seattle was insular and nonintellectual: "No opportunity outside Seattle has any appeal; they have little interest in other places and in the ideas of other communities."[4]

The smaller city of Cheyenne followed the same model. Its absentee owners saw little benefit and much peril in an expanding population. Dee Linford commented in 1949 that "the men who run Cheyenne incline to the thinking that their town is large enough. . . . The real leaders, those who dominate the city's economic life . . . do not want competition, and are constantly on the alert to block newcomers who might someday pose a threat to their vested position."[5] Economic development programs consisted of a few tourist facilities and the Frontier Days committee.

At the same time, most Western cities were marked by institutional openness. Narrow economies generated few new entrepreneurs on their own, but they did offer unfilled niches for new business initiatives. In Austin, for example, C. B. Smith found himself in somewhat the same position as Elwood Brooks. An auto dealer who moved to Austin in 1944, he was an outsider who saw opportunities for industrial growth despite the caution of many bankers and businessmen, who feared that new industry meant smokestacks and CIO organizers with un-Texan names. At the same time, a lack of competing activities allowed him to move aggressively to create an Austin Area Economic Development Foundation in 1948.

It was also possible for ambitious men to make a political mark in cities that lacked entrenched political machines and ethnic-group politics in the Boston or Chicago style. Western cities were fertile ground for the professionalization of local government in the 1940s and 1950s, and for the emergence of self-directed suburbs after 1960. Younger civic activists wrote new charters, organized reform campaigns, and defined a new consensus about the role of local government. To use the phrase of political scientist Amy Bridges, residents of many Western cities "refounded" their political communities in a generation of business-led reform.

Like the growth of the manufacturing and military sectors in Western cities, the modernization of municipal government was a trend that was accelerated by the events of the 1940s but whose roots predated the war. In Dallas, for example, the Citizens Council had called the shots since 1937. The adoption of a city manager form of government in the 1920s had led to a decade of political infighting rather than "businesslike" government, forcing the city's economic elite to play a direct role in outcompeting Fort Worth, Houston, and San Antonio for the Texas Centennial celebration of

Downtown Denver in the 1950s. The low-rise city of the early twentieth century fills the foreground in this view from the south. The new highrise downtown of William Zeckendorf and Clint Murchison has just begun to rise above the older skyline. (Courtesy of the Colorado Historical Society; neg. no. 35,268)

1936. The following year, banker Robert L. Thornton took the lead in making the informal alliance into a permanent organization of the men who had the real power to say yes or no. The Citizens Council included one hundred company presidents and board chairmen, with no substitutes allowed at the meetings. "If you don't come, you ain't there," was Bob Thornton's motto. For the next three decades the Citizens Council set the city's agenda and controlled politics through the Citizens' Charter Association, which picked or endorsed 90 percent of the successful city council candidates until the 1970s.

It was problems created by the wartime mobilization that spurred the Dallas leadership to undertake systematic planning for the city's future. Speaking for the Citizens Council, Mayor Woodall Rogers in 1942 urged the members of the American Municipal Association to prepare comprehensive postwar development plans. Practicing what he preached, Rogers engaged the nationally prominent planning consultant Harland Bartholomew to prepare a Dallas master plan. The plan took a comprehensive view of the metropolis and was tied to an active annexation effort that doubled the size of the city during the 1940s. The plan also called for $40 million in public improvements in anticipation of cutbacks in aircraft production. Local officials and the *Morning News* worked together to convince voters to approve a $15 million bond issue to fund the first projects on the master plan's list.

The Civic Affairs Conference played an analogous role in San Diego. Organized in 1935 to end factionalism at city hall, it worked to elect upper-middle-class councils and supported economic growth. By 1943, with the city past the most hectic period in the defense boom, San Diego found time to direct $25 million in local and federal funds to build sewers and other capital facilities in accord with an existing master plan. The first step toward a coherent program for postwar conversion was to prepare a report entitled *Planning for the Peace Era in San Diego County*. The second step was to form the Postwar Planning Committee, representing city and county governments, utilities, and other businesses. With help from the Chamber of Commerce, the committee commissioned what would ultimately be a 1,300-page report on industrial reconversion from the engineering consultants Day and Zimmerman, Inc. San Diegans were proud that their report added economic analysis to a traditional public works program. The committee defined a specific agenda of economic development projects, including downtown renewal, waterfront improvements, and the establishment of a port authority.

Cities throughout the West emulated Dallas and San Diego by developing postwar plans under the haunting fear of a "reconversion depression."

Many remembered the severe depression that had followed World War I. Since it was a second global war rather than the programs of the New Deal that had rescued many cities from the hangover of the Great Depression, leaders from Corpus Christi to Tacoma felt justified in worrying about the results of demobilization. Their first goal for postwar planning was to identify sources of new jobs for returning veterans and for the majority of war-industry workers who had announced their intention to stay in their new communities. A second goal was to develop efficient programs for the utilities, transportation systems, and other urban infrastructure that would help to promote economic diversification and catch up with wartime population growth.

Portland's deep worries about the city's ability to accommodate its new population and continue its windfall growth prompted the appointment of a Portland Area Postwar Development Committee, representing labor, industrialists, utilities, real estate interests, civic and religious leaders, and the press. The chairman was the current president of the local Chamber of Commerce and a past president of the National Association of Real Estate Boards, and the committee's membership overlapped the local chapter of the Committee for Economic Development. After several months of debate, it accepted the suggestion of Edgar Kaiser that it obtain $100,000 from the city, county, port authority, and school district to hire the advice of New York's Robert Moses, the country's leading advocate of systematic public works programming and pragmatic planning.

A man of commanding arrogance, Moses dispatched his advance team of engineers in September 1943 and arrived for six hectic days at the end of the month, brushing aside the mayor and trampling Portland sensibilities. The resulting plan, *Portland Improvement,* was a $60 million public works program designed to "stimulate business and help bridge the gap between the end of the war and the full resumption of private business." It proposed to employ up to 20,000 workers to build sewers, schools, public offices, a new airport, and a freeway loop around the business core. Implementation of the plan would give the city an efficient system of arterial highways, landscape the waterfront, modernize the railroad station, and create a civic center. Despite Moses's imperious style, Portlanders considered the report a bargain. The *Oregon Journal* printed thousands of copies, and the widely respected City Club added its endorsement. The result was overwhelming approval in 1944 of $24 million in special levies and bonds for schools, roads, docks, and sewers.

The experience of the San Francisco Bay area shows the same tendency toward pragmatic postwar planning with active business backing. There were, in fact, more bankers, utility executives, and Chamber of Commerce representatives than public officials at the first areawide planning meeting in August 1944, held under the auspices of the new California Reconstruction and Reemployment Commission. One outcome of the first session was the establishment of the Bay Area Council, a private organization headed by executives from the Central Bank of Oakland and Pacific Gas and Electric. Starting with a broad interest in promoting metropolitan economic growth and planning, the Bay Area Council evolved into a powerful lobby and important decision-making forum as its corporate members learned to translate their goals into specific projects that culminated in the Bay Area Rapid Transit system.

The cities of Oakland and San Francisco simultaneously appointed ad hoc committees to recommend public works projects. The San Francisco committee held fifteen hearings in 1945 and recommended capital improvements of $177 million. These included $20 million for a new airport, $23 million for streetcars, and huge amounts for streets and highways. Oakland's committee submitted a similar shopping list for new public investment. The entire regional effort matched the goals of the Reconstruction and Reemployment Commission: "to prevent unemployment . . . promote development of new industries, create new markets, promote the reemployment of discharged servicemen and readjustment of war workers, and the conversion of industry and commerce from war to peace standards."[6]

Plans are easier to make than to implement, however; follow-through required the consolidation of "progressive" business and professional leadership. The initiative for this consolidation came from two groups—aspiring entrepreneurs and professionals, and prominent business executives sympathetic to the goals of the national Committee on Economic Development (or CED, a new organization which represented the commitment of large corporations to strategic planning for continued economic growth). The first group had businesses and careers that stood to benefit directly from a growing population and an expanding market for cars, appliances, houses, and professional services. Many were newcomers to the West who found it difficult to understand how an older generation of property owners could be content with a steady-state economy. Ignored for appointive positions by the old elite, they were sometimes able to use membership organizations like the Chamber of Commerce to promote their agenda. In some cases they also found allies among more prominent businessmen who applauded the work of the CED.

The result of pent-up energies was a wave of municipal political reform between 1945 and 1955. During this "revolutionary" decade, civic activists created or reinstated local growth machines—development-minded alliances of major property owners, utilities, department stores, newspapers, and other local-market businesses. The activists replaced government by cronyism in cities like Albuquerque and San Antonio; they rationalized the chaotic pluralism that had given Phoenix thirty-one city managers in thirty-five years; and they eased out or bypassed caretaker administrations in cities like Seattle and Denver.

Like the progressive reformers of the early twentieth century, these neo-progressives captured the high ground by arrogating the rhetoric of progress and public interest. They painted their opponents as vice lords and crooked cops, corrupt political bosses, or, at best, small-timers unfitted to guide their city into the modern age. The immediate goal was often to update antiquated municipal administrations and provide a fuller range of city services at a lower cost. Beyond the classic progressive goal of efficiency, the reformers hoped to mobilize public and private resources to build the necessary physical facilities for economic growth. They wanted new docks and airports, an expanded supply of water, new highways, cheaper electric power, and a strong downtown as the core of a growing metropolis.

A typical example was San Jose, where ambulance operator and beer distributor Charles Bigley had put together a political organization in the late 1920s that controlled a majority on the city council into the 1940s. Like a political machine out of the textbooks, he earned the loyalty of low-income voters with favors and took payoffs from liquor and gambling interests through the police and fire departments. Excited by wartime opportunities, a group of younger, aggressive merchants, lawyers, and industrialists formed the Progress Committee in 1944 to throw the rascals out. Looking forward to the boom that they knew was ahead, they wanted to build "a new metropolis in the place of sleepy San Jose."[7] With the support of the newspapers, they brushed off the opposition of labor unions and large landowners, swept the city council election, and set out to clean house at city hall.

Although the Progress Committee disappeared as a formal organization soon after its 1944 victory, its business agenda and business interests dominated city government for the next three decades. City manager A. P. Hamann, hired in 1950 with business rather than government experience, pursued the goal of making San Jose "the Los Angeles of the North." The city recruited new industry. It built new streets, sewers, and an airport. It annexed rural territory in advance of urbanization—growing in size from 11 square miles in 1940 to 137 square miles in 1970—and it extended "shoestring" annexations along highways to reach attractive outlying districts. In the same way that Los Angeles had used its water supply to force annexations in the 1910s and 1920s, San Jose made annexation the price of hookups to its oversized sewer system built originally to serve the local canneries, giving cost advantages to annexed subdivisions. City officials justified their expansion on the grounds of efficiency—capturing a tax base for public services, coordinating capital improvements, and acquiring necessary land for parks and other facilities.

As Philip Trounstine and Terry Christensen have pointed out, San Jose boosters also fought to maintain the separate identity of their booming metropolis, resisting inclusion in the San Francisco—Oakland metropolitan area in 1950 and rejecting participation in the Bay Area Rapid Transit system in 1957. The prime beneficiaries and boosters of the Hamann regime were real estate developers and the *San Jose Mercury News*. Under the new ownership of Joseph Ridder after 1952, the *Mercury News* boosted growth and grew prosperous on growing advertising revenues. In Ridder's terminology, that translated into being "a constructive force in the development of San Jose and its territory."[8] An alliance of contractors, developers, and businessmen joined the *Mercury News* in selling more than $100 million in general obligation bonds to the voters during the 1950s and 1960s.

Like San Jose, Salt Lake City ended the 1930s with an embarrassing record of ineptness and corruption in city government. Both the mayor and the police chief landed in jail in 1938 for taking payoffs from three illegal lotteries, three bookies, sixteen brothels, and businesses with names like the Past Time Club and the Horse Show Card Room. Ab Jenkins, elected mayor in 1939, was a race-car driver rather than a politician. His well-meaning efforts to impose some fiscal discipline on the administrative departments of the other city commissioners paralyzed the city with public feuds and turned council meetings into shouting matches. Change came in 1943, when Jenkins stepped aside and voters turned to radio executive Earl Glade, who would serve as mayor for twelve years. With the support of the *Salt Lake Tribune* and the Chamber of Commerce, the mayor began to plan for postwar changes with the help of the National Resources Planning Board and gradually modernized the city administration.

The political revolution in Denver drew on the same cast of participants as San Jose but managed to emphasize administrative efficiency over headlong growth. Political change paralleled the opening of the metropolitan economy as a group of young reformers targeted Mayor Benjamin Stapleton for removal. Mayor since 1923 (with one four-year pause), "interminable Ben" maintained himself in office through his authority to appoint nearly all city employees and his willingness to adapt the tax structure in response to the suggestions of businessmen. In many ways an effective administrator who had taken good advantage of federal funds for parks and open space, Stapleton was also an easy target for caricature. The readers of *Time* and *Inside USA* found portraits of Stapleton "gliding on his oars" and mumbling through press conferences. When returning veterans began to compete with wartime migrants for scarce housing in 1945 and 1946, the mayor's solution was simple but not especially helpful: "If all these people would only go back where they came from, we wouldn't have a housing shortage."

The challenge to Stapleton in 1947 came from James Quigg Newton, a thirty-five-year-old Denverite who was returning home after years attending Yale, clerking for Supreme Court justice William O. Douglas, and serving in the navy. Newton had youth, dynamism, a cosmopolitan background, and ambitions for the city. With the strong backing of the *Denver Post,* he campaigned against the incompetence of an administration that tolerated dirty and rutted streets, awarded contracts to cronies, and contributed to the housing shortage with archaic building codes. He promised to seize the main chance and put Denver on the road to prosperity. New migrants, veterans, liberals, and small-business people turned out to give Newton the largest margin of victory in the history of Denver.

Quigg Newton's major impact during his two terms as mayor was to modernize Denver's municipal government. He brought in young professional administrators who were soon dubbed the "Michigan Carpetbaggers." He implemented competitive purchasing, a civil service system, and a sales tax. He reorganized city health services and Denver General Hospital. Although Newton reached out to broaden his coalition by appointing a leader of the Colorado Education Association to a city council vacancy, his sympathies lay with the growth of Denver as a white-collar metropolis. His successor, Will Nicholson, had been his chief lieutenant on the Republican side and continued to make Denver a pleasant environment for ambitious entrepreneurs. In the background were long court battles with farmers and western-slope counties over the diversion of Colorado River water across the continental divide and into Denver water mains. Nicholson also combined efforts with Governor Ed Johnson to gain the addition of a Denver–Salt Lake City link in the interstate highway system, eventually giving motorists the Eisenhower Tunnel beneath Loveland Pass.

In the Southwest, the Phoenix Charter Government Committee, the Albuquerque Citizens Committee, and the San Antonio Good Government League followed similar careers. Phoenix voters in 1949 responded to blatant corruption in city government by amending the charter to provide for at-large elections and to strengthen the city's council-manager government. When established politicians made it clear that they intended to maintain their influence on the city administration, prominent business and professional men organized the Charter Government Committee and assembled a full reform ticket that included department store executive Barry Goldwater. The committee swept the election of 1949 and repeated its success every other year for the next two decades.

In Albuquerque the immediate wave of postwar reform interrupted the dominance of Clyde Tingley in 1946. Tingley was an old-fashioned politician who had converted the position of city commission chairman into that of a partisan boss. After the 1946 vote, the memory of eight years of fragmented politics, a Tingley comeback, and "government by crisis" persuaded middle-class residents in Albuquerque's "Heights" neighborhoods to organize the Citizens Committee to back candidates who would return the city to the progressive ideal of efficiency. Like the Charter Government Committee, the Citizens Committee was a "slating committee" that functioned as an informal political party. It chose candidates, raised money, supported nonpartisan city manager government, and won elections.

San Antonians played out a story much like that in Albuquerque. A reform-minded administration that occupied city hall from 1943 to 1947 proved premature for cautious South Texans. From 1947 to 1949, San Antonio suffered under the inept guidance of Alfred Callaghan, the son and grandson of earlier city bosses who had a flair for saying the wrong thing. On one day he could propose saving money by having the three hundred animals in the city zoo stuffed, and on another he could refer to a rash of shootings by the police as "seven measly deaths" or refuse to spend money earmarked for industrial development. Voters in San Antonio booted out Callaghan in 1949 and managed to adopt a council-manager charter in 1951, but swirling factions and noisy political accusations blocked any semblance of efficient government. The city swept through five city managers in three years and ran through dozens of city council members in a series of recall campaigns.

In December 1954, fifty of the original advocates of charter reform met to do something about the chaos. The new Good Government League easily raised a war chest, recruited its council candidates, and won by a margin of two to one. The Good Government League wanted no sharing of power with the city's partisan leaders, for its goal—as stated in its publication *In Search of Good Government*—was "retention of the Council-Manager system, creation of good city government geared to community progress with efficient nonpartisan administrations, an end to factionalism, sectionalism, patronage politics, and maneuvering for special selfish interests." The Good Government League quickly evolved into another "nonpartisan" party that advocated a well-defined platform, maintained continuity of organization, used an anonymous committee to choose council candidates, and backed 77 of the 81 city council winners between 1955 and 1971. The "sectionalism" that it claimed to abhor often meant the interests of Mexican-American and African-American neighborhoods, which were given carefully selected token representation on the city council. Drawing most of its leaders from a few elite neighborhoods, the league, as Robert Lineberry has described it, was "a sort of upper class political machine, officing not in Tammany Hall, but in a savings and loan association."[9]

A third variation on the pattern of neoprogressive politics could be found in several of the West's oil cities, where strong growth coalitions from the 1920s and 1930s persisted into the 1940s and 1950s under the direction of tight cliques of businessmen. These cities had no need for a political revolution in the style of Denver or Phoenix. Neither were their power elites as formally and publicly structured as in Dallas. Instead, they were communities where the prewar elite was strong enough to consolidate its hold and sufficiently "growth-minded" to preempt challenges. Elected officials or civic organizations fronted for small coteries of businessmen who made the essential decisions. Minorities might receive token acknowledgement, but public dissent from the agenda of economic growth was scarcely tolerated.

The oil boom of the 1920s had given Oklahoma City a heady taste of growth. As the United States emerged from the Depression, the city already had its new development agenda in place. Mayors Robert Hefner (1939–47) and Allen Street (1947–59) presided over municipal administrations that pursued urban redevelopment and aggressive annexation. The city government articulated the forthright capitalism of Kerr-McGee Oil, Oklahoma Gas and Electric, the First National Bank, and especially E. K. Gaylord, who owned both daily newspapers and the first television station. While Gaylord's front-page editorials set the tone for the city, the actual plans and programs came from the Chamber of Commerce and its managing director, Stanley Draper. "Mr. Oklahoma City" by resolution of the Oklahoma House of Representatives, he dominated day-to-day policy from 1931 to 1969, just as Gaylord managed the larger climate of opinion.

Until well into the 1950s, many of the key decisions about the future of Houston were made in Suite 8F of the Lamar Hotel, the private suite of the construction tycoon George Brown. Over bourbon and a hand of cards, men like Jesse Jones, owner of the *Houston Chronicle* and Democratic party power broker, Gus Wortham of American General Life Insurance, James Elkins of the First National City Bank, and William Hobby of the *Houston Post* would pick their candidates and decide which causes would receive their contributions. With their minds focused on promoting the city's "good business climate," they held a veto power over the future of the city.

Houston experienced a carefully orchestrated Red Scare from 1950 to 1952. Its rapid growth and increasing cosmopolitanism during and after World War II brought a strong "fundamentalist" reaction against social change and modernization. Observers in the later 1940s noted its "nervous new civilization" and the uneasiness of the "people's collective nervous system." In a city where "the feeling of insecurity is running rampant," in the judgment of the *Houston Post's* 1950 New Year's edition, it was easy for the old elite of Jones, Brown, Wortham, and Hobby to use the *Chronicle* and the *Post* to steam up Houstonians about Reds, labor agitators, and liberal Yankees. By stifling dissent and defining an official "Houston line," they made sure that an expanded economy and electorate represented no threat to their power. They turned off the campaign in 1953 when the end of the Korean War and the inauguration of President Eisenhower seemed to have the Reds and the local liberals on the run.

In the context of the 8F crowd, historians have offered differing judgments on Oscar Holcombe, who served as Houston's mayor for twenty-two of the thirty-six years between 1921 and 1957. Amy Bridges emphasizes his independence as a political entrepreneur who built alliances with organized labor and the black community while pursuing the interests of the Houston elite with aggressive boosterism. Barry Kaplan, however, argues that Holcombe's defeat in 1952 and victory in 1955 depended on the withdrawal and restoration of support from the 8F crowd. Houston may best be understood as a Southwestern analog of Atlanta, where semi-independent political middlemen served the interests of the business elite, in part by coopting potential opposition blocs such as African-Americans.

The Los Angeles booster elite, led by long-established real estate syndicates and the *Los Angeles Times*, also had a history of stifling dissent from the left. As in Houston, the wartime boom brought new industries that did not depend directly on the downtown business leaders. It also brought a new population that did depend on defense industry jobs and that shared many of the same insecurities that made Houstonians open to patriotic appeals. The showdown in Los Angeles came over public housing, especially the Housing Authority's plans for redeveloping Bunker Hill. Located just northwest of downtown, the rundown housing of Bunker Hill was also a prime target for downtown expansion and the continued growth of the private real estate industry that bought so much *Times* advertising. Opponents of the Housing Authority used the tensions of the Korean War years to turn the issue into one of "communistic housing projects" and "housing pinks." Voters in 1952 rejected public housing by three to one. When Mayor Fletcher Bowron pushed ahead with the Bunker Hill project, to which the city was committed, the *Times* and the real estate tycoons looked for a substitute candidate. They ran Congressman Norris Poulson against a mayor whom the *Times* now accused of anarchism. As mayor from 1953 to 1961, Poulson managed to deny Nikita Krushchev the chance to visit Disneyland. He otherwise let members of the establishment write each year's municipal budget at a special retreat and took his cues from the *Times*.

Whatever the politics of the first postwar decade, the development programs of the second decade were remarkably similar. As basic services were put on track and physical infrastructure began to catch up with the growth of the 1940s, civic attention focused more and more narrowly on revitalizing central business districts. In the process, most Western cities followed the national pattern and turned to federal urban renewal programs. Urban renewal became a central policy issue of the 1960s, just as the professionalization of government had been a leading issue of the 1950s.

By national standards, Western cities were slow to sign up for federal renewal dollars, in part because of the conservative political values of the 1950s. Portland backed off its first urban renewal proposal in 1952 because of neighborhood resistance, and it was six years before politicians were willing to try again. Seattle held back from passing enabling legislation until 1957 because of the taint of socialism attached to any federal spending program, at least in the mind of Mayor Gordon Clinton. Salt Lake City voted 6 to 1 against accepting renewal dollars in 1965 after a campaign that described urban renewal as a violation of the divinely given right of property ownership. Omaha voters rejected urban renewal proposals on three different occasions. Dallas, Fort Worth, and Houston also saw no need to reinforce their booming private economies with suspect federal dollars.

Nevertheless, downtown renewal was the climax of two decades of business government in the majority of Western cities. The median starting date for nineteen major renewal projects in a sample of ten Western cities from Tulsa to Fresno was 1965. Advocates sold the program as a tool for enhancing the overall competitiveness of their city. The Oakland Planning Commission introduced redevelopment plans in 1959 with the forecast that the city could become the metropolis for central California. At the same time, cross-Bay leaders were working on plans to reassert San Francisco's role as a national metropolis. The Central Seattle Association looked for ways to confirm its edge over Portland, and Portlanders wanted urban renewal to fight back against Seattle. Boosters of renewal in downtown Denver hoped to create a "continental city" that could finally throw off the influence of Kansas City and Dallas.

Coalitions of downtown businesses and investors took the lead in selling urban renewal programs to city councils and voters in the years around 1960. In Portland and Tucson, business leaders were responsible for reviving urban renewal after initial defeats. Typical of the business coalitions were Downtown Tulsa Unlimited (1955), Downtown Denver Incorporated (1955), the Central Association of Seattle (1958), and San Diegans, Inc. (1959). With the backing of bankers and department store owners, the Tulsa group helped to pass bond issues in 1959 and 1965 for a $55 million civic center. It also supported an adjacent renewal project that cleared land for a hospital, a community college, and apartment and office buildings. Denverites developed and pushed through the Skyline Renewal Project in 1967, clearing thirty-seven blocks in the city's original business district— which in effect stockpiled land for the energy boom of the late 1970s.

San Francisco offers another example of the steps required to mobilize support for downtown renewal. The centerpiece was the Golden Gateway Center, which replaced the wholesale produce market near the ferry terminal with the Embarcadero Center's Hyatt Regency Hotel and its office buildings shaped like Nabisco vanilla wafers. The project also provided a Bay Area Rapid Transit station to bring suburban commuters to the Embarcadero Center and booming financial district. Industrialists C. B. Zellerbach and Charles Blyth got the project off the ground in 1955 by forming a business committee to advance planning funds to the city. Speedy implementation was backed by a new San Francisco Planning and Urban Renewal Association that formed out of the Blyth-Zellerbach committee in 1959. In the 1960s the Golden Gateway development triggered a private construction boom that Manhattanized the San Francisco skyline. The neo-Egyptian obelisk of the Trans-America tower was the most conspicuous among the dozens of buildings that added 10 million square feet of office space for bankers, corporate moguls, and other leaders of a national metropolis. Property owners enjoyed escalating land prices. Local market businesses had more customers. International corporations benefited from the growing concentration of attorneys, accountants, advertising agencies, and other business services.

If the process and products of the redevelopment impulse were the same

The Lovejoy Fountain in Portland. Designed by San Francisco landscape architect Lawrence Halprin, the Lovejoy Fountain marked a new interest in redesigning Western downtowns as centers of public life as well as business. (Courtesy of the Portland Development Commission and C. Bruce Forster)

from one city to the next, so were the costs. City officials sometimes routed new freeways through low-income neighborhoods, enlisting gas tax revenues to clear slums in an effort to sanitize the untidy fringes of Western downtowns. El Paso, for example, used a new expressway between the upper and lower valleys to remove many of the poor residents of South El Paso. Urban renewal projects also displaced minorities and remnants of immigrant communities—Mexicans in Los Angeles, Jews and Italians in Portland, blacks in San Francisco—and tore down old buildings that housed marginal businesses.

In cities like Tucson and Denver, urban renewal also tried to pave over skid road. Because of the nature of the regional economy, Western cities since the late nineteenth century had developed large districts to serve transient workers. Single men could find summer work at lumber camps and farms and on railroad gangs and return to winter over in skid-road districts with cheap hotels, flophouses, missions, bars, brothels, and labor exchanges. As the postwar economy rapidly made such districts obsolete, city officials tried to accelerate their demise. Novelist Louise Erdrich has described Fargo's North Pacific Avenue as "the central thoroughfare of the dingy feel-good roll of Indian bars, Western-wear stores, pawn shops, and Christian Revival Missions that Fargo was trying to eradicate." Singer U. Utah Phillips penned his own "Larimer Street Lament" for Denver's vanishing skid road:

> Your bulldozers rolling through my part of town,
> The iron ball swings and knocks it all down;
> You knocked down my flop-house, you knocked down my bars,
> And you black-topped it over to park all your cars.

> Old Maxie the tailor is closing his doors,
> There ain't nothing left in the second-hand stores;
> You knocked down my pawn shop and the big harbour light
> And the old Chinese Cafe that was open all night.

> And where will I go? And where will I stay?
> When you've knocked down the skid road and hauled it away?
> I'll flag a fast rattler and ride it on down, boys,
> They're running the bums out of town.[10]

At the same time that Denverites were saving two blocks of Larimer Street for a middle-class entertainment district, leaders in San Antonio and Seattle were planning the climax of the business revolution in the form of international expositions in 1962 and 1968. Like San Francisco in 1939–40, Seattle and San Antonio used their fairs to point toward new eras of prosperity. In Seattle, the leftovers from the Century 21 Exposition gave the city the convention center, museums, and theaters needed by every city that aspired to the big leagues. The Space Needle and the monorail that connected the 1962 fair to downtown gave Seattle nationally recognizable symbols. Even Elvis Presley helped to boost the city with a well-forgotten film called *It Happened at the World's Fair*. As Seattle's ticket takers and guides turned in their uniforms, San Antonio was focusing its own urban renewal program on preparing a site for the 1968 HemisFair. The renewal authority acquired 149 acres southeast of the Alamo for $28 million and resold it to the city for $3 million, evicting 1,600 residents and a number of active businesses. In turn, the city financed a theater, an arena, and an exhibition building, and leased the remaining land to HemisFair '68.

The exposition itself was a classic example of civic promotion—an "H-bomb of boosterism" in the words of one skeptic.[11] Support came from across the political spectrum. Businessman James Harris first proposed the fair, and Congressman Henry B. Gonzales picked up and publicized the idea. Liberal Senator Ralph Yarborough signed on to secure the federal participation necessary for designation as an official international exposition, while conservative Governor John Connally helped with state participation. A consortium of twenty-six local banks financed the operating corporation, which secured the loan with pledges from 480 San Antonio businesses. A pledge of $25,000 secured membership on the fair's board of directors (a who's who of Good Government League activists and old families).

HemisFair took as its theme the cultural and commercial ties between the United States and Latin America. Timed to coincide with the Mexico City Olympics, it hoped to impress its visitors with the unique heritage of San Antonio and to mark its arrival as a major modern metropolis. Six million visitors saw exhibits from twenty-four nations, though unfortunately they were housed in generic exhibition space rather than specially designed national pavilions. After the fair closed, the site remained in use as a convention center, federal building, Institute of Texas Cultures, and Tower of the Americas. At 622 feet, the tower just topped the 605-foot Space Needle. Between them, the two towers defined the corners of an American West that looked hopefully toward a second generation of continuing urban growth.

PART 2   GROWTH AND POLITICS IN THE POSTWAR GENERATION

3

FROM REGIONAL CITIES TO NATIONAL CITIES, 1950–1990

A century ago, Seattle and Portland had an equal partnership in the Pacific Northwest. With Portland founded just before the California Gold Rush (in 1843) and Seattle just after (in 1851), both cities grew in parallel as regional trade centers within a commercial and financial system dominated by San Francisco. In the common version of Northwestern history, the Klondike gold strikes of 1897 permanently upset the balance. Boosterism, luck, and previous trading connections made Seattle the entrepôt for the Far North. Portland and other West Coast cities had equal ambitions, but publicist Erastus Brainerd and the Seattle Chamber of Commerce identified Seattle with Alaska in the public mind. Once captured in the flush times, the story goes, Alaskan business stayed in the pocket of Seattle merchants, bankers, and boat builders and pushed the city into a commanding lead over Portland. "In Seattle," according to Murray Morgan, "gold spurred growth, and growth battened on growth."[1]

A closer look, however, shows that for another sixty years after the Klondike excitement the two cities retained more similarities than differences. Portland and Seattle were classic examples of regional cities whose economies were directly linked to the needs and prosperity of their hinterlands. As cities of wholesalers, bankers, and freight agents, they benefited between 1900 and 1930 from the timber industry's shift to the Northwest and from new railroad lines, irrigation projects, ranching, and dry farming in the Columbia Basin. As late as 1950, observers saw them as roughly equal rivals for the trade of the four-state region.

Thirty years later, the picture was strikingly different. Metropolitan Seattle held nearly double the population of Portland. A combination of federal spending and strategic decisions by Seattle's civic leadership had transformed the city into an important node for the long-distance exchange of goods, services, and ideas. Portland was welcome to serve regional functions like wholesaling and the export of agricultural products, Seattle's boosters believed; their own city was ready to join the big leagues of national and international life.

The engine that was obviously driving the new Seattle was Boeing. After the failure of the commercial Stratocruiser in the immediate postwar decade, Boeing survived on federal contracts for B-47s and B-52s until it introduced the immensely successful 707 in 1958. It followed with the 727, the 737, and the 747, which began to roll off the production lines in Everett in 1970 to serve as the flagships of major domestic carriers and national airlines around the world. Aircraft manufacturing jobs in metropolitan Seattle increased steadily from 1949 to 1958. For the next fifteen years, however, three quick boom-and-bust cycles culminated in the deep "Boeing depression" of 1969 to 1971, when the corporation's local employment fell from 105,000 to 38,000. Recovery with renewed air travel, however, again pushed employment in the 1980s to the level of the 1960s.

It took far more than Boeing to make Seattle a major player in national and international activities. Key growth sectors included tourism, higher education, scientific research, finance, and foreign trade. One step was the modernization of the Port of Seattle. A new growth-oriented majority of the port commissioners spent more than $100 million to modernize marine terminals and industrial land as a way to bypass Portland's historic advantage in raw-material exports and to compete directly with Oakland. The Port Commission gambled on long-distance trade, in which containerized cargoes would move through Seattle in transit between Asia and the Atlantic. A consortium of six Japanese shipping lines sealed the city's success in 1970 when they made Seattle their first port of call on the West Coast.

Seattle's second decision was the grand gesture of the Century 21 exposition. The successful fair brought hundreds of thousands of visitors and reams of publicity. In the course of planning for the fair during the later 1950s, its scope grew steadily—from a regional reaffirmation of the Alaska connection to "a means of recapturing prestige as the gateway to the Orient" and finally to the global theme of "the wonders of the 'space age' science and the future of Century 21." A federal appropriation of $9 million brought official recognition by the Bureau of International Expositions in Brussels, which in turn allowed planners to recruit foreign exhibitors and to draw on the best national expertise, ranging from the Walt Disney

The NASA Exhibit at Century 21, the Seattle's World's Fair, in 1962. The theme of the fair was the advancing frontier of science. Visitors stood in long lines at the NASA exhibit, which included John Glenn's space capsule. (Courtesy of the Special Collections Division, University of Washington Libraries; neg. no. 14118)

organization to an advisory board representing the National Science Foundation, the National Academy of Sciences, and the American Association for the Advancement of Science. The fair taught people outside the region that the Northwest's big city started with an *S*.

A third step was to transform the University of Washington from a provincial institution into a leading research university. After bitter internal battles during the McCarthy years of the early 1950s, the university secured a new president and a new agenda in 1958. Enrollment doubled during the 1960s, and University of Washington faculty members claimed a major share of the growing pot of federal research grants. In turn, the university attracted private research firms like Battelle Institute and laid the foundation for biotechnology and computer software companies. By 1977, Seattle stood eighth among all metropolitan areas in federal research and development dollars to universities and sixth in total federal research and development funds.

Seattle's new brainpower businesses recruited their workers from a national pool of talent. In both the 1955–60 and 1965–70 periods (the periods covered by U.S. census data), Seattle drew new residents from outside the Pacific states and the greater Northwest at twice Portland's rate. Newcomers stirred up Seattle's comfortable politics and supported massive spending on parks, pollution cleanup, and civic facilities during the 1960s. By the time Portland felt the same sort of civic energy in the 1970s, Seattle had a dozen-year lead in the race to evolve into a networked city, a race that has implications far beyond the Pacific Northwest. Historians and geographers have sometimes distinguished between "regional cities" and "network cities." Regional cities develop in step with their adjacent hinterlands, serving as economic and cultural centers for relatively limited contiguous regions. Network cities like medieval Venice and contemporary Singapore depend on long-distance trade, acting as gateways and links between national and world regions. In our comparison, Portland remained a regional or Northwest city, while Seattle evolved into a national city and a Pacific city.

By the 1970s, Seattle's networked economy was becoming the rule rather than the exception among Western cities. Geographer Allan Pred has compiled detailed data on the number and location of jobs controlled from selected Western cities. In 1974–75, for example, the small city of Boise held the home offices of a dozen large businesses, each of which had payrolls of at least 400 employees and operated in multiple locations.[2] The twelve companies controlled only 5,600 jobs in the Boise area but 57,400 in 102 other cities and towns in the United States and Canada and 14,300 in other countries. Phoenix's twenty-four large multilocational companies controlled more than a thousand jobs in seventeen different metropolitan areas from Boston and Allentown to Miami and Memphis.

As cities throughout the West reached for national and network functions between 1950 and 1990, they pulled the region into increasingly elaborate relations with the wider world. Networked cities have as much contact with each other as with their regional hinterlands, exchanging services, ideas, and—ultimately—decisions. Fourth-wave industries such as aerospace and information technology responded to national and international markets and drew their key engineering inputs from the national labor market. Industrial engineers and researchers responded to scientific breakthroughs from around the globe. Oil business executives in the age of telex and fax could deal with Edmonton and Aberdeen as quickly as with Long Beach or the Permian Basin of western Texas. The remainder of this chapter examines the expansion of national roles and functions for Western cities. The following chapter explores their deepening engagement with world networks and markets.

The most powerful force in nationalizing the cities of the American West was the federal defense budget. By definition, maintaining military bases and producing munitions are national functions. They may utilize local resources such as open space, cloudless skies, and ice-free harbors, but they respond to decisions by the president and Congress and they are intended to serve the general interests of the nation. Military personnel transfer back and forth among overseas bases and the various regions of the United States. Defense contractors know that the fate of their balance sheet is in the hands of Pentagon procurement officers.

Although the American defense budget dropped precipitously in 1946, 1947, and 1948 as the nation stood down from the wartime mobilization, spending edged up in 1949 with the onset of the cold war in Europe and surged after North Korea's invasion of South Korea in June 1950 and Chinese entry into the war in December. The national commitment to a dual policy of advanced and strategic defense held spending near or above 10 percent of the gross national product through the 1950s, and an increasing share of this defense budget went to the Western states. The three leading states of California, Texas, and Washington received 14 percent of prime contracts during World War II, 20 percent during the Korean War, and more than 33 percent by the end of the 1950s.

In particular, the United States, as a nation committed to the indefinite projection of power into the Pacific Basin and to continental defense through nuclear deterrence, depended on the development of nuclear weapons and their potential delivery by strategic bombers. Spending on the Air Force claimed nearly half the total budget of the Department of Defense by 1956 and 1957. The Korean mobilization found nearly three quarters of the airframe industry concentrated in half a dozen Western cities. Manufacturers used engines built in Hartford, Indianapolis, and New York, but the planes were designed, assembled, and tested in Dallas, Fort Worth, Wichita, Seattle, Los Angeles, and San Diego. The addition of ballistic missiles to the American arsenal in the later 1950s brought new facilities, like Thiokol's solid-fuel plant outside Salt Lake City and Martin Marietta's factory for Titan missiles in the Denver suburb of Littleton.

The growth of Los Angeles showed the ramifications of expanding defense production. The aircraft industry grew from 100,000 jobs in 1950 to 275,000 in 1955 and 350,000 by 1967, with another 150,000 in adjacent counties. In the early 1960s the *Los Angeles Times* estimated that a third of the area's jobs depended directly or indirectly on military spending. A similar study by the Bank of America found 12,000 firms linked to the aerospace giants, whose purchases accounted for 83 percent of the employment in electrical machinery manufacturing in the metropolis, 69 percent in photo equipment manufacturing, and even 12 percent in the production of cardboard containers. Lockheed's huge Burbank plant drew the parents of thousands of Valley girls to the subdivisions of the San Fernando Valley. Divisions of Northrop and Hughes Aircraft relocated from Los Angeles County to Orange County, helping to trigger a 230 percent increase in Orange County jobs during the decade.

The demand for thousands of warheads also urbanized the nuclear weapons industry. Isolated new towns like Los Alamos and Oak Ridge had met the research and engineering needs of the Manhattan Project, but the 1950s turned nuclear weapons into a big business. Under the contract management of Western Electric, the Sandia National Laboratory at Albuquerque took on the responsibility for the production engineering of nuclear bombs. It grew into the largest employer in its metropolitan area, with 5,800 workers by 1955. The Hanford Reservation continued to produce plutonium, and the Rocky Flats facility on the outskirts of Denver turned the plutonium into triggers for thermonuclear bombs. The new city of Richland and the older towns of Pasco and Kennewick grew together into a new metropolitan area, recognized officially by the Department of Commerce after the 1970 census.

Las Vegas became a fourth nuclear city with the opening of the Nevada Test Site on a bombing range sixty-five miles north of the city in 1951. The site offered plenty of space and a supportive city that already benefited from the tactical air combat training programs at Nellis Air Force Base. A year-round labor force of a thousand AEC workers played host to thousands of scientists, engineers, and military men during each series of test shots. Originally managed by the Atomic Energy Commission's Albuquerque office, the Nevada Test Site became a separately managed program in 1962. Test devices came from the Los Alamos, Sandia, and Lawrence Livermore national laboratories.

The Nevada Test Site had an immediate impact on Las Vegas. New subdivisions stretched northwest along the Tonopah highway to serve the test site's daily commuters. The Chamber of Commerce provided up-to-date schedules of test shots and gave out road maps that marked the best vantage points. Casinos and bars offered atomic cocktails (vodka, brandy, champagne, and sherry), Miss Atomic Bomb contests, and atomic hairdos molded around wire forms. The 1953 yearbook of Las Vegas High School, the Southern Nevada Telephone Directory for 1955 and 1956, and the official Clark County seal all featured mushroom clouds. By the time the Limited Test Ban Treaty of 1963 moved all testing underground, Las Vegas promoters had responded to public fears and had begun to downplay the city's atomic imagery. In the mid-1980s, however, the test site accounted for more than 7,000 direct jobs and 11,000 support jobs, or 9 percent of the work force in southern Nevada.

Supply depots, training bases, navy shipyards, and aircraft maintenance bases constituted the second leg of the Western military system. Admirals presided over naval commands headquartered at Seattle, San Francisco, San Diego, and Honolulu. Each city lay in the midst of a cluster of operating bases, shipyards, and air stations. Army and Air Force training facilities were especially prominent in Washington, Colorado, Texas, and Oklahoma. Employment at the six supply and repair installations in the Salt Lake City–Ogden area grew from 10,000 after World War II to more than 20,000 from the later 1950s into the early 1980s. The entire metropolitan areas of Vallejo and Bremerton revolved around navy facilities, and Killeen and Lawton around army bases.

Distinct from the operating and support bases were new activities built around the military's essential "Cs": command, control, and communication. The strategic offensive and defensive forces that formed the centerpiece of the cold war strategy were commanded from the national heartland of the Great Plains. The NORAD command post sunk deep beneath Cheyenne Mountain behind Colorado Springs coordinated North American air defense. General Curtis LeMay directed the B-47s and B-52s of the Strategic Air Command from Offutt Air Force Base outside Omaha. By the 1970s, solid-fueled Minuteman missiles were targeting Moscow and Beijing from unobtrusive silos spread across the rolling plains of the Dakotas and Montana. Malmstrom Air Force Base remade Great Falls from a trading and manufacturing town to the coordinating center for an ICBM complex scattered over a territory as large as Maryland.[3]

NORAD and SAC alike depended on the Distant Early Warning Line of radar stations across northern Alaska and Canada, which became operational in 1957. Construction of the DEW line, backup radar sites, and supporting bases added thousands of new residents to Fairbanks and Anchorage. Federal spending in the Anchorage-Valdez-Fairbanks triangle in central Alaska upgraded ports, highways, railroads, and airports. In Alaska's

1950 census, there was one uniformed member of the armed services for every 4.3 civilians. The Fairbanks construction boom peaked in 1951 and 1952, with $200 million in contracts and payrolls pouring into the city each year. As late as 1980, with the North Slope oil boom at full tilt, more than 20 percent of the payroll checks in Anchorage and Fairbanks came straight from the U.S. Treasury. By any reasonable economic multiplier, half of the cities' residents depended on the federal government for their livelihood.

The cumulative effect of cold war spending on the growth of the West can be gauged both in general and in detail. A city like San Diego summed up the urban impact of the armed peace. By one estimate, the navy alone was responsible for supporting 215,000 people in the San Diego area in 1957. Aircraft manufacturing supported tens of thousands more. Most residents had good reason to believe that what was good for Convair was good for the metropolis. Retired naval officers were an inescapable presence in clubs, yacht basins, and professional jobs. Off-duty sailors supported a classic downtown sleaze district of bars, tattoo parlors, and sex businesses. When cruising the harbor, as historian Roger Lotchin has pointed out, one would pass a submarine base, a carrier anchorage, dry docks, shipbuilding firms, ammunition bunkers, and barracks ships. The military was a constant presence in social life and civic activities. Scores of community organizations depended on military surplus goods to support their programs.[4]

Although aggregate data for the 1950s are most readily available at the state level, the numbers are a good proxy for the metropolitan impact because neither large contractors nor large bases could function without city workers and support services. The dark blue Air Force vans that carry shift change crews from Great Falls to the missile sites are simply one very visible example that could be multiplied by thousands. Examining federal defense spending by states for 1952 to 1962, Roger Bolton found that military procurement purchases and Defense Department payrolls accounted for at least 25 percent of income from out-of-state sources in Washington, California, Hawaii, Alaska, Utah, and Colorado. Another half dozen states—Nevada, Arizona, New Mexico, Kansas, Oklahoma, and Texas—depended on defense for 15 to 24 percent of outside income. A slightly different measurement of defense spending as a stimulus to growth during the 1950s would add Montana, South Dakota, and Wyoming.

Since the 1960s the Western share of national defense spending has been relatively stable. Its influence, however, has diffused even more extensively into the economic base of the region's cities. Two more surges of military spending extended the reach of the defense business into the growth industries of electronics, engineering research and development, and education. After dropping in relative importance from 1961 to 1965, defense spending grew from 7.6 percent of GNP to 9.7 percent from 1965 to 1969 as the United States supported a massive war in Vietnam. A gradual scaling down of the defense budget was again reversed with the so-called "Star Wars" buildup of the Reagan administration. From 1980 to 1987, military spending grew at more than four times the rate of other federal programs.

Civilian Department of Defense employment in 1980 topped 30,000 in greater San Francisco and Los Angeles; 20,000 in San Antonio, San Diego, and Salt Lake City; and 15,000 in Oklahoma City, Sacramento, and Honolulu. Half of the metropolitan areas in the West were net gainers from the defense budget during the Reagan administration, receiving more from federal defense spending than they paid in tax contributions for defense. The comparable proportion for the rest of the United States was 30 percent. San Diego, Dallas, San Jose, and San Antonio were the capitals of Pentagonia, each gaining at least $2 billion more in defense spending than they paid in taxes for defense in fiscal 1983. The biggest gainers on a per capita basis included Colorado Springs (with Fort Carson and the Air Force Academy), Killeen-Temple, Texas (with Fort Hood), and Santa Barbara (with Vandenberg Air Force Base).

The bursts of spending in the 1960s and 1980s reinforced the connection between defense and the West's new educational and information industries. A comprehensive definition of "high tech" industries, based on a high ratio of research and development to net sales, would include aircraft, guided missiles and space vehicles, computing machines, communication equipment, electronic components, and drugs. The federal government has been a primary customer for all but the last category. During the 1970s, Arizona, California, Washington, Kansas, Utah, and Colorado ranked among the top ten states for high-tech jobs as a proportion of total employment. All six states also made the list of defense-dependent states in the 1950s.

If San Diego exemplified the city as a direct military colony, California's Santa Clara County provided the setting for the creation of a more complex defense-science-industry alliance centered around electronics and aerospace. The central figure was Frederick Terman, dean of engineering and later provost of Stanford University. Having spent World War II working on radar systems in Cambridge, Massachusetts, Terman returned to Stanford determined to build university-industry alliances in basic research. His goals fit well with those of the Stanford administration, cash-poor but land-rich and determined to move its regional institution into the educational elite.

The university had already established the Stanford Research Institute in 1946 to promote the economic development of the West Coast. In 1951 it followed Terman's advice and established Stanford Industrial Park on surplus Stanford lands to generate cash and to provide sites for research-oriented industries that could benefit from ties to the university.

Stanford Industrial Park began to fulfill its promise in the mid-1950s, attracting a new company started by two of Terman's students, William Hewlett and David Packard, as well as research and development facilities for Xerox and Lockheed. ITT, IBM, Sylvania, Admiral, and similar companies established research facilities elsewhere in the county. The other key event was William Shockley's 1955 move from Bell Labs in New Jersey to Palo Alto to develop commercial applications of the transistor, which he had invented with John Bardeen and Walter Brattain. Within a year, a group of his own employees had moved to establish Fairchild Semiconductor in Mountain View, the county's first major semiconductor company. Easy access to San Francisco's venture-capital market facilitated electronics start-ups. Fairchild itself would spin off fifty other firms by 1979. The shared market for electronics companies in the Bay Area during this first decade was the rapidly evolving market for guided missile systems, which were remaking the American strategic and tactical arsenals.

Silicon Valley, incubated in Stanford Industrial Park and nearby research labs during the 1950s, took off as an industrial complex in the middle 1960s as civilian applications supplemented military markets. The farmlands of northern Santa Clara County were easily transformed into a "silicon landscape" of neat one-story factories, tastefully screened parking lots, and carefully tended research campuses. Silicon Valley itself cut a ten-by-thirty-mile swathe through Santa Clara County from Palo Alto to Mountain View, Sunnyvale, Santa Clara, and Cupertino. In 1950, Santa Clara County had 800 manufacturing workers, mostly in food processing. In 1980, it had roughly 3,000 electronics firms, 264,000 manufacturing workers, and annual sales of $40 billion. Executives and engineers found their expensive housing in the northerly towns and in the foothills of the Santa Cruz Mountains. Skilled workers with Filipino, Vietnamese, and Mexican backgrounds found more affordable housing in the level subdivisions of San Jose.

Colorado Springs is an example of the silicon clones whose economies have benefited from the effects of the electronics "product cycle." Firms in new and innovative industries—such as automobiles early in the century and electronics in the 1950s and 1960s—tend to cluster in a limited number of centers where competitors can benefit from common pools of technical

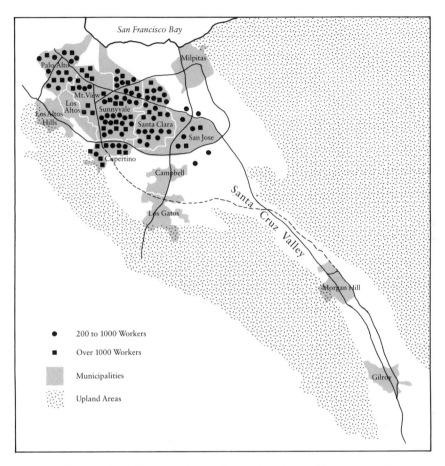

Silicon Valley. By the mid-1980s the small stretch of Santa Clara County from Palo Alto to San Jose counted more than a hundred large electronics firms. (Based on map in Everett Rogers, *The High Technology of Silicon Valley* [College Park, Md.: University of Maryland, Institute for Urban Studies, 1985], 26; courtesy of the Department of Urban Studies and Planning, University of Maryland at College Park)

expertise, market intelligence, and skilled labor. As a product moves from idea and innovation to mass production, increasingly standardized factories can be sited on the basis of labor costs and amenities rather than immediate access to research labs and headquarters staff. Hewlett-Packard and Ampex thus opened plants in Colorado Springs in the late 1960s. By the mid-1980s, the factories of the "Silicon Mountain" were divided roughly equally among the production of semiconductors, aerospace systems, and communications equipment. Several firms in the 1980s added microelectronics research and engineering design to routine production, becoming what geographer Amy Glasmeier identifies as "technical branch plants" that are responsible for continued research and development of a specific product line as well as for manufacturing and sales.

Similar spinoffs created the Silicon Prairie and Silicon Desert of the Southwest. Austin had tried something like the Stanford Industrial Park when it converted a World War II magnesium plant into the university-owned Balcones Research Center for defense work. The city's eighteen-year search for a new manufacturing base paid off in 1966 when IBM became its first large electronics corporation. The next fifteen years added production facilities for Advanced Micro Devices, Intel, Motorola, and other companies. In turn, the availability of trained technical workers and the engineering faculty of the University of Texas helped Austin in 1983 beat out San Diego, Atlanta, and Raleigh-Durham as the headquarters city for the Microelectronics and Computer Technology Corporation, a research and development consortium of twelve high-tech firms.

Phoenix has continued to benefit from Motorola's 1948 decision to open a facility specializing in defense electronics midway between the bomb builders of New Mexico and the aircraft companies of southern California. Motorola paved the way in the 1950s for Sperry Rand, General Electric, AirResearch, and Kaiser Aircraft and Electronics. The 1970s brought production facilities for Honeywell, IBM, DEC, Intel, and National Semiconductor. Dallas and Portland followed a slightly different model in which the homegrown instrumentation firms of Texas Instruments and Tektronix spun off smaller startup companies in the 1970s and attracted Silicon Valley giants, software companies, and U.S. branches of foreign firms to make use of the area's technically sophisticated labor force.

The "space" component of the aerospace industry was more concentrated than electronics, with its main impact coming from the Manned Spacecraft Center in Houston, the Jet Propulsion Laboratory in Pasadena, and the Ames Research Laboratory in Palo Alto. Houston turned itself into "Space City, U.S.A." with another business-university alliance. When NASA began to plan its new flight center, the strategic positions of Congressman Albert Thomas on the proper House appropriations subcommittee and Vice President Lyndon Johnson as chair of the National Space Committee assured that Houston would make the list of seriously considered sites. Morgan J. Davis (president of Humble Oil and Refining) and George R. Brown (leader of the 8F crowd, a principal in the huge Brown and Root construction firm, and chairman of the Rice University board of trustees) worked out the deal. Humble gave Rice 1,000 acres in the middle of a vast 30,000 acre tract of Humble property outside Houston. In turn, Rice donated the tract to NASA for its $60 million Clear Lake facility. Brown and Root got a design contract, Humble received a windfall boost in the value of its empty acreage, and Rice University emerged as a leader in aerospace engineering. Houston gained the prestige that went with the Manned Spacecraft Center, 5,000 new jobs at the height of the Apollo program, and scores of new companies and branch offices to work with NASA.

Western electronics and aerospace industries also built close alliances with other urban universities during the 1960s and 1970s. In one emblematic case, the huge defense contractor General Dynamics was a major force behind the creation of the University of California, San Diego, lobbying state officials and providing a founding donation to promote a high-tech research institution that obviously served the needs of the company. The UCLA engineering school was created in 1943 specifically to support the aircraft industry. The University of California, Cal Tech, and the University of New Mexico have also played special roles in nuclear and defense contracting. Between 1965 and 1977, San Diego, Seattle, and Houston joined San Francisco and Los Angeles as metro areas whose universities received the greatest amounts of federal research and development funds, followed by Austin, Albuquerque, Denver, and Salt Lake City.

The research and development establishment included directly operated federal labs; federally owned facilities operated by private or university contractors; on-campus labs run with federal and industry grants; and private corporations, which were paid first to design new weapons and then to produce them. In the Denver area, for example, the federal government operated the National Center for Atmospheric Research and a National Bureau of Standards lab in Boulder, and the Solar Energy Research Institute in Golden. Beginning in 1953, a series of corporate contractors ran Rocky Flats just outside Denver with scant regard for safety or environmental damage from fugitive plutonium and tritium. Universities in Denver, Boulder, Fort Collins, and Greeley competed for federal grants. High-tech companies that were enticed by life near the Front Range included IBM, Hewlett-Packard, Sundstrand, Ball Brothers Research, and Beech Aircraft. The new industries and labs accelerated the dispersal of the metropolis, shunning Denver's old industrial core along the South Platte River for suburbs like Littleton and Golden, satellite communities like Boulder, Longmont, and Loveland, and nearby cities like Fort Collins.

NASA's Lyndon B. Johnson Space Center in Houston. Located twenty-five miles southeast of Houston, the Johnson Space Center symbolizes both the political clout and the emerging high-tech economy of Southwestern cities. (Courtesy of the National Aeronautics and Space Administration; S-78-36570)

By the early 1960s, Western corporations, universities, and think tanks were receiving half of all federal research and development funds. Los Angeles was far and away the leading metropolitan area in this respect in 1977, with more than twice the contracts of number two, Washington, and number three, San Francisco. Other standard metropolitan statistical areas in the top twenty were Seattle, Albuquerque, San Diego, Dallas, Salt Lake City, and the nuclear metropolis of Richland-Pasco-Kennewick. The pattern persisted in the next decade, when 60 percent of Star Wars contracts for 1983 to 1986 went to California and New Mexico, and another 10 percent went to Texas, Washington, and Colorado.

The massively expanding participation of Western cities in the national defense and scientific research systems was supplemented by other activities that used Western locations to serve national markets. In particular, the 1950s and 1960s saw Westerners create entire urban landscapes of leisure—specialized communities to serve needs that had previously been filled within the comprehensive metropolis.

Demographic data confirm the popular notion of a retirement migration to the Southwest, especially from the Middle West. The easily tracked subgroup of military retirees make up at least 1 percent of the total population of Washington, Hawaii, Nevada, Colorado, Arizona, and New Mexico. The majority have clustered in military base cities like Denver, San Diego, Honolulu, San Antonio, and Phoenix, which offer familiar surroundings and access to clubs, medical facilities, and old friends. More generally, California, Texas, and Arizona were the destinations of winter migrants and permanent retirees. Between 1940 and 1950 the migration of active workers to wartime and postwar jobs obscured the demographic impact of workers reaching retirement age. For the period 1955–60, however, California ranked second only to Florida in the number of immigrants from other states aged 60 or over. Texas and Arizona joined it in the top five states in 1965–70 and 1975–80. During the 1960s and 1970s, metropolitan Phoenix and Tucson saw their proportion of residents aged 65 or older grow at nearly twice the national rate. Albuquerque and San Diego also exceeded the national increase.

Phoenix and Los Angeles developers created age-segregated new towns in the 1960s. "Retirement new towns" like Leisure World and Sun City were fully specialized environments for people aged fifty or older. They were possible because of the presence of open space for development and the absence of close community ties among many older migrants. The pioneer was the Del E. Webb Company of Phoenix, a large construction and

The Monorail and the Space Needle at the Seattle world's fair. Built for the 1962 world's fair, Seattle's Space Needle observation tower and monorail symbolized Western cities as frontiers of the science-based economy. Like the Alamo and the Golden Gate Bridge, they became trademarks for a city. (Courtesy of the Special Collections Division, University of Washington Libraries; neg. no. 4904)

real estate development firm that opened Sun City Center outside Tampa and Sun City outside Phoenix in 1960. It was the Phoenix community that caught the national imagination, even though it was a real estate development first and a social experiment second. It was soon followed by Ross Cortese's Leisure World communities in Seal Beach, Laguna Hills, and Walnut Creek in California, confirming the Southwest as the home of complete retirement cities. In 1960 no Arizonans and only 70,000 Californians lived in towns with senior populations of 21 percent or more. Twenty years later, the numbers were 460,000 Californians (in fifty-eight separate communities) and 117,000 Arizonans (in fifteen communities).

Built on the site of a cotton ranch twelve miles northwest of downtown Phoenix, Sun City was firmly embedded in the growing metropolitan area as a source of shopping, entertainment, and medical services. Its target market consisted of older migrants to Phoenix who were settling primarily in conventional neighborhoods or in trailer parks and apartments set aside for the elderly. As John Findlay has noted, Sun City was a subtly controlled environment. Its physical characteristics and relentless national advertising for it helped to define retirement as a distinct stage of life, offering "an unending treasure of perfect days, filled with interesting activities." Like other successful promoters of supersubdivisions, Webb put in its golf courses and shopping centers before he began to build and sell houses, assuring that the community projected the image of active recreation. There were 7,500 Sun Citizens by 1963 and 38,000 by 1990. The attractions were presumably the same as those for Laguna Hills Leisure Worlders—golf, clean air, low-maintenance housing, and an escape from urban minorities. As Sun City built more and more expensive housing after the late 1960s, it also began to acquire not only a range of income groups but also its own spread of generations from early retirees in their fifties to the "old elderly" in their eighties. The result was a true innovation. As Frances FitzGerald has commented, "the Sun Cities and Leisure Worlds are without precedent; no society recorded in history has ever had whole villages—whole cities—composed of elderly people . . . deliberate creations—places where retired people have gone by choice to live with each other."[5]

Where Sun City was a landscape of leisure, Las Vegas consciously created a specialized environment for high-intensity entertainment. The city had prospered in the 1930s by serving the licit and illicit demands of workers at Boulder Dam, and then of the tourists who began to add the dam to their the must-see list of Western sights. The election of reformer Fletcher Bowron as mayor of Los Angeles in 1938 pushed California entrepreneurs of vice to Las Vegas in time to capitalize on the war boom. New investment in the 1940s upgraded many of the small downtown clubs and built the first resorts on the Strip south of town. Through World War II and immediately after, however, the entertainment theme was the Wild West. The Frontier, Pioneer, Boulder, and El Cortez clubs competed in the neon gulch of Fremont Street. The first hotels on the Strip were the El Rancho and the Last Frontier, decorated with wagon wheels and cattle horns.

The big change in the Las Vegas ambiance came with Bugsy Siegel's Flamingo Hotel, whose opening in 1947 was intended to put Las Vegas in the same league with Miami and Havana. As Eugene Moehring has noted, the Flamingo "combined the sophisticated ambiance of a Monte Carlo casino with the exotic luxury of a Miami Beach–Caribbean resort. The Flamingo liberated Las Vegas from the confines of its Western heritage and established the pattern for a 'diversity of images' embodied in future resorts like the Desert Inn, Thunderbird, Dunes, Tropicana, and Stardust."[6] By the 1960s Las Vegas was trying to define itself as a universal and generic resort rather than simply a Western gambling den.

Business in the hotels and casinos reflected the changing image. Growth slowed in the later 1950s as the market for weekenders from southern California was tapped out, but it took off again after 1960 with a growing national convention business and easy air access. The city government helped by pouring funds into a new convention center and oversized airport. By the 1970s, Las Vegas was attracting nearly 3 percent of the total convention attendance in the United States. This proportion was more than Washington and Miami attracted and was comparable to the much larger cities of Houston and Denver. Direct employment in hotels, motels, and resorts more than doubled from 1958 to 1967 and doubled again to 47,000 workers by 1980. The businesses of entertainment, lodging, eating, and drinking accounted for 35 percent of the entire Las Vegas work force.

Las Vegas as the special creation of the federal government and cheap air fares can be contrasted with Reno, where tourism and gambling have been longer established but slower growing. Reno was originally a regional city created by railroads, mines, and ranches—the city that Las Vegas had hoped to become between 1905 and 1930. Despite its special divorce industry and gambling clubs, Walter Van Tilburg Clark could describe Reno after World War II as a "state city," small for the United States but big for Nevada, "communally bound into the state interests."[7] Its downtown casinos are interspersed among run-of-the-mill office buildings. Its suburban gambling hotels tower above the low-rise rail yards, trucking companies, warehouses, and light industrial parks of a regional city.

Another city to mix and match some of the Las Vegas elements has been

Honolulu. If Las Vegas uneasily married the Air Force and AEC communities to its casino strip, Honolulu merged three cities—the Navy city
around Pearl Harbor, the tourist city along Waikiki, and the regional trade
and finance center in between. Statewide, income from the defense industry
surpassed income from sugar and pineapples in the 1950s. Tourism, in turn,
passed defense in the early 1970s as jet travel dropped the real costs of quick
vacations from California. Much of Honolulu's tourist business at the end of
the 1960s had come from military personnel on R & R and their visiting
families. The clientele grew increasingly international in the seventies,
when the inventory of hotel rooms in Honolulu passed 30,000. Nevertheless, Honolulu's 58,000 military personnel and 19,000 civilian defense
workers in 1980 totaled twice the direct employment in tourism.

The rapid growth of the metropolitan-military complex, the research industry, and nationally marketed retirement communities and leisure complexes
supported broader expansion within each metropolitan economy. Booming
cities required a greater volume and variety of goods, services, and management skills to meet the needs of growing populations and business markets.
At the same time, the growing variety of industrial suppliers, business
services, and transportation options reduced costs in previously isolated
Western cities. The expanding social infrastructure of universities and urban
services in the larger cities also supported economic concentration, allowing
local firms to produce goods previously hauled in by locomotive or trailer
truck.
    The process was apparent in the first decade after the war. Cities such as
Denver and Salt Lake City attracted smaller manufacturing operations to
serve local markets, while accessibility to the entire West brought a number
of larger firms. The Pacific, mountain, and Southwestern states all received a
disproportionate share of new manufacturing investment compared to prewar factory capacity, with particularly large increases in Texas and Oklahoma. The number of new or expanded manufacturing plants in Los Angeles was 50 percent higher for 1945–48 than for the war years of 1942–44,
and southern California absorbed an eighth of all new investment in U.S.
manufacturing in the immediate postwar years. By the 1950s, Los Angeles
was second only to Akron in the production of tires and second only to
Detroit in the number of auto assembly plants. The role of Western cities as
distribution centers also grew with the size of regional markets, the increasing variety of local products, and the rise of new high-tech industries.
Dallas, Houston, Phoenix, and Portland showed particularly rapid growth
in wholesaling between 1948 and 1977. Denver, Tulsa, Oklahoma City,

Omaha, and Salt Lake City wholesaling also grew faster than their metropolitan populations.

Managers began to follow mass production to the urban West in the 1960s. Despite the huge quantities of war supplies produced in the West, only twelve of the one hundred largest wartime defense contractors had been headquartered west of the Mississippi. In the first years after the war, much of the Western economic base continued to develop as a regional market within a national economy directed from the Northeast, with branch factories of companies like U.S. Steel, General Motors, and Goodyear. Duncan Aikman's description of El Paso in 1949 was apt for many other Western cities as well. Citing companies like Phelps Dodge, Standard Oil, and American Smelting and Refining, he commented that "El Paso *is* metropolis for its never-quite-surveyed hundreds of thousands of square miles of more or less relative emptiness. But at the same time it is not 'big metropolis.' . . . It is chiefly a convenient operational stage through which bigger interests back East, or wherever they are, function regionally."[8]

Between 1955 and 1975, however, the United States experienced significant shifts in its industrial mix and in the preferred location for corporate headquarters. By the 1970s the ranks of corporate giants headquartered in Western cities included not only homegrown technology and resource companies like Boeing, Boise Cascade, and Morrison Knudsen but also companies that explicitly relocated to the western Sunbelt—Greyhound from Chicago to Phoenix, Cities Service from New York to Tulsa, Johns-Manville from New York to Denver, and GTE from Stamford, Connecticut, to Dallas. Overall, the proportions of total assets of the 500 largest industrial corporations that were controlled from major Western cities increased in fifteen cases and decreased in only two. The biggest increments were in the oil cities of Tulsa and Houston, but increases were spread from Wichita to San Antonio to Seattle.

Modern corporate management is a fully networked activity. The essential job of large business executives is to make important decisions on the basis of limited information. The more comprehensive the flow of data and analysis, the greater the edge a particular firm will have. Much of the internal staffing of a large corporation is designed to assemble and funnel information to decision makers. In addition, large corporate centers offer a full range of "producer services" and "consulting professions" from law to engineering and architecture. Abundant business services encourage and support new and smaller firms, as with the explosive growth of Silicon Valley. In turn, professional services can become an important "export" business for a metropolitan economy.

From a world perspective, the cumulative result of the growth of such network activities has been the emergence of an information-based or "transactional" economy. The information economy had its origins back in the organizational revolution of the late nineteenth and early twentieth centuries. The growth of big business and big government coincided with the cumulative effects of the telegraph, telephone, the railroad, and the typewriter, which allowed the physical separation of control and production. The size of organizations and the specialization of information-consuming activities have continued to increase with electronic data storage and communication. "Transactional cities" are the sorting points in information flows. As junction points in economic networks, they concentrate the political and economic decision-makers and the occupations and industries that center on the generation, processing, distribution, and recombination of information.

The relative commitment of specific U.S. cities to transactional functions can be judged with an additive point system that measures white-collar employment (0 to 3 points); employment in finance, insurance, real estate, and corporate administration (0 to 2 points); proportion of all major corporate headquarters (0 to 2 points); and role as a federal administrative center (0 to 2 points). With this system we can assign point totals for each factor at the beginning of the 1960s and measure change through the 1980s. Cities gain points by having percentage employment increases greater than the average for all U.S. metropolitan areas, by gaining an increased share of all major corporate headquarters, and by substantial absolute increases in federal roles.

The results are shown in table 5. In 1960, San Francisco was the most important transactional center in the West, followed by Dallas, Los Angeles, and a set of regional centers such as Seattle, Denver, Salt Lake City, San Diego, Sacramento, and Oklahoma City. Dallas, Los Angeles, Phoenix, and Houston made the biggest gains over the next two decades. Although San Francisco maintained its lead, it was seriously challenged by Los Angeles and Dallas. Los Angeles has increased its share of corporate headquarters by two-thirds since 1960 and has passed the traditional headquarters city of San Francisco. Eleven of the twelve largest U.S. banks with main offices outside California now have their primary branch office in Los Angeles. Dallas has built on its underlying function as a regional city by offering first-rate air connections and a prime location for regional offices and subsidiaries of national and international companies. By the 1980s it ranked fourth among U.S. cities in the number of companies traded on the American and New York stock exchanges.

Table 5. Importance of the Information Sector in Western Metropolitan
Areas Since 1960

	Point Total	
	1960s	1980s
San Francisco	8	10
Dallas	6	9
Los Angeles	5	8
Seattle	4	6
Denver	4	6
Salt Lake City	4	4
San Diego	3	4
Sacramento	3	4
Oklahoma City	3	4
Phoenix	2	5
Houston	2	5
Honolulu	2	4
Portland	2	3
San Antonio	2	2

SOURCE Adapted from Carl Abbott, "Through flight to Tokyo: Sunbelt Cities in the New World Economy, 1960–1990," in *Urban Policy in Twentieth-Century America,* ed. Arnold R. Hirsch and Raymond A. Mohl (New Brunswick, N.J.: Rutgers University Press, 1993), 183–212.

The regional urban system that had emerged by the 1980s was dominated by a dozen major metropolitan areas, which fell neatly into three sets. The big four were greater Los Angeles, the San Francisco Bay area, Houston-Galveston, and Dallas–Fort Worth, with metro populations in 1990 ranging from 3.7 million to 14.5 million. The "second four" of Seattle-Tacoma, San Diego, Phoenix, and Denver counted between 1.8 million and 2.6 million people. The "third four" of Portland, Sacramento, San Antonio, and Salt Lake City all ranged between 1 and 1.5 million.

The system displayed remarkable stability over the forty years. The top five metro areas in 1990 had also been the top five in 1950. The top twelve had been in the top fifteen, with Sacramento and Salt Lake City nudging ahead of Omaha, Honolulu, and Oklahoma City. Measures of "urban primacy"—the degree to which a region's urban population is concentrated in its largest city—showed absolutely no change over the four decades. The commonly used Ginsburg Index (the population of the largest city divided by the total population of the four largest) remained at 0.51, indicative of a fully developed urban system.

The network connections of cities like San Francisco, Dallas, and Seattle are obvious to any visitor downtown. The "third four" of Portland, Salt Lake City, Sacramento, and San Antonio, in contrast, have each operated in the shadow of a larger city that has tended to arrogate network and control functions. Local businesses and economic development officials have had to struggle to find their own direct entry into the networked economy. Salt Lake City has emphasized scientific research and development and the creation of a Biotech Valley at the base of the Wasatch Mountains. This context helps to explain the eagerness of the university and the state to believe the best about cold fusion when its achievement was announced at the University of Utah in 1989. Portland has labored to keep up with larger West Coast cities as a world port and contact point with the industrial nations of the Pacific Rim. San Antonio has proposed to promote itself as a center for biotechnology, tourism, business telecommunications, and Latin American finance. In addition to its role as the capital and administrative center for the nation's most populous state, Sacramento has benefited from the inflation of land and living costs and growing commuting times in the Bay Area. As the subdivision frontier crossed the Mount Diablo range from the East Bay in the 1980s, Sacramento began to look like a reasonable alternative to the coastal cities for national and international firms looking for a California location, and even for Silicon Valley companies that wanted to cut costs.

The spread of major-league sports since 1950 has reflected the progress of networked urbanization. Major-league teams operate by definition within a national system of associated clubs. The teams may depend on local fans and local broadcast revenue, but they judge success against highly pub-licized networks that are national or even international in scope. They also allow their boosters to make the cherished claim of being a "big league" city.

The first Western franchises in the major leagues of football, baseball, and basketball were the Los Angeles Rams and the San Francisco 49ers of the National Football League. The Rams moved from Cleveland in 1950, the same year that the Forty-Niners entered the NFL after four years in the upstart All-American Football Conference. Baseball followed eight years later, when the Dodgers and Giants left New York City for Los Angeles and San Francisco, and expanding leagues have given Western cities more and more teams since then. The region's four largest metropolitan complexes are complete major-league cities, with NFL, NBA, and major-league baseball franchises. The second four have struggled to acquire or hold all three sports—Phoenix gains a football team; San Diego loses the NBA; Denver joins the big four by gaining an expansion franchise in the National League; Seattle simultaneously worries about dropping out of the top rank by losing its American League team for the second time. The third quartet, in contrast, were solely NBA cities through the 1980s.

A less colorful but more comprehensive way to identify the location of high technology industries, related research activities, and big business managers is the concentration of brainpower. A good indicator of a networked city is one in which more than 20 percent of the residents aged 25 or over had finished at least four years of college. Washington, D.C.—the home of the high-priced lawyer and lobbyist—ranked first in 1980 with 32 percent, but next in line were Austin (28 percent) and Denver (26 percent). The list includes unexpected cities such as Grand Forks, North Dakota; Midland, Texas; and Anchorage, Alaska, in addition to likely candidates from Colorado Springs and Albuquerque to San Diego, San Francisco, and Honolulu. More than half of the fifty-four metro areas that met the cutoff were Western. For large metro areas with 500,000 or more residents, the Western share was 10 out of 16, or 63 percent of the most highly educated cities.

Networked functions had become ubiquitous in Western cities by the end of the twentieth century. Anchorage is a city of federal civil servants rather than bush pilots and mining outfitters. The first San Francisco fortunes were made by supplying the needs of regional development in the Sierra goldfields and the central valley. They are now generated by companies like Bechtel, which sells professional advice to customers around the world. Albuquerque's poor and sparsely settled hinterland by itself could scarcely support a city of half its present size. The difference comes from scientists, civil servants, and managers. The transformation of Orange County from a farming district to an industrial giant sums up the power of the networked economy. The first aerospace firms of the 1950s were followed by more research-oriented subsidiaries of Douglas Aircraft, North American Rockwell, and the Ford Motor Company. The new missile and electronics plants called up an electrical equipment and supply industry with a specialization in advanced communication and detection equipment. New service, information, and consulting industries appeared in the 1970s and 1980s in medical technology, software, and energy development.

In the networked world, of course, tall buildings are the most visible symbol of a city's importance. They rise as proxies of corporate standing and meet the particular demands of financial industries, with their thousands of bank vice-presidents, brokers, accountants, and attorneys. In the 1920s, tall buildings spread from New York and Chicago to the Midwest and West. Los Angeles built a high-rise city hall. Lincoln and Bismarck added high-rise state capitals. Seattlites could admire the gleaming white pyramid of the Smith Tower. Even Albuquerque sprouted a nine-story skyscraper in 1922. The steel-frame mania began to catch hold again in the late 1950s and exploded in the later 1970s and the 1980s. By 1985, Houston, Dallas, San Francisco, and Los Angeles ranked 3, 4, 5, and 6 in the country in the number of buildings over 500 feet tall—two-fifths of all the tall buildings outside the big two of New York and Chicago and including two thousand-footers in Los Angeles and Houston.

In the cities of the American West, however, it is equally important to remember that networked cities can be built on the suburban model of the Stanford Industrial Park and Silicon Valley. The networked industries that have given Orange County a larger output of goods and services than the entire state of Arizona are housed in pastel research campuses and mysterious buildings that camp by the San Diego and Newport freeways behind protective skins of bronzed glass. Thomas Pynchon could well have had them in mind when he described the high-tech Yoyodyne corporation, whose engineers and programmers saluted its "pink pavilions bravely shining" in a company anthem sung to the tune of the Cornell alma mater. Joel Garreau has identified "edge cities" around Anaheim, Newport Beach, Irvine, and the John Wayne Airport. Costa Mesa, say its promoters, has become "South Coast Metro . . . the shape of the future."[9]

4

GATEWAYS TO THE WORLD

Like an accomplished repertory actor, Houston played a variety of roles in the movies of the 1980s. It was America's boomtown in *Urban Cowboy*, crammed with blue-collar workers trying to become instant Texans. It was Space City USA in *Terms of Endearment*, a town in which it seemed natural to find a lecherous astronaut as a next-door neighbor. The city's most telling appearance, however, came in the film *Local Hero*, an ironic comedy that transports a quintessential yuppie from the high-rise offices of an international energy company to a sleepy village on the coast of Scotland. A master of the transoceanic telex, the wheeler-dealer is supposed to incorporate the town into a Houston oil empire. Although he fails (of course), the film's closing cut from the North Sea beaches to a Texas condo tower reminds us that the distance between Houston and the world is no greater than the distance between Houston and Baytown or Texas City.

The internationalized environment of Houston and other Western cities in the 1980s was the result of three key events of the early 1960s: a boom in American foreign trade, the opening of immigration from Latin America and Asia, and prosecution of the nation's third Asian-Pacific war in three decades.

The expansion of foreign commerce dated from the General Agreement on Tariffs and Trade in 1947, followed by the Trade Expansion Act of 1962. Although both measures originally looked across the Atlantic, their liberalized trade regulations provided the basis for a tilt of American overseas commerce toward Asian and Pacific partners and ports. The total value of American imports and exports grew from 6.8 percent of the gross national product in 1960 to 14.6 percent by 1987—the heaviest orientation of the economy to foreign trade since World War I. The unplanned corollary was a shift of trade to the ports of Texas and the West Coast, which together accounted for 25 percent of American imports and exports by 1970 and 38 percent by 1980. The value of U.S. trade across the Pacific pushed past trade with Europe at the start of the 1980s—$121 billion versus $116 billion in 1982, according to Los Angeles's Security Pacific Trading Corporation.

The Immigration Reform Act of 1965 had a comparable effect on patterns of immigration. By removing Eurocentric quotas for immigration, the measure opened the door for newcomers from Latin America and Asia who made the cities of the Southwest and the Pacific states their primary destinations. Legal migration to the United States grew from 3.3 million in 1961–70 to 4.5 million for 1971–80 and 6 million for 1981–90. Nearly 5 million of the people who arrived in the 1980s were Latin Americans (37 percent) and Asians (47 percent), the two groups that also furnished the majority of immigrants without legal documentation.

The third event that connected the American West to the "Far West" of Asia was the Gulf of Tonkin incident and the resulting congressional resolution in the summer of 1964 that opened the door to the escalation of the American war in Vietnam. The 17,000 American military personnel in South Vietnam at the beginning of 1964 ballooned to 539,000 by the end of 1968. The cost of maintaining the American presence in Southeast Asia grew a hundredfold. The gateways between the United States and Indochina were the same coastal cities that had felt the most intense effects of the first Pacific war of 1941–45. As they had been twenty-five years earlier, San Diego, San Francisco, Seattle, and Honolulu were the last stops before Asian bases and battle zones. In the late 1960s, the 5,000 GIs who flew to Honolulu each week for five-day sessions of Rest and Recuperation accounted for one fifth of the city's tourist business.

Robert Stone's prize-winning novel *Dog Soldiers* offered a compelling summary of the effects of the new Pacific connections on Western cities. Writing in the early 1970s, Stone presented both the war and the international trade in drugs as sources and symbols of the erosion of national character. With Vietnam and Thailand only a few hours away, the most ordinary streets and residents of San Francisco and Oakland were forced into the front lines of moral choice. Stone's metropolis is one in which Samoan immigrants muster out of the Coast Guard to manage pornographic movie theaters for the junior Mafia; San Francisco stewardesses smuggle pot from Bangkok; East Indian women spin topless in seedy bars;

and Japanese military brides work for Filipino dentists. The story itself careens from Saigon to San Francisco to Mexico.

We need not share Stone's vision of moral decline to agree that war, immigration, and trade all pulled the West out of itself after 1960. The most prosperous Western cities now look outward as well as inward. They not only define and structure relationships within the region but also mediate between the West and the world. They are points of settlement, financial centers, targets for investment, and crossroads for a series of transnational regions. They tie together four great circles that loop outward to the points of the compass—east to Atlantic America, south to Mexico, Central America, and South America, north to Canada, and west to the Pacific islands and Asia. The first of these circles was the subject of the previous chapter, which examined growing network roles in the national economy. The others are the topic of the present chapter.

The Mexican/American West is constructed in three tiers—the binational borderlands of intensive interaction, a larger cultural region of Hispanic settlement, and a still larger area of substantial contact. This description adapts Donald Meinig's terminology of *core, domain,* and *sphere* to an analysis of cultural regions. The core is the area of greatest homogeneity of cultural features. The domain is an area in which a cultural group has a dominant or substantial presence. The sphere is an area of attenuated influence in which only selected cultural features are present, usually in a minority role.

American border cities from Brownsville to San Diego and their Mexican twins dominate the borderlands region in which daily interaction is possible between the two countries. The region extends perhaps seventy-five miles south of the border, the distance at which the Mexican government has established its checkpoints for visas and tourist cards. On the north it coincides with the areas covered by the Southwest Border Regional Commission in 1976 and the "border economy" analyzed by Nils Hansen in 1981. It contains the four American metropolitan areas that had Hispanic majorities in 1980, including Laredo at 92 percent—an "international city" in fact rather than just in booster literature. Like W. H. Timmons's characterization of El Paso and Juárez, the cross-border communities are "Siamese twins joined together at the cash register." Green-card workers cross from Mexico to the United States, many of them to work as domestic servants. American popular culture flows southward. Bargain hunters and tourists pass in both directions. Mexican and U.S. manufacturers exchange products, workers, and managers. D. W. Meinig's description of El Paso and Juárez could apply to other border cities as well: "The two linguistic cultures live in intimate association or at least daily awareness of one another. Every day thousands of Mexican workers, shoppers, and those seeking various special services (such as schools and hospitals) cross the several bridges to El Paso, and every day thousands of Americans—local residents, sojourners (such as military personnel), and tourists—cross those same bridges. . . . Spanish and English newspapers, radio stations, television stations, and cinemas serve the whole area."[1]

The borderlands cities share retailing and recreation. The American cities have attracted heavy Mexican shopping, especially during the Mexican oil boom of 1970s, when the peso enjoyed a high value relative to the dollar. Just as Venezuelans and Colombians filled the stores of downtown Miami, Mexicans crowded into San Diego. San Diego State University researchers estimated that Mexican citizens spent $400 million in San Diego County in 1978. A major shopping center in Chula Vista reportedly made 60 percent of its sales to Mexicans, and downtown San Diego stores nearly a quarter. Developer Ernest Hahn conditioned the construction of Horton Plaza in downtown San Diego on the completion of the "Tijuana Trolley," the new light-rail transit line from San Diego to the Mexican border, presumably to compete better for Mexican shoppers. Going the other direction, most of the signs for roadside attractions for dozens of miles south from Tijuana are in English rather than Spanish.

Border cities share labor pools as well as consumers. After the end of the *bracero* program in the mid-1960s, the Mexican government began to encourage the development of a "platform economy" by allowing private companies along the U.S. border to import industrial components duty-free as long as 80 percent of the items were re-exported and 90 percent of the workers were Mexican nationals. The idea was to encourage American corporations to locate assembly plants south of the border. A series of further incentives followed, such as allowing total foreign ownership of the factories and exempting them from currency regulations. American firms that want to take advantage of the Mexican *maquiladora* program utilize Sections 806.3 and 807 of the U.S. tariff code, which date back to the 1930s and which charge duty only on the value added to American-made components assembled in Mexico. For Mexico, maquiladoras have become the second largest earner of foreign exchange, trailing oil but ahead of tourism.

The impact of the program has been most substantial in El Paso. The city was already a major clothing manufacturer because of its access to Mexican workers. In the 1950s, clothing firms discovered that they could get the

Third World advantages of inexpensive labor and right-to-work laws without leaving home. Ninety percent of the job growth in manufacturing in El Paso from 1954 to 1968 was in the garment industry, which was largely staffed with green-card and Mexican-American women. It is not surprising that the first industrial park specifically for maquiladoras was built a few miles away in Juárez in 1969. Maquiladoras grew explosively after Mexico devalued the peso in 1982, lowering the effective cost of Mexican operations. By the 1980s, many managerial employees lived in the United States and commuted to Mexico. New El Paso factories made automobile parts and other components. In 1988, 8,000 Americans in El Paso worked in jobs directly tied to maquila industries, and thousands of others provided indirect support in transportation, finance, and services. Across the border, 100,000 Mexicans, most of them women, worked in routine assembly operations.

From the Gulf of Mexico to the Pacific Ocean, the 600 maquiladora plants with 125,000 workers of 1982 grew to 1,800 plants with 500,000 workers by 1990. On the northern side of the border, more and more local factories have begun to supply maquila components in close consultation with plant managers. Seven binational urban clusters in the borderlands house 4.8 million Americans and 3 million Mexicans. Ranked by the number of maquila employees, the most important is Las Cruces/El Paso/Juárez. Following in order in 1990 were San Diego/Tijuana; Brownsville/Matamoros; McAllen/Reynosa; Nogales, Arizona/Nogales, Sonora; Imperial County/Mexicali; and Laredo/Nuevo Laredo.

The larger Mexican-American cultural region is best defined by concentrations of Spanish-surnamed population rather than cross-border contacts. It includes all of New Mexico, most of Arizona, and substantial portions of Texas, Colorado, and California. The boundaries were sketched out by Spanish settlement in the seventeenth and eighteenth centuries. They have remained stable since the 1940s, but the intensity of the Hispanic presence has grown with northward migration, creating what Joel Garreau calls the binational region of Mexamerica. The Mexican-American population also moved rapidly from country to city. In 1980 the five states held twenty-five metropolitan areas or consolidated metropolitan areas with 50,000 or more Spanish-surnamed residents, up from five in 1950 and ten in 1960. Such cities are now found as far north as Sacramento, Denver, and Dallas.

The cultural region includes two cities whose historic biculturalism survived into the second half of the twentieth century. The "Spanish" cities of Santa Fe and Tucson partially balance the "Midwestern" cities of Albuquerque and Phoenix in northern New Mexico and southern Arizona. Tucson and Santa Fe were centers for Spanish-speaking settlement regions before the arrival of the English-speaking Americans. Their Hispanic residents supported substantial merchant classes that held onto property through the nineteenth century and intermarried with the newcomers. The mass migrations of Mexican workers in the 1910s, 1920s, and 1940s largely bypassed Santa Fe, while Tucson drew most of its migrants from its historic hinterland in the adjacent state of Sonora.

In the mid twentieth century, of course, Santa Fe and Tucson actively sold multiculturalism and sunshine as the essentials of their tourist packages. One commentator in 1949 described Tucson's chief industry as the exhibition of its quaint "folk" and their products. Santa Fe's daily *New Mexican* in 1926 listed its city's "special assets" as antiquity, old landmarks, a stirring history, a foreign flavor, a Spanish atmosphere, a unique type of architecture, and picturesque traditional customs. The promotion of tourism by the Santa Fe Railroad and the revival of Spanish colonial crafts in the 1930s helped to preserve Santa Fe's bicultural character. In the 1970s and 1980s, a booming city carefully cultivated its distinctive character by strict design controls that forced new building into imitations of old Santa Fe styles.

In contrast to Tucson and Santa Fe, the cultural pluralism of Los Angeles and San Antonio resembles that of El Paso. As staging grounds for Mexican-American immigrants and migrant farm workers and as centers of Mexican-American institutions, the cities have continually re-created and re-balanced their biculturalism. East Los Angeles is a huge city within a city that stretches twenty miles eastward from downtown Los Angeles and that houses more than 2 million Mexican-Americans. By the 1979–80 school year, two-fifths of the school children and half the first-graders in Los Angeles County were Hispanic. In San Antonio the expansion of civilian jobs at the army and air force bases in the 1940s and 1950s helped to create a substantial Hispanic middle class. At the same time, peripheral growth on the Hispanic west side involved the scattering of mobile homes and cheap housing on poorly drained land. The interpenetration of low-income housing with the crop and grazing lands of southern Texas provided a symbol of San Antonio's historic role as refuge and reservoir for Spanish-speaking farm workers.

The Hispanic West has also pushed northward since the 1950s. In particular, the permanent settlement of Hispanic farm workers has changed the ethnic character of communities in the central West. The boundary of the sphere of contact can be marked by the location of communities in which

Mexican-born residents outnumbered Canadian-born. In 1950 the line ran somewhere between San Jose and San Francisco, Pueblo and Denver, and Topeka and Omaha. By 1980 the northward movement of Latin America added Omaha, Denver, Casper, Reno, San Francisco, Portland, Yakima, and Richland to the Mexican-American sphere. In the realm of popular culture, it turns out, this zone of contact roughly coincides with the area in which Mexican restaurants outnumber Chinese and Italian restaurants as the most common ethnic cuisine.

Ties between the cities of the western United States and western Canada are more clearly economic than cultural. Each country is the other's largest customer, with the United States buying 75 percent of Canadian exports and Canada buying 25 percent of U.S. exports. Migration back and forth across the open border has always been easy but essentially invisible, since cities like Winnipeg, Regina, and Vancouver drew their residents from the same ethnic groups that predominated in Fargo and Seattle. As late as 1980, however, Canada remained a more important source of immigrants than Mexico or Asia in Bismarck, Billings, Great Falls, Spokane, Bellingham, Provo, Medford, and Redding.

The new Canada–United States Free Trade Agreement of 1989 opened economic channels even wider than before, moving the two countries in the direction of a North American common market. The Conservative govern-ment of Canada, elected in 1984, worked toward free trade in a reversal of a generation of Canadian policy designed to limit American control of Cana-dian assets and markets. The 1989 agreement lowered tariffs and assured Canadians of reliable access to U.S. markets without the fear of sudden protectionist upsurges. New American businesses in Canada will be able to compete without special restrictions, essentially on the same basis as Cana-dian firms.

The results of the free-trade agreement may be most substantial in the Pacific Northwest. The cosmopolitan port cities of Vancouver and Seattle have a long list of similarities, ranging from their economic base to their physical setting. In 1988 the state of Washington and the province of British Columbia established a Pacific Northwest Economic Partnership to market Vancouver and Seattle cooperatively as investment opportunities and to promote the regional biotech, aerospace, software, and environmental en-gineering industries. The Seattle Chamber of Commerce held its 1990 con-ference in Vancouver, while the Vancouver Board of Trade proposed a joint business association. *The New Pacific,* a Seattle-based magazine founded in 1989, has tried to articulate a sense that "Cascadia" is a single economic and social region jointly anchored by its two regional capitals (or three, if a more provincial Portland cares to come on board).

In the prairie provinces, the cities of Alberta are part of a continental energy empire. The American oil industry crossed the border after World War II, particularly after the opening of Alberta's Leduc oil field in 1947. American companies controlled 70 percent of Canadian oil production at the end of the 1950s and took a leading role in the 1970s in exploring the Athabasca tar sands of northern Alberta. Tulsa oil companies found themselves hiring experts to analyze Canadian culture. While Edmonton grew as an operations center and the base for Canadian oil firms, Calgary became a second Denver, with scores of administrative offices for American-owned oil operations. Ironically, by 1981 Canadian investors were responsible for half of the new office construction underway in downtown Denver as they looked for a repeat of the Calgary boom in which American dollars had primed the pump for Canadian fortunes.

In 1950, Mexican-born or Canadian-born residents outnumbered Asian-born in *every* Western metropolitan area. By 1980, Asians had grown into the largest of the three groups in thirty-five metropolitan areas. What happened in between was immigration reform and an explosive growth in immigration eastward across the Pacific. Asians constituted 6 percent of all newcomers to the United States in 1965, 40 percent by 1980, and nearly half by the end of the decade. They made New York state their second most popular destination, but California, Hawaii, and Washington were their first, third, and fourth. Historically, Chinese were the dominant Asian community in San Francisco, and Japanese in Los Angeles. The migrations of the 1970s and 1980s, however, brought Asian ethnic variety to every Pacific Coast city. Honolulu by 1980 had more than 50,000 Japanese, Chinese, and Filipinos. San Francisco had more than 50,000 Chinese, Vietnamese, and Filipinos. Los Angeles had more than 50,000 of all four groups. Observers could easily distinguish new ethnic neighborhoods of Koreans in Hawthorne, Japanese in Culver City, Chinese in Monterey Park, Vietnamese in Westminster, Samoans in Carson and Wilmington, Cambodians in Lakewood, and Thais in Hollywood. Only New York, with its densely packed Chinatown, had a single Asian community of comparable size. Beyond the coastal states, Asians by the 1980s were also the dominant immigrants in mountain cities like Salt Lake City, Boise, Denver, and Reno and in seventeen plains cities from Fargo to Wichita Falls. The pattern reflected the location of military bases and large universities, but it also included more general cities like Omaha and Topeka.

The most publicized of the Asian immigrants were the refugees from the war in Indochina. The first arrivals in 1975 and 1976 tended to be highly educated professionals who had been associated with the American war effort. Another three-quarters of a million Vietnamese, Laotians, and Cambodians have arrived since 1976 via refugee camps, with the peak coming between 1979 and 1982. Nearly all settled in metropolitan areas, especially in California, Texas, and Washington. Special concentrations of ethnic subgroups include the Mien, a highland people from Laos, many of whom settled in Portland, and the Hmong, one third of whom settled in Santa Ana and many others in Denver.

Half of the 700,000 Vietnamese-Americans now live in California, with their numbers increasing due to a steady relocation from other states. Sixty-five thousand lived in San Jose in 1990. The fifteen Vietnamese newspapers, weekly magazines, and regularly scheduled TV programs in the Bay Area are filled with advertisements for Vietnamese lawyers, car dealers, insurance agents, auto repair shops, and home improvement companies. This entrepreneurship is emblematic of the rapid acculturation of the early refugees. Indeed, the 130,000 immigrants of 1975 now have average adjusted incomes higher than the nationwide average for all Americans. Although they have smaller numbers and wield far less political power, the economic adjustment of Vietnamese in San Jose is analogous to that of Cubans in Miami.

Taiwanese, Filipinos, and Koreans have followed the classic model in which immigrants tend to be younger adults voluntarily looking for economic opportunity. The 15,000 Koreans in Portland owned 500 businesses in 1990, ranging from groceries and laundromats to appliance stores and video outlets. They supported eighteen churches, twenty public associations, and three language schools. The Olympic Boulevard area in Los Angeles had approximately one third of the area's Korean households in the early 1970s but relatively few long-term residents. Instead, it was a place of initial adjustment, much like the European immigrant neighborhoods of earlier generations. "Koreatown serves as a launching pad for many Korean newcomers," according to demographer Eui-Young Yu. "Very few of them stay very long. The zip code analysis of the Korean directories also shows that growth rates of the Korean population are much faster in the outlying and suburban areas than in Koreatown. The Koreatown of Los Angeles will probably develop into a primarily Korean shopping and service area."[2]

Outside their own ethnic communities, Koreans, Vietnamese, and other foreign-born business owners have filled retail vacuums in central-city neighborhoods that have been abandoned by chain stores. They have quickly occupied the role of a "middleman minority" that buffers Anglos from blacks and Hispanics. For example, the number of Korean-operated businesses in greater Los Angeles grew from 1,300 to 7,000 between 1975 and 1983. A first generation of immigrants from India in the 1960s were predominantly persons with scientific and technical training, but the members of a second generation in the 1980s were much more likely to find their economic role as business proprietors. The ubiquitous Los Angeles mini-mall, which appeared in the hundreds in the 1970s, is often a case of Asian entrepreneurship.

The number of ethnic Chinese in the United States jumped from 236,000 in 1960 to 1,079,000 in 1985 and transformed stagnant Chinese communities in the process. New Chinatowns appeared in Houston, Oakland, and San Diego. Immigrants from Taiwan, Hong Kong, overseas Chinese communities in Southeast Asia, and all parts of the People's Republic of China joined the old families from Guangdong in the historic Chinatown of San Francisco. Social and economic divisions appeared between upwardly mobile and assimilating students and professionals, Chinatown businessmen, and an insular labor force in Chinatown's sweatshops and service jobs.

There was also a new tension between the old elite, which operated through family associations, district associations, and the Chinese Consolidated Benevolent Association, and newcomers with a wide range of political experiences and ideas. John Keeble tried to capture the differences in his 1980 novel *Yellowfish*, which starts in San Francisco's Chinatown, visits the environs of Spokane, crosses the international border to Vancouver's Chinatown, and returns to San Francisco by way of a Chinese-owned casino in Reno. Set in 1977, the story involves the smuggling of a probable Chinese political agent and three illegal Chinese immigrants (the "yellowfish") from Canada to California. The plot pivots on a struggle for power between factions and generations in Chinatown. The immigrants themselves endure the dangers of the backcountry to obtain the expected security of cities that are fully engaged with the emerging system of trans-Pacific trade.

A low-paid immigrant labor force supports not only Chinatown's shops, restaurants, and factories but also the West Coast electronics industry. Silicon Valley millionaires are supported by thousands of low-paid but skilled manual workers, many of them immigrants from Mexico or Asia. Hewlett-Packard was known in the mid-eighties as a "Little Vietnam," and Advanced Micro Devices as a "Little Manila." Personal hiring networks allowed women with virtually no English to work effectively for more assimilated supervisors. Portland's electronics firms have similarly attracted a community of several thousand Koreans to the city's Silicon Forest suburbs.

The feminization of routine jobs, with a consequent lowering of relative wages, has presumably helped to prevent greater "offshoring" of production.

The Los Angeles garment industry has also depended on low-wage nonunion workers, often distressed immigrants and women. In 1975 only 10 percent of Los Angeles County's 2,200 garment firms were unionized. Few had more than a few dozen employees, most of whom worked in lofts, storefronts, and basements without health or pension benefits. By one estimate, two-thirds of the workers were undocumented Latina or Asian immigrants. Many of the entrepreneurs are from Hong Kong, Taiwan, Korea, and Latin America. The sales are arranged and the fashions set in the vast California Mart at the intersection of Olympic and Main in downtown Los Angeles, where retail buyers from around the world can visit hundreds of showrooms and wholesalers. Factory spaces cluster around the California Mart and just south of the Santa Monica Freeway to allow small businesses to benefit from the same suppliers.

Much more glamorous than rooms full of sewing machines has been the increasing importance of Japan and the "four tigers" of Korea, Taiwan, Hong Kong, and Singapore as trading and investment partners. In 1970, California's import and export trade was just short of $9 billion. By 1985, it was $94 billion—one-fifth of the gross state product. The state's leading trading partners in descending order were Japan, Taiwan, Korea, Canada, Germany, Hong Kong, Australia, Mexico, and Singapore. Japanese automakers choose Los Angeles and Orange counties for their United States headquarters. Japanese real estate investors at the end of the 1980s put Los Angeles, New York, San Francisco, Honolulu, and San Diego at the top of their list of favorites and included Dallas, Phoenix, and Seattle also in the top ten.

Western cities look south to Mexico, north to Canada, and west to Asia. They are also connected to worldwide networks of trade and information. In the jet-age eighties, one measure of a city's global attraction is international tourism. In 1988, Texas, Arizona, California, Washington, and Hawaii each hosted more than a million foreign visitors. Western cities among the top ten destinations for foreign travelers to the United States include both specialized tourist cities and the leaders in the same hierarchy defined in the last chapter. Twenty-one percent of foreign visitors visited Los Angeles in 1988 (second only to New York), 17 percent visited San Francisco (third), 13 percent visited Honolulu (fourth), 7 percent visited Las Vegas (eighth), and 6 percent visited Dallas (tenth).

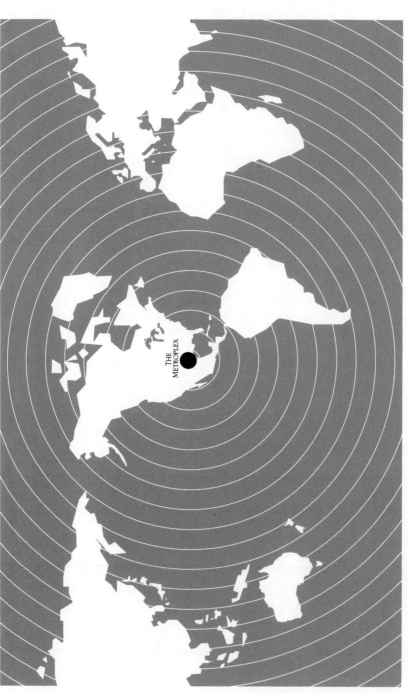

Dallas, Fort Worth, and the world. By the 1980s the Dallas–Fort Worth "Metroplex" had joined the many Western cities that were trying to illustrate their centrality for world commerce. This promotional graphic was published in *The Metroplex: Dallas/Fort Worth Profile* by a consortium that included the Dallas Partnership, the Fort Worth Chamber of Commerce, the City of Garland, the City of Carrollton, the North Texas Commission, and the Dallas–Fort Worth International Airport.

With or without substantial foreign tourism, nearly every Western city saw itself as being an international city in the 1980s. Anchorage argued that it was the natural midpoint and air hub between North America and northern Asia. Cities battled for through flights to Tokyo, Osaka, Frankfurt, and Paris. Denver committed billions of dollars to a new airport to challenge Dallas as a travel center. San Francisco after World War II continued to enjoy its status as the chief international contact point for the Western states, with every expectation that it would continue to "benefit as a focal point for increased trade with hitherto underdeveloped countries in the Pacific Basin and South America."[3] Indeed, as R. B. Cohen and H. C. Reed have independently shown, San Francisco in the postwar decades was one of three major international banking cities in the United States. It was the best place west of the Mississippi to find lawyers versed in trade law and international negotiations. It accounted for 3.2 percent of total sales by the largest American manufacturing corporations and 5.4 percent of their foreign sales, for a "multinational index" of 1.69. The care and feeding of these global ties remained a key element in the development program of Mayor Diane Feinstein, who sold an "Invest in San Francisco" program to Asian businesses on her numerous trips to Seoul, Shanghai, Hong Kong, and Manila.

To sort out the competing claims of trade offices, development agencies, and globe-trotting mayors, a comprehensive assessment of the growing international connections of Western cities can be developed in a manner parallel to their ranking as domestic transaction centers. The comparative index needs to take into account the diverse impact of Mexican green-card workers in El Paso, Filipino immigrants in San Jose, Korean auto shipments through Portland, Japanese ownership of Los Angeles banks, and Canadian shoppers in Seattle. The additive index utilizes the six categories of foreign-born population (0–2 points), foreign trade (0–2 points), presence of foreign banks (0–2 points), importance of foreign investment (0 or 1 point), importance of foreign markets for local businesses (0 or 1 point), and role as a global information center (0 or 1 point). Changes from 1960 to the 1980s are measured by percentage increases in foreign-born population greater than those for all U.S. metropolitan areas, by an increased share of the national total of foreign trade and banking, or by substantial absolute increases. The results are shown in table 6.

Despite the diversification of San Francisco's global ties between the 1960s and the 1980s and its continuing prominence as a financial center, booming Los Angeles shouldered ahead as the West's most international metropolis. Reflective of its importance is the emergence of the *Los Angeles Times* as one of the nation's three global newspapers, with six bureaus in

Table 6.   Relative Importance of International Connections for Western
            Metropolitan Areas Since 1960

	Point Total	
	1960s	1980s
San Francisco	6	9
Los Angeles	4	10
Houston	3.5	5
Honolulu	2	6.5
Seattle	2	5.5
San Antonio	1.5	2
San Diego	1	4
Phoenix	1	2
Portland	1	2
Sacramento	1	2
Salt Lake City	1	1
Dallas	0.5	4.5
Denver	0	0
Oklahoma City	0	0

SOURCE See table 5.

Europe, five in Asia, five in the Middle East and Africa, and five in Latin
America as of 1990. Behind the California giants, San Diego, Honolulu,
Seattle, Houston, and Dallas pushed forward as the West's second-level
international cities. In contrast, Portland, Denver, Oklahoma City, and Sacramento remained dependent on their regional and perhaps national functions.

The international dimension of Honolulu is apparent to any casual visitor. With a limited and isolated commercial hinterland, Honolulu has developed significant foreign connections at the mass-market level through tourism and immigration. The city's ethnic variety was set in the late nineteenth
and early twentieth centuries, when sugar kings brought in thousands of
Chinese, Japanese, Okinawan, Filipino, Portuguese, and Puerto Rican
workers. Honolulu was the first and is still the only American city in which
Asians and Pacific Islanders constitute the majority of the population. The

city was the port of entry for an average of 438 immigrants per year from 1929 through 1954, for 10,692 from 1955 through 1965, and 39,269 from 1966 through 1979. The 1970s and 1980s also brought extensive marketing of Honolulu as a tourist destination for newly wealthy Japanese, who thronged to the beaches and hotels of Waikiki.

Street-level connections helped to pave the way for new international roles for Honolulu. Its big corporations diversified out of sugar and pineapples in the 1960s. Castle and Cooke moved into banana production in Costa Rica, Honduras, and the Philippines, and into manufacturing in South Korea, Thailand, and Singapore. By the early 1970s, at least 160 Honolulu firms were operating in Asia, and Honolulu corporations controlled more than 25,000 jobs in other nations around the Pacific. The Dillingham Corporation, wrote Francine du Plessix Gray in 1972, "has built water-treatment plants in Vietnam, condominiums and power plants in Korea, harbor facilities in Singapore, underwater pipelines and ship berths in Thailand; it has undertaken construction work in Guam and Micronesia, dredging operations in Colombia and Guatemala, mineral explorations in Malaysia, Thailand and Australia, and transport and construction work in New Zealand, New Guinea, and Australia."[4]

This cross-Pacific activity set the stage for an economic strategy emphasizing Honolulu's pivotal location between America and Asia. Residents by the 1960s could think of Honolulu's downtown office core as the "Plaza of the Pacific." Honolulu's large Asian-American populations have made it an attractive destination not only for Japanese tourists and hotel builders but also for Japanese seeking to invest in second homes. Japanese real estate investments of $6 billion by the end of the 1980s put Honolulu third behind New York and Los Angeles as a Japanese investment target. Executives of multinational corporations place a high value on Honolulu's quality of life and infrastructure for their regional offices. State officials defined a Pacific Rim strategy in the 1960s and reaffirmed it after the election of Governor John Waihee in 1986. It envisions Honolulu as an information exchange center that will function as a Geneva of the Pacific. The state planned to build on existing information exchanges such as the East–West Center, the Pacific Forum, and the Japan-America Institute of Management Sciences. Its goals have included encouraging air hub operations and developing a stock exchange to take advantage of the trans-Pacific time lag.

In contrast to Honolulu, the international dimension of Dallas is still most apparent in its boardrooms and in boarding areas at the vast Dallas–Fort Worth Airport. A growing international role has been built directly on the city's earlier functions as a regional center. Through the 1950s and

The Port of Long Beach. The port, which calls itself the "trade center for the world," and the immediately adjacent facilities of "Worldport LA" (just to the west of this scene) constitute the largest port complex in the United States. The Port of Long Beach continues to expand its container terminals on filled land. Oil fields and downtown Long Beach are shown in the middle background. A container ship is steaming along the breakwater. (Photo by Metivier Photography, courtesy of the Port of Long Beach)

1960s, Dallas was clearly the leading center for the "near Southwest" between the Mississippi River and the Rocky Mountains. Originally a product of the railroad, Dallas secured a central position on the new Interstate Highway System in the 1960s. Its warehouse workers and paper pushers provided transportation, finance, distribution, and administrative services for much of Texas, Oklahoma, and Arkansas. In the 1970s and 1980s, Dallas businesses capitalized on their educated workers, distribution and communication systems, regional banks, and business services. As also with Atlanta, the revolutions in telecommunications and air travel have enabled Dallas to grow into a hub for international businesses seeking access to American markets.

Economic development leaders in Dallas eagerly joined the growing international economy in the 1980s. The Dallas Partnership talked about a future as "a preeminent center of world commerce in the twenty-first century." This aggressively American city cooperates with its self-consciously Western neighbor Fort Worth to publish maps showing the "metroplex" as the navel of the world. Publicists now distribute promotional materials in French, German, Italian, Chinese, and Japanese, and define a list of continental rather than regional rivals—Mexico City, Los Angeles, and New York rather than New Orleans and Oklahoma City. Foreign corporations employed 35,000 area workers by the late 1980s, and foreign bank offices made it a secondary center for international finance. Its economic development executives continue to work to acquire foreign firms, trade offices, professional consulates, and business agents to support the social infrastructure of translation services, specialized retailers, schools, and social organizations that make life easier for non-Americans.

Houston has been a very different sort of "world-class city" since the 1960s. The Bayou City, said official propagandists in the 1980s, was "an international city with a dazzling future," a city whose "global consciousness" was attracting "world attention." Behind the puffery was a city that specialized in being a global center for the distribution of oil tools, oil-field technology, and petroleum production expertise. The oil industry helped to multiply the value of trade through the Port of Houston by a factor of ten during the 1970s. Houston's leading trade partners were the oil countries of Mexico and Saudi Arabia. Exceeding even agricultural products and petrochemicals, its leading export group, at $1.7 billion, was construction, mining, and oil-field machinery.

Houston's global reach involved high levels of personal interaction. The metropolis hosts more than six hundred international companies and more than seventy-five branches and agencies of foreign banks, placing it ahead

The Dallas–Fort Worth airport. Shown under construction in the 1970s, the new Dallas–Fort Worth airport was a key element in the ambitions of the Metroplex. Boosters point out that its site covers as much land as the entire island of Manhattan. (Courtesy of the Dallas/Fort Worth International Airport)

of San Francisco and close behind Chicago as a world financial center. Houstonians returned the attention by playing a major role in developing the oil fields of the Middle East, Indonesia, Malaysia, and the North Sea. Before the recession of the 1980s, a hundred Houston companies operated in oil fields around the South China Sea and a hundred in the countries around the North Sea. The plot of *Local Hero* may have seemed quaint to many Americans, but it reflected daily life in Houston.

5

THE POLITICS OF DIVERSITY

On August 11, 1965, a California Highway Patrol officer working in the Watts district of South Central Los Angeles stopped Marquette Frye's ten-year-old Buick and booked Frye for suspicion of drunk driving. On March 3, 1991, members of the Los Angeles Police Department ended a high-speed chase by apprehending, kicking, and beating Rodney King, whom they suspected of robbing a pizza shop. The law enforcement officers in both cases were white, and the suspects were black. In 1965 the incident itself triggered a fierce race riot. In the King case, it took the acquittal of four police officers on April 29, 1992, to set off a comparably violent outbreak in South Central. The similarities between the two incidents illustrate some of the ongoing tensions as Western cities have slowly adjusted to their multiracial character. The differences show the effects of twenty-six years of increasingly pluralistic politics in Western cities.

In 1991 every American who watched the evening news was soon aware that the arrest and beating had been videotaped by a bystander. Replay after replay brought an outpouring of protest and comment, much of it focused on the attitudes of Los Angeles police chief Daryl Gates. Demands for his resignation came from city council members and from Mayor Tom Bradley, who had been a Los Angeles police lieutenant himself before entering politics and reaching the mayor's office in 1973. Gates finally agreed to step aside after a blue-ribbon panel concluded that the institutional values of the police department condoned racist behavior in spite of official policies. After a decade in which Western cities had appointed African-American and Hispanic city managers and school superintendents (in places like Dallas and Oakland) and had tried both African-American men and white women as police chiefs (in Houston and Portland), midcentury values still seemed to be flourishing in the Los Angeles Police Department.

The Los Angeles police chief who found himself so beleaguered in 1991 would nevertheless have seemed the epitome of conciliation compared to William J. Parker, his predecessor in the early 1960s. Outspoken and tactless, Parker despised anyone who interfered with the ability of the police to enforce his understanding of public order. He regarded it as only a coincidence that the police arrested twice as many people for each crime in black districts as in white. Criminals, civil rights demonstrators, Communists, and black activists all seemed to Parker to show disrespect for the law. In response, a fifteen-page booklet with his most outrageous statements circulated in the black community under the title *Chief William H. Parker Speaks*. Parker's stance was reinforced by Mayor Sam Yorty, a political opportunist who simultaneously played on white fears and claimed right up to the summer of 1965 that Los Angeles blacks were immune to the civil rights activism sweeping other parts of the country. There was no need, he said, for even the public gesture of a human relations commission when blacks lived in such harmony with white Los Angeles.

Attitudes like those of Yorty and Parker, of course, set the context for violence in Watts in 1965. Although it involved a purely routine police action, the arrest of Marquette Frye occasioned the best-publicized race riot in American history. A crowd had gathered around the car, and its mood turned ugly after Frye's loudly protesting mother was also taken into custody. The arrival of the Los Angeles police incited the crowd, and an angry mob was soon stoning passing cars, threatening the police, and attacking white-owned businesses with a reputation for exploiting the community. Rioting, looting, and arson spread through the entire Watts community the following day, with the police powerless to intervene. The California National Guard arrived on the evening of August 13 and effectively laid siege to Watts. It completed its occupation of a now quiet neighborhood on August 15. The riot damaged at least six hundred buildings, four thousand people were arrested, a thousand were injured, and thirty-four killed.

Watts was one episode out of hundreds in the series of riots that hit U.S. cities between the summer of 1964 through the spring of 1968. Police set off disturbances in Omaha in 1966 by breaking up an illegal fireworks display. San Francisco's riot in September 1966 capped years of mounting tensions in the Hunters Point district. Again, the trigger was police action—

the shooting of a teenaged robbery suspect. The stoning, looting, and arson spread to the Fillmore district on the second day before two thousand national guardsmen quieted the disturbance. The summer of 1967 brought other smaller disturbances to cities like Phoenix and Portland.

The initial response of public officials was to blame the riots on the riffraff. Most Negroes, said Mayor Yorty, deplored the violence, which he said was perpetrated by unemployed youths roaming the streets. The rioters were "mad dogs," said California politician Ronald Reagan. "One person threw a rock," said Chief Parker, "then, like monkeys in a zoo, others started throwing rocks."[1] In fact, the participants were an accurate cross section of the potential rioters. Average participation ran between 10 percent and 20 percent of people aged fourteen to fifty-nine who lived in the riot areas (about 15 percent in Watts). Almost all the participants were neighborhood residents. If many were unemployed or had criminal records, so did many nonrioters in the same communities. Later studies showed that many black residents of Watts approved of the riot whether they had watched it on the streets or on television.

In the most obvious way possible, the protest riots in cities like Los Angeles and San Francisco were political statements. Fundamentally they were protests about the national circumstances of white racism identified by the National Advisory Commission on Civil Disorders in 1968. The police officers and white businesses that were the frontline targets were immediate symbols of white authority. On the local scene, the protests also signaled the unraveling of postwar growth coalitions as the guardians of the general public interest. They made it unmistakable that significant segments of the community actively rejected a unitary statement of community goals. Even blacks who sat out the riots recognized that they were an effort to force local establishments to pay serious attention to minority communities.

In this political interpretation, the disorders were part of a larger dialectic in the political evolution of Western cities. Powerful postwar growth coalitions eroded in one city after another between 1965 and 1980. The neo-progressives often failed to reproduce themselves by recruiting new leaders to replace an aging generation. More important, they were challenged by newly mobilized constituencies with new ideas about minority rights and community conservation. In the 1980s this era of ethnic and neighborhood revolt yielded in turn to a revised version of growth politics. At best, cities went beyond rainbow coalitions to support new rainbow growth coalitions, which pursued economic expansion with a list of community goals that included the empowerment of ethnic minorities. In other cases, the changes may have updated the rhetoric and broadened the leadership pool without changing basic political goals.[2]

Political scientists since James Madison have recognized that large government units tend toward pluralistic politics. Even without shifts in public issues and community values, Westerners might have expected to hear more political voices in a Phoenix of 800,000 people than one of 100,000 or a San Jose of 625,000 people rather than 65,000. In fact, several distinct tendencies came together after 1965 as African-Americans, Hispanics, middle-class Anglos, and women all learned to use spatial concentration and neighborhood networks as political resources. The challengers to the growth coalition, with its claim to speak for the all-encompassing public interest, therefore created city council districts, neighborhood organizations, and community groups that could use their geographic bases to articulate a variety of public interests.

Many of the "antigrowth" activists were members of the postindustrial middle class. Professors, engineers, government workers, and executives of national corporations depend on the national demand for their talents rather than on local markets for goods and services, which they do not produce. They are, says sociologist Harvey Molotch, cosmopolitan in their ideas and careers. They therefore tend to see their cities as residential environments rather than economic machines. As salaried employees caught in the inflation of the 1970s, they were deeply concerned about preserving neighborhoods with affordable and convenient housing.

The introduction of new issues into local politics was a product of generational as well as structural change. The extraordinary wartime migration of people in their twenties and thirties intensified the impact of the national postwar baby boom in Western cities. As the first of the Western boomers reached voting age in the mid-1960s, they found new ideas being articulated by slightly older men and women whose personal and public consciousness was shaped by the Great Prosperity from 1945 to 1970. These activists came of age and progressed through high school, college, and their early careers during the great era of American optimism, when economic and political power on the world scene underlay a sense of expanding possibilities at home. Within the United States, of course, that prosperity and optimism were especially characteristic of Western cities. The new voices pushed aside the more cautious generation whose ideas had been shaped by the Great Depression and the Second World War and whose agendas started and stopped with economic development.

In the study *The New Urban America,* first published in 1981, I described the newly mobilized activists as "quality-of-life liberals." In many ways, quality-of-life liberalism was the urban manifestation of the growing environmentalism that is often dated to Earth Day 1970. In a manner that ironically recalled the prewar elites of Cheyenne or Denver, these middle-class city people worried that breakneck development was fouling the air, eating up open space, sacrificing neighborhoods to the automobile, and deferring the huge costs of remediation to future decades. Their agenda included environmental clean-up, the promotion of public transportation, and the renewal rather than abandonment of older neighborhoods. With their own political values formed during the civil rights decade of 1956–65, many of these city liberals also shared the national liberalism associated with the antipoverty programs of the Kennedy and Johnson administrations. Neighborhood liberals sometimes found that the neoprogressive coalitions of the 1950s had already been weakened by the rise of new suburban industries whose owners and managers thought very little about the needs of central-city businesses. New aerospace, defense, and electronics companies cared far more about suburban highways and world markets than about fading downtowns, older neighborhoods, and public transportation. Spencer Olin, Jr., has analyzed the Industrial League of Orange County, which has represented the major defense and high-technology corporations in their search for national and world markets, finding that it has consistently overriden local efforts to slow the pace of growth. Philip Trounstine and Terry Christensen wrote in 1982 that "downtown San Jose has simply not been a serious concern for the major corporate interests who have built their low-rise headquarters in Silicon Valley cities to the north."[3] The corporate merger mania of the 1970s and 1980s further undermined the old elites by transferring thousands of banks and businesses from local to absentee control.

The growth of political power among Hispanics and African-Americans in the 1970s complemented and amplified the impact of middle-class activism. During the decades of growth politics, the business establishment in cities from San Antonio to Dallas to Phoenix tried to satisfy minority demands for influence on public decisions by consulting informally with carefully chosen community leaders and by running single black or Hispanic candidates on citywide tickets. The bargain was minority votes for the growth coalition in return for possible gains in legal treatment, city jobs, or public housing.

In the mid-1960s, the Community Action Program of the Office of

Economic Opportunity (1964) and the Model Cities program (1966) added a new element to the mix. The federally funded programs were important training grounds for a younger group of black and Hispanic leaders. Over the course of their existence, however, the programs usually remained under the control of mayors and city councils. Mayor Joseph Alioto of San Francisco used the federal War on Poverty to fund hundreds of jobs in the Hunters Point district, giving himself a tool to freeze out opponents and reward supporters in the black community. He also used federal contracts and jobs to force competition between the Hispanic Mission Coalition and the Hunters Point Model Cities program. The well-entrenched business establishment in Oakland used antipoverty and Model Cities programs "to insulate city hall from minority demands," letting black community activists battle with black administrators for control of programs that were isolated from the key points of decision making.[4]

Despite the manipulation and organizational dead ends of the 1960s, however, the next decade brought a fundamental shift in power as African-Americans and Mexican-Americans gained substantial direct representation on city councils and other policy-making bodies. The change was especially radical in the Southwest, where it followed roughly sixty years in which white majorities had gerrymandered local electoral systems to dilute the effect of minority votes. The adoption of city-manager and commission systems of local government in the early 1900s was usually accompanied by at-large elections and small councils, both of which favored well-known majority candidates (that is, progressive white business leaders). Growing minority populations and civil rights activism began to threaten the status quo after World War II, however, and cities manipulated their electoral systems to stave off change. The Texas legislature made it possible for school districts as well as cities to adopt the place system, which prevents minority voters from concentrating their support behind a single candidate.[5] Waco moved to at-large council elections in 1950, immediately after a black candidate nearly won a city council seat, and Houston abolished its five districts in 1955 in favor of pure at-large voting for its council members.

By the 1960s such actions had resulted in the discouragement of minority voters and the absence of black or brown faces from city councils. As late as 1980, 12 percent of all Texans, but only 0.8 percent of elected officials, were African-Americans. Hispanics were underrepresented by a factor of three in Texas and California and by a factor of two in Colorado (table 7). Even more telling was the case of Abilene, a West Texas city of 100,000 whose political life was dominated by an Anglo-American slating group called the Citizens for Better Government and whose council candidates ran

Table 7. Minority Population and Elected Officials in the Southwestern
          States, 1980

	Ethnic Group as Percent of Population	Percent of Elected Officials from Ethnic Group
Blacks		
Texas	12.0%	0.8%
Hispanics		
Texas	21.0	6.3
Colorado	11.7	5.5
Arizona	16.2	13.2
California	19.2	6.6

SOURCE Data from U.S. Commission on Civil Rights as reported in Chandler
Davidson, ed., *Minority Vote Dilution* (Washington, D.C.: Howard University Press,
1984).

at large. In Abilene's 1979 city council election, only seventy-six Mexican-
Americans and thirty-one African-Americans bothered to vote out of a
minority population of roughly 19,000.

A lack of political clout meant inequality in the provision of public
services. In the 1960s, Houston's black and Hispanic neighborhoods were
still contending with unpaved streets, inadequate public health services,
and often a complete lack of sewers. Another notorious example was San
Antonio's Hispanic west side, short-changed for generations by the city
government. Structural problems of poverty and dilapidated housing were
compounded by long-standing municipal neglect. It was west-side streets
that the city failed to pave or repair. It was low-lying west-side neighborhoods that lacked storm and sanitary sewers and that caught the runoff
from downpours over the affluent Anglo neighborhoods on hills to the
north. Parks on the west side were more likely than elsewhere to lack
recreational equipment and maintenance. Fire stations got neither the new
equipment nor the crack crews.

The most effective response to the dilution of minority voting has been
the use of Section 5 of the Voting Rights Act of 1965 to force cities to
establish district systems. Along with the Nineteenth Amendment and the
National Labor Relations Act of 1935, the Voting Rights Act was one of three

key steps in expanding the inclusiveness of American democracy during the twentieth century. Section 5 allows the U.S. Justice Department or the U.S. District Court for the District of Columbia to review proposed changes in election systems in specified states for their effects on minority voting. The federal authorities may disallow the changes or require compensatory actions. A sympathetic Justice Department helped with enforcement during the Carter Administration, and in 1982 Congress renewed the legislation and restored provisions weakened in the courts. Minorities can also argue in federal courts that electoral systems violate equal protection and voting rights guaranteed under the Fourteenth and Fifteenth amendments.[6]

In the typical case of Houston, the Justice Department invoked the preclearance process, which allows a federal veto of changes in local electoral systems, in 1979 in response to major annexations in 1977 and 1978. The department ruled that the annexations diluted minority voting strength and could go forward only if the city modified its at-large council elections. The acceptable plan included five council members chosen at-large and nine from districts. The new council elected in November 1979 included three blacks, two white women, and a Hispanic. As described by Richard Murray, it was far more outspoken and ideologically diverse than the city councils of the 1960s and 1970s, although it was far from revolutionary in its impact.

The annexation of 55,000 Anglo-American suburbanites to San Antonio in 1972 also fell under the preclearance provisions. The change to district elections in 1977 came in a city where the Good Government League (GGL) had just collapsed under its own contradictions. It had grown old without recruiting new leaders to replace the veterans of the stormy politics of the 1950s. In addition, suburban north-side developers and businessmen with new fortunes had little patience with the old-money GGL, with its focus on the health of the central business district. Victories by the "Texas A&M clique" of enthusiastic suburban developers in 1973 put the GGL in the minority on the city council for the first time since 1955.

Mexican-American voters had already been mobilized by an organization called Communities Organized for Public Service (COPS). A coalition of neighborhood groups and parishes, COPS had grown steadily with the help of the Catholic archdiocese and community organizer Ernesto Cortes, who employed the tactics developed by Saul Alinsky. COPS channeled citizen frustrations by taking on concrete and winnable issues like traffic safety and the allocation of federal Community Development funds. After a flash flood covered most of the west side on August 7, 1974, COPS had a visible and inarguable issue that drew in more and more participants and forced the city to dust off a thirty-year-old plan for storm sewers. Although COPS did not take a direct role in the 1975 council campaign, the demise of the GGL and the new west-side activism helped to elect an independent black, two independent Mexican-Americans, and a third Latino who soon began to leave behind his GGL endorsement.

In the same year, extension of the Voting Rights Act to Texas allowed the Mexican American Legal Defense and Education Fund to challenge the 1972 annexations. In 1976 the Justice Department disallowed voting in the annexed area, an action that disfranchised thousands of middle-class San Antonians and threatened the city's ability to borrow money. Under federal pressure, the city council submitted a plan for ten council districts to the voters in January 1977. The Anglo-American north side, homeland of the old neoprogressives and the new suburban frontiersmen, voted 20–1 in opposition, but a 20–1 margin in favor from the Hispanic west side proved just enough to carry the plan. The first election under the new charter in May 1977 brought a council balanced among five Mexican-Americans, one African-American, and five Anglo-Americans (including mayor Lila Cockrell).

Other Texas cities that shifted to partial or full district systems in the 1970s and early 1980s included Corpus Christi, Fort Worth, El Paso, and Dallas. In the case of Dallas, the federal courts in 1975 ruled that citywide voting diluted the effective voting power of African-Americans, who made up a quarter of the city's population. The city shifted to an eleven-member council with eight district seats and three at-large. In the first election under the new system, the Citizens Charter Association was able to win only six seats instead of securing its accustomed sweep. Statewide, twenty-one city councils shifted to districts during the 1970s. The effect was roughly to triple the number of black and Hispanic council members.

A number of other Western cities adopted district elections because of grassroots campaigns rather than a federal mandate. The impetus in Sacramento (1971), Stockton (1971), Albuquerque (1974), San Francisco (1977), San Jose (1980), Oakland (1981), and Phoenix (1982) came from local variations on a labor, liberal, and minority alliance. Each group saw itself gaining an enhanced voice through small-area representation. Denverites carefully expanded their city council in 1971 to create two "black" seats and two "Chicano" seats. Sacramento's white Democrats made explicit commitments to well-organized minority groups in a successful 1969 campaign against a dominant conservative coalition. The insurgents then instituted district elections to secure their political position. Stockton's liberal-minority alliance narrowly pushed through district elections in the face of an entrenched conservative coalition, allowing the election of the city's first black and Hispanic council members. In both cities the change brought blacks and Hispanics a larger share of city jobs and greater membership on appointive boards and commissions. In the early 1980s the councils included men like Joe Serna in Sacramento and Ralph White in Stockton, both of whom had been militant minority-community organizers fifteen years earlier. At the same time, the degree of change should not be overestimated, for the *Sacramento Bee* in 1979 found that the city's fifty "most powerful" people included only two minorities.

European-Americans, of course, were often less concerned about structural reforms than about specific issues. With their college degrees and good jobs, quality-of-life liberals could assume that they had entry to the corridors of power and could focus on efforts as freeway fighters, neighborhood preservationists, and advocates of pleasingly designed cities. Their specific concerns ranged from fear of smog in San Diego to a defense of the old Pike Place Market in Seattle. In some cases the political change may have amounted to little more than sloganeering, as with San Diego's replacement of "City in Motion" with "America's Finest City." Although Pete Wilson won the first of his three terms as mayor in 1971 on a platform of managed growth and comprehensive planning, breakneck development would continue until it ran headlong into neighborhood resistance in the later 1980s.

Fear of rapid growth was also the underlying issue in Denver's grassroots battle to rescind the city's commitment to host the 1976 Winter Olympics. The Chamber of Commerce, Governor John Love, Mayor Bill McNichols, and nearly every other mover and shaker agreed that the Olympics were a symbol of progress, capable of "breaking Denver from the shell of provincialism . . . and catapulting it before the world as a truly international city."[7] Ballooning cost estimates that rose from $14 million to $92 million and fears of environmental damage to the Rockies raised popular doubts. Opponents gathered 77,000 signatures to place on the November 1972 ballot a state constitutional amendment and a Denver city charter amendment prohibiting further use of public funds for the Olympics. The group Citizens for Colorado's Future (CCF) reiterated that the primary beneficiaries of the Olympics would be the tourism and construction industries, while ordinary citizens would bear the costs through higher taxes. Counterattacks on the CCF as a group of political amateurs were more accurate than insulting, and the measures carried by substantial margins. The community mobilization of the 1972 campaign launched Patricia Schroeder's national political career and enabled Richard Lamm, a leader of the anti-Olympics effort, to move from the state house of representatives to the statehouse in 1974.

The transformation of Austin politics built directly on student activism at the University of Texas. As late as an open housing referendum in 1968 and the city council elections in 1969, Austin came down solidly on the side of property rights. Two years later, however, antiwar activists and environmentalists led a referendum that rejected city participation in a nuclear power project. The Coalition for a Progressive Austin was organized in 1975 to back liberal candidates for the city council, and it maintained a somewhat uneasy alliance with homeowners, whose vocal neighborhood associations were fighting intensive development. The Progressive Austinites were essentially a slow-growth group in opposition to the business agenda of the Greater Austin Association.

The Coalition for a Progressive Austin won a majority on what was quickly termed the People's Council. UT student activist Jeff Friedman became the new mayor, but it quickly became apparent that the liberal coalition was suffering from internal contradictions as it tried to please middle-class slow-growthers, radical university populists, and minorities who were happy with economic development if they could get a fair cut. After Friedman was unable to define a middle ground between the radicals and a hostile business community, the coalition's ability to govern rapidly dissipated. Nevertheless, the episode did add neighborhood and environmental issues to the city's political agenda.

In contrast to the somewhat utopian hopes and disappointments in Austin, Portland's neighborhood revolt worked by increments over the decade from 1966 to 1975. Originating with a score of self-defining neighborhoods scattered around the city, it brought a new city planning policy that directly linked the conservation of older neighborhoods for young families, expansion of downtown employment, and stronger public transit. The ferment also changed the terms of Portland politics by legitimizing neighborhood associations as participants in the policy process. As in Austin, the movement drew on men and women in their twenties and thirties and brought a new generation to political leadership—notably Neil Goldschmidt, elected mayor in 1972 at age thirty-two. Between 1969 and 1973, the average age on the Portland City Council dropped by fifteen years, with similar shifts on the Multnomah County Commission and in the state legislative delegation. The new Portland leadership reflected demographic changes typical of Western cities. Portland was younger in 1970 than it had been in 1950 or 1960. Indeed, the proportion of its residents aged fifteen to thirty-four increased from 22 percent to 30 percent during the 1960s.

The origins of the neighborhood movement were different in every section of the city. Portlanders now tend to remember the group with which they were directly involved as the first to storm the barricades of the city hall establishment. In fact, the process of neighborhood mobilization began with the Model Cities program in northeast Portland and the community action program in low-income white neighborhoods in the southeast quadrant of the city. It gained its most articulate spokespeople among the middle-class "colonists" of physically deteriorated neighborhoods that lay in a crescent around the western margin of the central business district. These neighborhoods were prime targets for institutional expansion and urban renewal, which had already taken out the city's old Italian and Jewish immigrant neighborhood of South Portland. They were also vibrant communities with affordable housing and energy-efficient locations within walking distance of downtown. In 1969, 1970, and 1971, their residents organized to fight a long list of development proposals, arguing the need to preserve older housing and mixed neighborhoods. The city's response under Mayor Goldschmidt was to create the Office of Neighborhood Associations, which offered city assistance to independent neighborhood groups. Unlike top-down systems of neighborhood consultation, Portland helps neighborhood groups set their own programs, sometimes in opposition to ideas emerging from city hall.

Two other decisions at the start of the 1970s had both a symbolic and a practical impact. One was the "deprogramming" of the Mount Hood Freeway, a five-mile connecter that would have displaced 1,700 households and devastated half a dozen struggling neighborhoods in southeast Portland. Resistance started with neighborhood groups that challenged the environmental impact statement for the freeway, giving time for Goldschmidt and his allies on the County Commission to work out an acceptable alternative that emphasized better bus service and an east-side light-rail line. At the same time, the city tore up a six-lane expressway that blighted the downtown waterfront, replacing it with a riverside park that has anchored a revitalizing downtown.

Omaha's formal planning process displayed the same shifting goals as did planning for downtown Portland. The Omaha Plan of 1956 had scarcely recognized the downtown as a problem and emphasized investment in the city's infrastructure. Ten years later, the Central Omaha Plan recognized special downtown needs but placed its faith in interstate highways and urban renewal. The next seven years, however, brought a generational transition in civic leadership and a willingness to focus on the multiple experiences that the downtown had offer. A new central business district plan in 1973 divided the city center into eight "neighborhoods." As in Portland, planners hoped to bring a younger generation of Omahans back downtown with a variety of functions and attractions, including a Central Park Mall, completed in 1980.

The rise of neighborhood liberals in cities like Austin and Portland was closely associated with the increasing importance of women as direct participants and leaders in local politics. An obvious indicator has been the long list of women elected mayor of major Western cities. Portland voters chose attorney Dorothy Lee to head a reform administration as early as 1948. Patience Latting followed in Oklahoma City in 1971. In the last twenty years, the list has expanded to include Dallas, Fort Worth, Austin, Houston, Galveston, San Antonio, Corpus Christi, El Paso, Phoenix, Santa Barbara, San Jose, San Francisco, Modesto, Stockton, and Spokane. In 1987, women served as mayor in twenty-six Western cities of at least 50,000 residents, just under half of the national total. Since Western states took the lead in granting voting rights to women before the Nineteenth Amendment, it is not surprising that women constituted at least 15 percent of state legislators in thirteen of the nineteen Western states, compared with fourteen of thirty-one Eastern states.

This ease of access to leadership positions, especially after 1970, reflected the same institutional openness that assisted neoprogressive reform after World War II. We can derive several hypotheses about political empowerment and capacity-building from the special character of Western cities and their impact on middle-class women. First, the cities of the postwar West were communities filled with newcomers who lacked ties and obligations to extended families, churches, and other community institutions. Women who had satisfied their responsibilities to their nuclear families were therefore relatively free to devote time and energy to political activity. Second, the spreading suburbs of Western cities were "frontiers" that required concerted action to solve immediate functional and service needs, like adequate schools and decent parks. Since pursuit of the residential amenity package has often been viewed as "woman's work" (in contrast to the "man's work" of economic development), burgeoning suburbs offered numerous opportunities for women to engage in volunteer civic work, to sharpen their skills as political activists, and finally to run for local office. Their work in behalf of neighborhood amenities, of course, could easily overlap with the issues of quality-of-life liberalism. Third, Western cities had fewer established political institutions such as political machines and strong parties. In the same way that it had helped the neoprogressives, a system of personal, nonparty politics was open to the influence of energetic women.

San Jose and Santa Clara County showed the specific impact of these processes in what some called "the feminist capital of the nation." Voters in 1980 made women a three-to-two majority on the Santa Clara County Board of Supervisors and a seven-to-four majority on the San Jose City Council. That majority included Mayor Janet Gray Hayes, elected in 1974 with the slogan, "Let's make San Jose better before we make it bigger." By 1982, fourteen of the fifteen cities in Santa Clara County had women on their councils, and four had a woman as mayor. Mainstream as well as radical candidates hoped for endorsements from the major women's political organizations.

The roots of political achievement lay in grassroots organizing in the 1970s that blended issues of neighborhood quality and environment, equal services for Chicanas, and feminist issues such as comparable worth and shelters for battered women. Janet Flammang has argued that women and their organizations such as the League of Women Voters, the National Women's Political Caucus, the National Organization for Women, and the Chicana Alliance filled a political vacuum in the nonpartisan arena of Santa Clara County. They defined issues, educated the electorate, recruited candidates, raised campaign funds, and rang doorbells for candidates. The same training grounds were present in comparable cities like Sacramento. In affluent Silicon Valley, the lead in the 1970s came from slow-growth environmentalists and neighborhood activists whose husbands had secure professional careers. These middle-class women joined an informal coalition of minority and labor groups to convince the citizens of San Jose to switch to district council elections. By lowering the cost of campaigning and increasing the relative importance of door-to-door canvassing, district elections helped women as well as minority candidates.

Women's participation in local politics also drew on their success in filling high-level professional and managerial jobs. The relative openness of Western cities to the economic advancement of women can be measured by women's share of executive, administrative, and managerial positions— jobs such as accountants, labor relations specialists, transportation planners, insurance underwriters, and purchasing managers. Among large metropolitan areas nationwide in 1980, the proportion ranged from 23 percent in Scranton, Pennsylvania, to 38 percent in Washington, D.C. The West accounted for eight of the top ten metropolitan areas and had only one metropolitan area under 30 percent. Opportunities were especially good in San Diego, San Francisco, San Jose, Sacramento, and Honolulu. Statewide census data show that the West is also hospitable to women entrepreneurs, as measured by the ratio of woman-owned businesses to population. Eight of the top ten states in 1987 were Western, and all nineteen Western states were in the top twenty-five.

There is no doubt that the events of the 1970s brought permanent changes in the political life of Western cities, especially by empowering women and members of minority communities. As blacks and Hispanics grew to a majority of potential voters in Oakland, for example, Anglo-American liberals became a luxury rather than a necessity in the electoral coalition that elected Lionel Wilson mayor in 1977. Wilson emphasized minority employment over the environmental concerns of his white allies and increased the share of city contracts going to minority firms. He pushed successfully for district elections that gave blacks a majority on the city council by 1983. Wilson also gave key appointments on the civil service commission, the port commission, and similar agencies to blacks and Hispanics. His choices had "long experience, considerable skill, and good standing in the political networks of the city" and helped to signal the arrival of Oakland's African-American middle class.[8]

The changing political landscape also seems to have opened new economic opportunities for minorities. The previous chapter discussed the entrepreneurial success of Asian immigrants. In addition, a U.S. census survey of minority-owned businesses in 1982 found that Western cities supported large numbers of black and Hispanic businesses relative to the size of their black and Hispanic populations. Los Angeles, San Francisco–Oakland, and Houston were the top three metropolitan areas for black businesses, followed closely by San Diego and Dallas–Fort Worth. Although the top spot for Hispanic businesses was Miami, Southwestern cities—starting with McAllen, Texas, and Santa Barbara—occupied the third through twenty-fourth slots.

The 1980s brought a synthesis between the ethnic and quality-of-life revolts of the 1970s and the growth coalitions of the earlier decades. In fact, Western cities converged on the center from two directions. On the one hand, cities like Dallas and Houston moved gradually toward the political middle as business leaders decided to co-opt rising minority populations and project a progressive image in the era of international trade and information industries. At the same time, the neighborhood and ethnic rebels of the 1970s discovered that they needed business allies in Ronald Reagan's 1980s. With declining federal funds for social services, housing, and pollution control, they needed to generate local economic growth to provide both jobs and tax dollars. At the same time that quality-of-life liberals were

aging into quality-of-life consumers and the yuppie was replacing the gra-
nola eater as the standard image of urban thirty-year-olds, the recession
years of the early 1980s occasioned some particularly sharp rethinking of
public priorities.

If any Western city was open for business in the 1980s, it was Diane
Feinstein's San Francisco. The "hyperpluralist" city experienced a brief
triumph of the neighborhood revolution in the late 1970s. George Moscone
won a narrow victory in the mayoralty race in 1976 with votes from white-
collar liberals, Latinos, blacks, and gays. The same coalition supported the
adoption of district elections, which allowed direct representation of ethnic
minorities and gays on the board of supervisors. However, the changes were
supported by only a precarious electoral majority. The murder of Moscone
and council member Harvey Milk by former council member Dan White in
1978 brought to the surface the city's deep social divisions among its
liberals, minorities, and residents of working-class neighborhoods.

As the city's new mayor, Feinstein led the return to citywide elections for
the board of supervisors in 1980. By restoring an electoral system that
dampened the impact of neighborhood agendas, commented Frances
FitzGerald, "she could proceed to steer the city back to a more conservative,
pro-business course. Though she was a liberal Democrat, she would not be
out of step in the eighties." A nationally applauded downtown plan adopted
in 1984 was a serious effort to preserve the special aesthetic of downtown
San Francisco, but it also made full provision for the continuing growth of
office facilities. As Feinstein told journalist Neal Pierce, "the plan recognizes
that growth has to take place. Without growth you get dropping retail sales,
vacancies, and blight."[9]

Cities in the desert Southwest also moved toward the political center.
Terry Goddard entered Phoenix politics as a neighborhood rebel but turned
into an alliance builder soon after his arrival in the mayor's office. He owed
his election in 1983 to voters in new white neighborhoods and minority
groups, both of which felt that doors were closed at city hall. His campaign
took the offensive against big developers like Charles Keating, Jr., who were
bankrolling his opposition. By the time of his reelection in 1985, however,
Goddard had proved to be a friend of downtown revitalization and had
made peace with much of the development industry, preparing for an
unsuccessful run for governor in 1991.

Albuquerque's Citizens Committee had lost its influence as early as 1966
because of disaffection among Hispanic voters and lackluster leadership.
Seven years later the city replaced a commission-manager charter with a
new council-mayor system involving district elections. In 1977 the city

LEGEND

Census Tracts Over 25%

Black   Chinese   Filipino   Hispanic

Ethnic neighborhoods in San Francisco. The city has a long heritage of ethnic
neighborhoods such as Chinatown and Italian-American North Beach. The national and international migrations of the later twentieth century have added
African-American, Mexican-American, and Filipino neighborhoods, all of which
affect the mix of local politics. (From Brian J. Godfrey, *Neighborhoods in Transition:
The Making of San Francisco's Ethnic and Nonconformist Communities*. Copyright ©
1988 The Regents of the University of California)

adopted its first comprehensive plan, and voters elected Mayor David Rusk on a platform of neighborhood preservation, public transit, downtown revitalization, and planned growth. "I can't get hysterical," he commented, "about big factories not going up all over the countryside."[10] Four years later, however, Rusk's identification with environmentalist rhetoric fueled his defeat by the more business-oriented Harry Kinney.

Houston was a decade behind many of the other Western cities. The more broadly based Houston Chamber of Commerce had succeeded the 8F crowd as the guardians of development interests. Moderately liberal Roy Hofheinz, mayor from 1974 to 1978, accepted federal community development funds and nudged the city closer to the American mainstream. A further slide toward the center came in 1981 with the election of Kathy Whitmire with wide liberal and ethnic support. Whitmire was far from a "no-growther," but she looked moderate when compared to opponents like former mayor and Chamber of Commerce president Louis Welch. Whitmire's appeal spanned gays, yuppies, and blacks. In office, she earned overwhelming black support in return for improving public services and signaling a new direction in law enforcement by hiring African-American Lee Brown as police chief. In working to modernize and expand Houston's minimal public sector and incorporate the black middle class, Whitmire was essentially offering an updated version of the neoprogressive agenda that had worked so well for Atlanta in the 1950s and 1960s. In concert with the restructured city council, she helped to give Houston its first decade of genuine pluralist politics in the postwar era. However, she was forced to de-emphasize social issues in favor of economic development as the Texas recession deepened and after voters rejected an equal employment opportunity measure for homosexuals in 1985. By 1989, Whitmire was firmly in the business camp, speaking in behalf of the privatization of public services, low taxes, and a good business climate. That she has been interpreted variously as a coalition builder, an agent of change, and a business-oriented conservative shows the synthesizing nature of 1980s politics.[11]

The politics of Los Angeles can likewise be read both ways. Tom Bradley's election as mayor in 1973 depended on a coalition of blacks, white liberals, and environmentalists who supported community development and affirmative-action programs that were a breath of fresh air after the Yorty administration. Massive downtown redevelopment was sold to the same alliance as a form of job creation in 1975, but the new programs gave downtown business and real estate interests a growing voice at city hall. By the 1980s, claims critic Mike Davis, the largesse of land developers had eroded any real distinctions between a Bradley administration and the entrenched Republicanism of the burgeoning suburbs.

The attractions of the political center were most visible in Denver and San Antonio, where Federico Peña and Henry Cisneros promoted what might be called *neo*-neoprogressive agendas. In each case, a young Hispanic politician brought new ideas into city government. Cisneros defeated a representative of San Antonio's downtown establishment in 1981, and Peña ousted crusty, fourteen-year incumbent Bill McNichols with the help of three thousand volunteers. If the campaigns had come a decade earlier, they might well have split their communities. In the 1980s, however, Peña and Cisneros were able to run simultaneously as technocrats and neighborhood advocates. Their administrations accepted the primacy of economic development policies but also took minority concerns far more seriously than had their predecessors. They were explicit that economic development should justify itself by producing jobs and other benefits for the poor.

Peña took office in a city with a leadership vacuum not too different from that of 1947. Like Ben Stapleton a generation earlier, McNichols had grown indifferent to any but routine services. The energy industry building boom was largely guided by the private Denver Partnership rather than the city, allowing the greatest beneficiaries of downtown development to plan its course. Peña's campaign tapped neighborhood activism that had been dormant under McNichols but also enlisted major business backers. His slogan "Imagine a Great City" was broad enough to encompass a rainbow of groups and interests. Controversy over the siting and cost of a new convention center undermined some of Peña's credibility and forced him to struggle to a narrow reelection victory in 1987. In his second term, Peña concentrated on easily identifiable projects. These included a $242 million bond issue for public works infrastructure, a comprehensive plan that paid attention both to neighborhoods and the downtown, and a new multibillion-dollar airport to compete head-on with the Dallas–Fort Worth airport. The range of the 1980s coalition is defined by two of Peña's statements. "What you heard today from the voters was the sound of Denver taking off," he commented after the voters approved the airport in May 1989. At the same time, he has claimed that his greatest achievement was breaking down barriers against citizen access to city government: "Now environmentalists are not fighting the planning board; they are serving on it. That's going to have a lasting effect."[12]

Henry Cisneros gave San Antonio its new political center six years after the collapse of the Good Government League. A pragmatic liberal with experience in Washington, he had carefully followed economic development issues as an urban studies professor and as a city council member since 1975. Overwhelming reelection margins in 1983, 1985, and 1987 gave him the chance to develop a systematic growth strategy outlined in his own report *San Antonio's Place in the Technology Environment: A Review of Opportunities and a Blueprint for Action*. This "orange book" defined five key growth sectors and served as the springboard for "Target '90," a strategic plan on which several hundred civic leaders signed off. Cisneros was described as a "state of the art civic entrepreneur," trying to link government and business and to project a new national and international reputation for his city. Underpinning his agenda was a desire to expand job opportunities for Hispanics and to build up the Hispanic middle class from which Cisneros himself had come. By 1988, burnout from more than twenty years on the fast track and a crisis in his personal life forced Cisneros to opt out of a fifth term as mayor. In eight years, however, he had managed to unite a deeply polarized community around his vision of San Antonio as a leading city of the twenty-first century.

An important national impact of the centrism of the 1980s was President Clinton's choice of Cisneros as Secretary of Housing and Urban Development and Peña as Secretary of Transportation. Its visible symbols on the Western landscape were massive downtown development projects built for public or semipublic purposes. Downtown development offered politicians the enticement of pleasing nearly everyone by giving profits to landowners and retailers, entry level jobs to minority groups, public amenities to the middle class, and a focus for civic pride to the entire community. The list of development projects in which the public sector took the lead or facilitated private investment was standard nationwide. Denver, Anchorage, Phoenix, San Jose, and Boise built centers for the performing arts in the 1980s. Albuquerque, Tulsa, San Diego, San Antonio, Portland, and Sacramento assisted festival markets and mixed-use office-retail complexes. Most costly of all were new or vastly expanded convention centers. The first wave of convention center development had been tied to urban renewal programs during the 1960s. The second wave, in the 1980s, expressed the desire to compete in the transactional economy and to find a substitute for entry-level factory jobs. As advocates of a new San Diego convention center argued in 1981, "the visitors' industry . . . puts to work young people who otherwise might be seeking welfare or be on the streets adding to the crime problem." Visitors to Seattle, Portland, San Francisco, Oakland, San Jose,

Los Angeles, San Diego, Boise, Denver, Albuquerque, San Antonio, Austin, and Houston can all find new or greatly expanded centers built since 1980.

In pursuing convention center politics, the coalition regimes are doing what Western cities have done best for nearly half a century. Political scientists often distinguish between the developmental policies of city governments and their allocative policies. The first set of policies has to do with efforts to expand the city's economic base. Since most Western cities now have forty or even fifty years of practice at economic development, it has proved relatively easy for broadened regimes to continue with programs like downtown revitalization on the venerable theory that a rising tide lifts all boats. Indeed, it has often been the white-dominated real estate establishment that has fought the greatest battles over convention center siting. Denver business interests, for example, spent six years battling between a site near Union Station and one near the existing Currigan Center. The first would have given a windfall to property owners on the northern edge of the downtown, while the second will benefit landowners in the established city core. Similarly, Seattle debated for years before rejecting the expansion of the Seattle Center (left over from its Century 21 world's fair) in favor of a new site adjacent to downtown hotels and department stores.

Allocative politics, in contrast, have to do with how the costs and benefits of growth are shared among different districts and groups within the larger community. The political revolts of the 1960s and 1970s were in direct response to neoprogressive politics that allocated benefits to the white business class and diverted costs to older neighborhoods and minority groups. On the surface, the new, improved development agenda takes explicit notice of previously neglected groups and tries to adapt the service economy to their needs. New ethnic leaders have been among the consistent advocates of convention centers as development tools, with backers including Tom Bradley and Lionel Wilson, as well as Henry Cisneros and Federico Peña.

In the years to come, Western cities face two related political challenges. As seen in the 1970s and 1980s, city administrations fall into political trouble when voters perceive downtown revitalization and neighborhood services as opposite choices in a zero-sum game. Neighborhood disaffection with growth agendas has given San Francisco fifteen years of flip-flopping politics and Seattle a moratorium on downtown development.[13] Rapid diversification of the Los Angeles City Council since 1985, reflecting neighborhood discontent with developer politics, eroded Tom Bradley's political coalition.

The second and more serious challenge comes from the incipient emergence of what we can call the "party of order." In 1991, San Franciscans elected Frank Jordan to replace incumbent Art Agnos, and Houstonians replaced Kathy Whitmire with Bob Lanier. Both of the new mayors ran law-and-order campaigns that played to middle class voters fed up with high rates of property crime, gang violence, highly visible homeless populations, and other signs of social disorder. Jordan, who served as San Francisco's police chief from 1985 to 1990, promised "clean and safe streets." Lanier promised to add 655 officers to the police force immediately. At their extreme, the racial fears of majority society may fuel the politics of hatred that have been growing beneath the surface of American society like a giant fungus that has been ignored by national leaders. The last decade brought not only former Ku Klux Klan leader David Duke to the fore as a viable political candidate in the South but also a new visibility for antiblack groups in southern California and racist appeals in mainstream state politics in Arizona. It also brought the coalescence of white supremacist groups in the rural Northwest and racially motivated assaults by white-power skinheads in cities like Portland.

It remains to be seen whether the riots in Los Angeles, San Francisco, Seattle, and other cities following the acquittal of police officers charged with using excessive force against Rodney King will promote social reform or strengthen the party of order. The 1992 disturbances in Los Angeles recapitulated the scenario of 1965—defiance of largely white authority, assaults on police and passersby, looting of white-owned (and now Korean-owned) stores, and burning of stores along Crenshaw Boulevard. The outbreak of sympathetic disturbances in many of LA's Hispanic neighborhoods and in other Western cities mirrored the riots that followed the assassination of Martin Luther King, Jr., in 1968. More people died in the 1992 riot, however, than in any single disturbance of the 1960s. In the 1960s, after initial finger-pointing and efforts to place the blame on a small criminal element (efforts at denial repeated in 1992), seeing the riots as political actions helped to show the exhaustion of postwar growth coalitions and to open American cities to a decade of populist initiatives. Concerned citizens can hope that the riots of 1992 opened the door to a similar recognition of economic inequalities and a strengthening of pluralistic politics rather than to repression in the name of public order.

**PART 3   CITIES AND THE SHAPING OF THE
MODERN WEST**

6

MULTICENTERED CITIES

In Cyra McFadden's novel *The Serial: A Year in the Life of Marin County,* her fictionalized "refugees" from San Francisco reflect on their move to the suburbs:

> Now they lived in Mill Valley . . . a tract house on the Sutton Manor flatlands; it was big enough, comfortable, and just barely affordable. Besides, the first time they'd seen it, a racing green '63 TR-4 was parked in the driveway, a strong indication that the house's present owners were okay people. If they could live in a tract house, so could Kate and Harvey. . . . And it was still Marin, though just barely; Kate still hated to tell people, when she gave directions, to stay on East Blithedale all the way out, as if they were heading for 101, turn left at the Chevron station, go past the Red Cart, and turn right at the carwash.[1]

Kate and Harvey were not the only people who were confused about the character of the urban West. As the region's residential communities spread over the landscape in the boom years that followed World War II, Americans struggled to define the character of the highly suburbanized cities of California, Colorado, Arizona, and Texas. Over the last half-century, we have slowly come to realize that Western cities can best be understood as characteristic products of twentieth century America. They seem incoherent if we try to fit them into the mold of Glasgow, Toronto, or Boston, for they lack the sense of closure that lies at the heart of European urban design. They are simple to read, however, if we see them as clear expressions of the new technologies of movement and communication. They cluster straight-

Horizontal Los Angeles. The community of Westchester, photographed in 1949, epitomized the national image of Los Angeles as a city of endless horizontal sprawl in look-alike subdivisions. (Courtesy of the California Historical Society/Ticor Title Insurance, Los Angeles, Department of Special Collections, University of Southern California Library)

forwardly along their highways. Their residents are tied together by long-distance networks of travel and communication. Their streets and houses tell how Americans have constructed their everyday lives in the postwar decades. Approaching the southern California city of "San Narciso," one of Thomas Pynchon's fictive characters knew how to read the Western city as she "looked down a slope, needing to squint for the sunlight, onto a vast sprawl of houses, which had grown up all together, like a well-tended crop. . . . The ordered swirl of houses and streets, from this high angle, sprang at her now with the same unexpected, astonishing clarity as the circuit card had."[2]

For Americans after 1945, Western cities certainly *looked* like the future, especially in their California manifestations. The Association of American Geographers devoted a special 1959 issue of their scholarly journal to the thesis that greater Los Angeles "epitomizes the recent dominance of the city" in American society. San Diego journalist Neil Morgan in 1963 restated the nineteenth century idea that exuberantly growing Western cities led the nation's westward tilt. Two years later, *Fortune* described Los Angeles as the "prototype of the supercity." Richard Austin Smith found "a scaled-down, speeded-up version of the process of urbanization" and concluded that Los Angeles "may now be emerging as the forerunner of the urban world of tomorrow." To other writers of the decade it was a "leading city" or even the "ultimate city." Journalist Richard Elman traveled to the Los Angeles suburb of Compton "with the thought in mind that this was the future . . . what lies in store for all the new suburbs of all the big cities of America."[3]

Many found the prospect both intimidating and appalling. William H. Whyte offered Santa Clara and San Bernardino counties as extremes of uncontrolled sprawl. Peter Blake used a photographic sequence on the construction of Lakewood, a new community in Los Angeles County, to illustrate the contribution of large-scale subdivisions to the spread of *God's Own Junkyard*. A distinguished historian found Los Angeles a nebulous entity that remains "the least 'legible' of the great settlements of the world." To an anonymous journalist it was "topless, bottomless, shapeless and endless . . . random, frenzied, rootless, and unplanned." Its suburbs were "formless." It was a "violently aggressive organism" with no pattern but "helter-skelter" growth. Like Phoenix and Houston, it frequently attracted epithets like "noncity" and "nowhere city."[4]

Despite the attacks on smog-shrouded subdivisions and amoeboid sprawl, the 1960s also brought growing attention to the idea that Western cities—complete with their cars and drive-ins—represented not merely the unavoidable American future but a new urban form that had to be judged on its own terms. In 1967, for example, Robert Riley tested urban myths against the new cities of the Southwest. In Tucson, Albuquerque, Las Vegas, Phoenix, Odessa-Midland, and similar metropolitan areas, he found that the national processes of mobility and affluence were operating without an older urban fabric to get in the way. "It could even be," he argued, "that what we are seeing emerging is the third major stage of urban development—a post-industrial city as different from the industrial city as that city was from pre-industrial urban settlements."[5]

Working from a home base of Berkeley, James Vance and Melvin Webber extrapolated general models of the new metropolis from close observation of the booming environs of the San Francisco Bay area. Vance suggested in 1964 that large metropolitan areas were subdividing into largely independent and isolated urban realms that developed side by side with little social or economic connection. The East Bay and South Bay realms needed little contact with the presumed central city of San Francisco. Webber took the same word and posited an even looser metropolitan structure. In his conception, the "nonplace urban realm" was replacing the physically centered city with a complex set of social and economic networks. As instant communication made central location a choice rather than a necessity, new Western cities could take a far looser and more open form.[6]

In the 1970s and 1980s, a group of urban specialists in southern California developed a Los Angeles–based equivalent of the historic "Chicago School" theories of urban growth and change. They pointed to the decentralization of the metropolis, its multiple independent centers, its influence over vast urban fields, its international connections, and its shifting employment patterns as models of future urban development. In neomarxist language, Los Angeles is the "paradigmatic expression of late capitalist industrialization, urbanization, and social life." Historian Sam Bass Warner, Jr., has agreed that it is "par excellence a city of the past half century" and Dolores Hayden that it is "the largest, most complex, mid-to-late 20th century city in the U.S." and is representative of American culture and values.[7] A logical next step has been to introduce Orange County as the test case of an even newer "postsuburban" environment whose own self-sustaining economy and social life repeat and expand the patterns of Los Angeles.

A key for understanding the complex interactions of appearance, form, and function in Los Angeles and its Southwestern cousins is Reyner Banham's 1971 book *Los Angeles: The Architecture of Four Ecologies*. A British architect and critic, Banham came to California with a fresh eye. His book mixes a traditional discussion of Los Angeles architects and buildings with an effort to define subareas or "ecologies" characterized by distinctive inter-actions between the natural landscape, architectural choices, and prevailing lifestyles. The seventy miles of "surfurbia" make Los Angeles "the greatest City-on-the-Shore in the world."[8] The region's foothills neighborhoods, its suburbanized valleys, and its "autopian" freeways constitute the other ecologies. The book has become a point of reference that is directly cited and unconsciously quoted by critics and journalists alike.

Behind the several ecologies, Banham found two essential characteris-tics: movement and linearity. As many observers have noted, Los Angeles is structured around individual control over personal travel. It functions be-cause its citizens are able to utilize its freeway system for access to all of its subareas. In turn, a city based on automobiles becomes a linear city, with Wilshire Boulevard as the first linear downtown. Neighborhoods are de-fined by freeways. Every parallel highway and every adjacent neighbor-hood carries equal weight in the city's design. Life in Los Angeles means choice and circulation within an open environment that is spatially and perhaps even socially egalitarian.

Many of the traits of Los Angeles are drawn even more clearly in Las Vegas. At the same time that Banham was learning to drive the southern California freeways, Robert Venturi, Denise Scott Brown, and Steven Izenour were leading a class of Yale architecture students through a seminar called "Learning from Las Vegas." The resulting book defines Las Vegas as a national model of an emerging urban form, an exaggerated example of emerging patterns. It is presented as the cultural expression of the Sunbelt Southwest—a New Florence to the New Rome of Los Angeles. Its central component is the commercial strip, a new main street made up of separate nodes of activity separated by parking lots, announced by huge signs, and connected by automobiles. Like Los Angeles, it is a city designed around high speed, with spaces created by billboards and traffic signals rather than buildings.

The Sprawl City of Las Vegas, in turn, led to a startling comment by John Brinkerhoff Jackson, the founding editor of *Landscape* magazine and one of the most creative thinkers about the ways in which Americans have adapted the natural environment to everyday use. Writing a few years ago, he commented that "almost all up-to-date American cities west of the Mississippi are variations on a basic prototype, and that prototype is Lub-bock, Texas. . . . There is a new kind of city evolving in America, chiefly in the Sunbelt, and on a small scale Lubbock tells us what those new cities look like." Jackson's point is that what we learn from the Las Vegas Strip we can also learn from other cities built around the automobile. Throughout the Southwest, Jackson points out, highway strips are as old as the cities themselves. Residential areas fill in as repetitive, low-density units within the framework of the thoroughfares. Lubbock and its sister cities tell us "how the street, the road, the highway has taken the place of architecture as the basic visual element, the infrastructure of the city."[9]

Taken together, Lubbock, Las Vegas, and Los Angeles offer consistent lessons about the form and visual character of most Western cities. They are vernacular environments that have responded to the tastes and demands of middle Americans, with only sporadic and often *post facto* attention to comprehensive planning and urban design. These ordinary cities are linear rather than centered and hierarchical. The ideal model has no privileged locations comparable to the downtowns of turn-of-the-century American cities or the public centers of historic cities. With the automobile reducing the time and inconvenience of distance, each district has approximate equality of position along the axis or within the grid. As John Gregory Dunne has asserted, "the freeway is totally egalitarian, a populist notion that makes Los Angeles comprehensible and complete."[10]

We have to be careful, however, when we move from critical analysis to measurement in defining the distinct character of Western cities. On several obvious dimensions they have tended to converge on the national average. At the end of World War II, for example, a number of smaller cities such as Tucson and Albuquerque concentrated higher-status residents in the central city and relegated the poor and uneducated to the fringe in a pattern reminiscent of medieval Europe or colonial Latin America. During the 1950s and 1960s, however, Western suburbs came increasingly to match those of older cities as the homes of a disproportionate share of upper-status residents. The suburban ring shifted from lower to higher status during the 1950s in Denver and San Antonio, and during the 1960s in Tucson.

Nor do Western cities "sprawl" more than those of the American mid-lands, at least as measured by such factors as automobile use, commuting patterns, and population density. The West in 1980 contained thirty-five metropolitan areas with populations of 300,000 or more. They can be matched with twenty-five metropolitan areas located from the Mississippi River eastward (but excluding the extremely low density cities of Florida and the extremely high density cities of the North Atlantic seaboard). The results are clear: Western cities are not markedly different from those of the nation's nineteenth-century heartland on two-dimensional measures of density and the decentralization of activities. As measured by the median value for each regional set of cities, Western downtowns have held a slightly higher proportion of total metropolitan-area retail sales (4 percent compared to 3 percent for Eastern cities) and a roughly equal proportion of sales of "big ticket" comparison goods (5 percent of metro area sales). Hospital services remain more centralized in Eastern cities, presumably because of the inertia of heavy capital investment in older, centrally located hospitals. Residential patterns actually reverse our expectations, with Western cities showing higher population densities (2,680 persons per square mile compared to 2,539) and a lower proportion of single-family houses (65 percent of housing units compared to 70 percent).

Western city dwellers are also similar to Easterners in their transportation choices. Westerners are as likely as other Americans to get to work on foot and nearly as likely to utilize public transit, although the median percentage for each option is distressingly small at 3 to 4 percent of all commuters. Indeed, Western cities have often been in the forefront of efforts to curb the impact of the automobile. Planner Victor Gruen chose Fort Worth as the test case for an auto-free downtown, but after Fort Worth balked at the cost of Gruen's plans, he helped Fresno to become the first large city to exclude cars from its major downtown shopping streets in 1964. Portland in 1977, Denver in 1982, and San Antonio in the 1990s have led in the development of downtown transit malls in which buses are funneled along auto-free streets to speed mass transit. Seattle has buried its own peculiar version of a transit mall in a $400 million, 1.3-mile bus tunnel beneath its central business district.

There is little truth to the popular myth that the auto dependency of Los Angeles is the product of a corporate conspiracy. The story line in *Who Framed Roger Rabbit?* notwithstanding, the big red cars of the Pacific Electric trains disappeared because of poor service and consumer preference, not conniving by General Motors and Firestone. The frequently cited but seldom read antitrust decision against GM in 1948 found the company guilty of putting the squeeze on other bus manufacturers rather than undermining rail transit. In 1993, Los Angeles opened the first 4.4 miles of a 23-mile Wilshire Boulevard subway running west from downtown. The opening of a 22-mile light-rail line to Long Beach in 1990 had already brought Los Angeles into line with San Francisco, Sacramento, Portland, San Jose, and San Diego (as well as Vancouver, Edmonton, and Calgary) as Western cities with new rail transit systems.

If there is scanty evidence that Western cities are especially dependent on automobiles or spread their people and activities more thinly over the landscape than Midwestern cities, what is it that makes observers consistently *think* that they are different? To discover the answer, we need to look at three dimensions rather than two—at cityscapes rather than street maps. The skylines of the cities of the greater Southwest have stayed close to the ground. They have spread *evenly* rather than thinly across their sites. Design choices have combined with natural environments to create cityscapes marked by openness in three dimensions. Similar design characteristics extend from the northern plains and the northern Rockies southward to California and Texas. Denver, said one commentator, drapes over the Colorado plains and foothills like a "lumpy pancake." Los Angeles, agreed architecture critic Brendan Gill, has "hugged the ground on which it was built."[11]

The standard model of American cities assumes that the intensity with which land is used decreases steadily with distance from the downtown. A high-rise central business district gives way first to a zone of multistory factories and warehouses left over from earlier generations, then to a ring of mid-rise and walkup apartments, then to multistory single-family residences, and finally to postwar tracts of split-level and single-level houses. The regular decline of population density as we move outward from the center allows us to define standard density gradients that describe straight lines or continuous curves.

In the greater Southwest, in contrast, land use does not taper gradually in intensity from the edge of the typical downtown. It plunges abruptly from a glimmering set of new high-rises to a low-rise, usually one-story, city that stretches away to the horizon. In the 1840s, Frederick Engels described *The Condition of the Working Class in England* by "walking" his readers through the neighborhoods of Manchester. The modern equivalent is to "drive" the reader from the airport to the central business district. Leaving Los Angeles International Airport for the center of the city, we turn from Sepulveda onto La Tijera, La Cienaga, Stocker, Crenshaw, Coliseum, Rodeo, and Figueroa. There are one-floor commercial strips, one-story bungalows on tiny lots, blocks of two-story apartments, a failed first-generation shopping center, more one-story retailing, and a handful of multistory business buildings in a rudimentary light-manufacturing zone just south of downtown. The stranger's drive into Los Angeles repeats the experience of a character in Alison Lurie's novel *The Nowhere City*: "She gestured at Mar Vista laid out below the freeway: a random grid of service stations, two-story apartment buildings, drive-ins, palms, and factories; and block after block of stucco cottages."[12]

What some observers have taken to be a cityscape peculiar to Los Angeles is typical of much of the West. The region's characteristic styles in residential architecture have had their roots outside the traditional sources of Great Britain, the North Sea littoral of Europe, and the northeastern United States. Spanish colonial styles, bungalows, ranch houses, and twentieth-century modern houses evolved and flourished in response to the region's particular physical and social environment. Their common traits have included low profiles; prominent horizontal lines established by flat or sweeping shallow-angle roofs; wide porches and patios for protection from the sun in the days before air conditioning; and openness to the outdoors through porches, wide windows, and open floor plans.

Even before the arrival of Anglo-Americans, with their North Atlantic architectural heritage, Spanish colonists in the Southwest had established a one-story vernacular that adapted the urban courtyard design of Spain and Mexico to the circumstances of the frontier. Settlers filled a town like Tucson with "low-profile, flush-front rectangular cluster houses built on a single level." Early sketches of San Antonio, Santa Fe, and Los Angeles show similar assortments of low-built structures set in rows or arranged around courtyards. Agricultural settlers on the Hispanic frontier in New Mexico and Colorado adapted the same forms, starting with one-story houses around a plaza and later adding correlleras—terraces of houses flanking the roads into the plaza. When migrants arrived in smaller groups, they usually built a *placita,* using low adobe sheds, workshops, and houses with common walls to encircle a hollow square.

Ranch houses of the nineteenth century cattle frontier and ranch-style tract houses of the twentieth century are the direct descendants of the Hispanic buildings. Ranchers usually started with a set of directly connecting rooms, sometimes wrapped around a courtyard or growing incrementally at the ends. In more elegant versions, ranch houses were separated from their auxiliary buildings and turned outward through wider windows and broad porches. In turn, the gentleman's ranch house inspired the suburban versions of the mid twentieth century, with their low profiles, flowing interior spaces, and orientation to the outdoors. A book on *Western Ranch Houses* published in 1945 by *Sunset* magazine, the great proponent of the California idyll, emphasized the Spanish origins of the newly popular style. More recently, critic Brendan Gill has stressed the regional character of a style brought into being by the climate and culture of the Pacific.

The early decades of the twentieth century were the era of the bungalow in Western cities. The style derived in part from British colonial buildings in India, where *bangla* meant a low house with galleries or porches on all sides. Although one American adaptation was the sophisticated "rustic" country or recreational home for the Northeastern elite, the bungalow as a popular middle-class style found its home ground in California. The word was scarcely known in 1900, yet by 1910 it had become a vastly popular generic term, considered both on the West Coast and elsewhere as a southern California phenomenon. The typical bungalow rose one or one and a half stories, often disguising the second floor with a long, projecting, low-pitched roof. Interior and exterior space interpenetrated through large front porches and numerous windows. Interiors offered few barriers between the first-floor rooms.

Bungalows matched the social and physical environments of the West. Informal interiors and an emphasis on the outdoors seemed appropriate to the new middle-class cities of the Pacific Coast. Porches and overhangs provided shelter from summer heat. As Clifford Clark has commented, bungalows were "easily adapted to the low, sculptured hills and flat valley areas, helping to maintain the contour line of the landscape. In such an environment, small, single-family houses could be packed relatively closely together without creating a sense of crowding or congestion."[13] Bungalows spread quickly through the greater Southwest. An architect recently relocated from California built Boise's first bungalow in 1904, and the style caught on quickly as the city boomed during the next few years. White-collar householders in Salt Lake City filled the "Avenues" neighborhood northeast of Temple Square and the state capitol with bungalows that reflected the thrifty lifestyle of the Mormon middle class. Denverites in the 1910s and 1920s built their own version, using brick rather than wood and leaving usable sunlit basements for partial protection from the extremes of the Great Plains climate.[14] Along the Northwest Coast, the eight-month drizzly season and the ubiquity of the lumber industry brought special modifications in Portland and Seattle. The early decades of the century saw the proliferation of frame bungalows and two-story houses that wore exposed rafters and wide shingled roofs like the ribs and fabric of a giant umbrella.

The final characteristic style of Western cities—the "modern" or "contemporary" house—has parallels to the bungalow. It, too, is an imported style, brought to the United States by members of the European avant-garde in the 1920s and 1930s. With horizontal lines, flat roofs, low profiles, open interiors, and large windows, modern houses seemed especially appropriate to California society and California light. European-born architects such as Richard Neutra and Rudolph Schindler helped to establish the style with a series of commissions for showplace houses that stretched close to the ground or cascaded over vertical sites. A study of the international style in

Housing the Western middle class. From the Pacific to the Midwest, variations on the California bungalow dominated middle-class housing from the Progressive Era to the Great Depression. The bungalow's horizontal lines helped to define the character of Western cityscapes. These examples from the Washington Park area of Denver are typical of the Colorado version, with a low roof and usable basement with natural light to fight the climate of the Great Plains. (Photograph by the author)

1940 found the largest number of examples in California, with increasing popularity elsewhere in the southern tier of states through Arizona, Texas, and Florida. The California-based magazine *Arts and Architecture* helped to publicize the style after World War II by publishing a long series of "Case Study Houses." The northwest variant shared the rectilinearity, the open, functional floor plans, and the sheltering roof projections, but substituted naturally finished wood for wide expanses of glass.

The preference for low-slung, horizontal styles has created neighborhoods and commercial strips very different from those of the Northeast and Midwest. The sprawling working-class neighborhoods on the west side of

San Antonio, with their blocks of one-story houses, stand in sharp contrast to Milwaukee or Chicago, where successful immigrant families built two-story houses over raised basements and beneath steeply pitched roofs to shed the heavy snows of the Great Lakes states. They contrast even more sharply with the vertical row houses of Baltimore and Philadelphia, which stacked two narrow floors, an attic, and a basement. For a more recent period, the Cape Cod houses of Levittown, New York, with their strong vertical emphasis, offer the same contrast to the contemporaneous hip-roofed ranch houses of Lakewood, California.

Another case in point is the contrast between Broad Street in Columbus, Ohio, and Colfax Avenue in Denver. Both are commercial strips that form parts of U.S. Route 40, but they are very different in appearance. Lined with converted mansions, institutional headquarters, old storefronts, and new strip development, Broad Street reflects generations of use and adaptation. Colfax is a street of the mid twentieth century that grew simultaneously with Denver's transformation into a regional metropolis. Its endless procession of low-rise commercial buildings testifies more than anything to the growth of Denver from the war boom of the 1940s to the opening of I-70 in the 1960s.

Impressionistic evidence is supported by a systematic comparison of popular housing choices in Ohio and California. Richard Fusch and Larry Ford counted single-family housing styles within corridors leading outward from the centers of Columbus and San Diego. The results are clear. Ohioans have preferred to live on two levels. Depending on the decade, they built steep-roofed Queen Anne houses, two-story American basic and four-square houses, European colonial revival houses, Cape Cod bungalows, and two-story "colonial moderns." San Diegans built exactly what we would predict—low-set bungalows, Spanish revival houses, and ranch houses.

Multifamily housing shows the same contrast between vertical cities in the Northeast and horizontal cities in the Southwest. The apartment house was a European import to the United States after the Civil War, but until well into the twentieth century, high-rise housing for both the upper and lower classes remained largely a phenomenon of New York and other large Northeastern cities. An apartment boom of the 1920s had much greater impact on the northern half of the country than the southern. In eight northern-tier cities in 1960, the proportion of dwelling units located in structures with ten or more units ranged from 9 to 43 percent, with a median of 14 percent. In eleven Western cities, the same proportion ranged from 2 to 14 percent, with a median of 6 percent. When Southwesterners did build multifamily housing, moreover, they often used the distinctly regional style of the one-story U-shaped apartment court. Whether they are carefully designed buildings by Los Angeles architects Irving Gill and Rudolph Schindler from the 1910s and 1920s or speculative units thrown up for low-income renters, the origins of the apartment court obviously lie in the Hispanic terraces and *placitas* of the previous century.

The same low-rise preference was expressed in public housing projects of the 1940s and 1950s. The high-rise public housing warehouses of New York, Chicago, and St. Louis have become notorious as architectural and social mistakes. Western cities during the same decades commonly built public housing in one-story or two-story blocks, as with Seattle's pioneering Yesler Terrace. The practical result could sometimes be a confusing discrepancy between Eastern expectations and Western cities. In search of a motel in the southern reaches of Los Angeles, Richard Elman reported finding "a greenish low building of stripped-down cinder block with a sign in front on which only the word 'Gardens' was legible." He was looking for the rental office when a passing policeman pointed out in no uncertain terms that it was a *housing project* for *poor people*. "Never mind my embarrassment," Elman continues, "if that was a housing project I was now completely disoriented. There weren't more than eight tiny units with little boxy windows and a wooden stoop in front, no trees anywhere. It looked just the way motels used to look."[15]

A new apartment boom since the 1960s has brought the proportion of multifamily housing in Western cities even with national levels. Much of the new construction, however, has been in garden apartments and two-story apartment blocks scattered through older districts. We can establish the similarity with the help of the American Housing Survey of the United States Department of Housing and Urban Development, which gathers data for selected cities on the proportion of housing units in buildings of four or more stories. Information is available for the years around 1980 for twenty of the thirty-five Western cities used in previous comparisons and for thirteen of the Eastern cities. The proportions in the East range from 0.7 to 9.1 percent, with a median of 2.7 percent. In the West they range from 0.2 to 19.0 percent, with a median of 1.55 percent. If the unusual case of Honolulu is omitted, the Southwestern range is 0.2 to 6.7 and the median slips to 1.5 percent.

The openness of the natural environment in the West underlies and accentuates the horizontality of their built environments. In the simplest terms, we can appreciate their special form because we can see it. We can take in smaller cities like Santa Fe or Cheyenne at a single glance. We can see enough of most larger cities to comprehend them as units in a way that is impossible in the East.

Southwestern and mountain cities are held together by a high sun and bright air. It is this clarity of sight that makes the region special—not the brown earth, and not flowing water or its absence, but open horizons. Alison Lurie took light as the symbol of the intrusive newness of Los Angeles. The California sun shines with "impartial brilliance" on the trans-planted New Englanders in *The Nowhere City*, filters through the drawn drapes of their new house, floods them at the beach. The central character stands on his front walk and looks up at the "intense blue overhead, crossed by trails of jet vapor, dimming to a white haze at the horizon." His letters home talk about "the dry light, the white-walled houses with their orange and lemon trees, the Santa Monica Mountains rising smoky green and brown against the north edge of the sky."[16]

Perhaps most obviously, Western cities are open to view because so many of them offer natural vantage points. Baltimore and Milwaukee can only be experienced as a series of neighborhoods and a succession of scenes unfold-ing at eye level. We can see Los Angeles (or at least a substantial part of it) all at once. "Once in the fall of '64," wrote Christopher Rand, "I got a fine view of the whole West Side [of Los Angeles]. . . . I was walking southward in the Santa Monica Mountains, and suddenly I rounded a peak and saw the ocean. . . . Small waves were breaking on the beach, which ran off below me, in a graceful curve, to the dune-shaped, hazy height of Palos Verdes, twenty miles away. Inland from the beach, from all twenty miles of it, lay the sprawling city, stretching on to the interior and finally meeting the distant faint brown hills that rimmed the L. A. Basin."[17] Versions of this view of Los Angeles from its mountains have become a cliché in magazine photo spreads and advertisements for new Buicks, but it is a cliché because it forms and confirms our image of how we view and understand the urban complex of southern California.

Other Western cities are also open to inspection. San Francisco, wrote Jean-Paul Sartre, is "a city of air, salt, and sea, built in the shape of an amphitheatre." Santa Barbara and Oakland are built against coastal hills, Honolulu against the central peaks of Oahu, Tucson below the Santa Cata-lina Mountains, Albuquerque, Santa Fe, and Colorado Springs at the base of the Rockies. Salt Lake City lies as Richard Burton saw it 130 years ago, occupying "the rolling brow of a slight decline at the western base of the Wasach . . . stretched before us as upon a map." The mass of the Franklin Mountains thrusts at the center of El Paso. From its slopes we can overlook the length and breadth of the city. "As it widens out south eastward into its valley," wrote Duncan Aikman, "El Paso looks almost as big as Indianapolis and certainly bigger than Peoria."[18] Other river cities—Denver, Cheyenne, Casper, Boise, Billings, Bismarck, Grand Junction—sweep up broad, shallow slopes from the stream at their center. When we find the proper vantage points on the ridges and escarpments that mark the margins of their valleys, we can see them as single metropolitan units.

Walter Van Tilburg Clark opened *The City of Trembling Leaves,* his 1945 novel about coming of age in Reno, with a summary of the special openness of Western cities. Built along the Truckee River as it pours out of the Sierra Nevada, Reno is defined by "the vigor of the sun and the height of the mountains." From the hills that line the north side of the city, "you look down across the whole billowing sea of the treetops of Reno [and] . . . see the tops of downtown places, the Medico-Dental Building, the roof sign of the Riverside Hotel." Beyond to the south the city slopes upward again from the river, "a high region of new homes, bungalows, ornamented brick structures of greater size, a number of which it would be difficult to describe fairly, and white, Spanish houses. This region seems to become steadily more open, windy and sunlit as you move out." To the east the city spills into the widening valley, where "the light spreads widely."[19] Like the other cities of the West, Reno is built to be seen.

The corollary of the open city is the unbounded city. The typical Western city is capable of indefinite extension by adding easily reproducible units pulled from the box of urban Tinkertoys. The structure of the city itself presents no arguments against placing one more casino at the end of the strip or one more subdivision beyond the last. In such extensive cityscapes, Americans have been especially likely to create order by building new and independent nuclei to serve as alternatives to the historic city center. The result of this planned polycentrism is a metropolis that equalizes locations in terms of political and economic power.

We can, if we want, continue the pattern we have started with Lubbock and Las Vegas and call this new understanding "learning from Las Colinas and Costa Mesa." What experts have variously termed "outer cities," "out-towns," "mini-cities," "megacenters," or "technoburbs" are loosely connected and substantially self-sufficient suburban realms in which hundreds of thousands of residents may orbit around newly created concentrations of employment, retailing, and services. Examples range from the Denver Tech Center to Orange County employment nodes to the "Contra Costopolis" around Walnut Creek northeast of Oakland.

Although Houston boosters like to claim the Post Oak–Galleria district as the tenth largest "downtown" in the United States, it offers few reminders of historical city centers. It takes on many of the elements of a downtown but spreads them over four or five times the space. The sixty-four-story Transco Tower sits in a sea of parking near an interchange of West Loop 610. The huge Galleria shopping mall, opened in 1970 and later doubled in size, is one of the largest on the continent. A daytime population that tops 60,000 works in isolated clusters of high-rise offices and hotels. A few of the pieces are connected by pedestrian walkways (but not sidewalks). Most are tied together only by automobile.

Las Colinas near the Dallas–Fort Worth airport has been an effort to plan more systematically in the new suburban style. Massive investment in infrastructure and amenities transformed a nineteen-square-mile ranch by adding a broad lake, canals, and plenty of carefully tended green space. Las Colinas had reached half its projected work force of 100,000 by 1986. Its inventory of office space supposedly matched that of downtown Dallas in the 1950s. The neat and tidy environment has been especially attractive for corporate regional offices of firms like IBM, Xerox, DuPont, and AT&T. At the same time, most of the office workers commute from other suburbs. Journalist John Louv has noted that Las Colinas has no street life or social life outside the athletic club and the carefully segregated shopping. In addition, the development went into receivership during the Texas real estate depression of the 1980s. The location of choice for entrepreneurs rather than organization persons has been the bustling chaos of the Golden Triangle area sprawling along the freeway loop in the north Dallas suburbs.

Located across Lake Washington from Seattle, downtown Bellevue offers another type of self-conscious alternative to the typical freeway-based out-town, with its unrelated pieces of showoff architecture. Only two bridges link the fast-growing eastern suburbs of King County to Seattle, giving Bellevue an enormous advantage in accessibility. Beginning in the late 1970s, Bellevue faced a proposed freeway shopping mall and a volley of scattershot office development that threatened to Houstonize the city's neighborhoods. Its response was to zone for a high-rise core. New office towers have to pass a design review and must build to the sidewalk rather than cower behind parking lots. A new retail center and a transit terminal anchor the ends of a pedestrian axis. Plans require that a third of downtown workers arrive by car pool or bus. The goal is a suburban center that offers the intensity and critical mass of a traditional downtown.

The Las Colinas and Bellevue experiments with careful planning for alternative downtowns are steps toward fully articulated satellite cities. The availability of large tracts of empty land in single or limited ownership near Western cities has made New Towns relatively easy to create as real estate deals. The roots of Irvine, California, for example, date to the 1860s and 1870s, when James Irvine acquired title to several ranches in the southern portion of the future Orange County. The Irvine Company moved from agriculture to land development in the 1950s, leasing lots in expensive coastal subdivisions around Newport Bay. By 1960 the spread of Orange County suburbia was bringing frequent offers for other portions of the property. Rising property tax assessments that valued the ranch's agricultural land at its potential for urban use were another pressure for urbanization. Between 1959 and 1964, architect William Pereira and Irvine Company employees developed a plan for a 40,000-acre tract between Newport Bay and the site of a new University of California campus. They envisioned a set of communities, each with a mix of housing, schools, and shopping centers. The residential communities would be linked to two major industrial sites and a Newport Center "downtown." Large builders erected the new housing on leased parcels, leaving the company in clear control of long-term development. Success in attracting upper-income residents in the 1960s led to a 1970 plan revision, which divided 53,000 acres among twenty-four residential "villages." Covering only part of the Irvine Company lands, the incorporated city of Irvine counted over 110,000 residents by 1990.

The Woodlands is another of the new-town experiments. George Mitchell, a futurist and energy king, viewed his development fifteen miles north of Houston International Airport as a new kind of "cluster city." Unlike Irvine, the Woodlands was designed to include low-income housing, in part to obtain a HUD guarantee for $50 million of development costs. Set among lakes and pine woods, the city sells a combination of small-town nostalgia and high-tech communications infrastructure. From initial design work in 1966 until 1975, its future was in doubt because of lagging demand for housing, lax internal management, and the inability of HUD to deliver on its commitment. Only a corporate reorganization, the Houston energy boom of the latter 1970s, and George Mitchell's own money finally rescued the Woodlands Development Corporation.

The obvious danger of planned communities is social segregation. With the requirements of federal aid, by the early 1980s the Woodlands itself had achieved creditable progress toward a social and racial mix (9 percent minority) and development of its employment base. With unfortunate frequency, however, the builders and residents of other new communities have tried to lock the gates against undesired outsiders. Dozens of "minimal cities" were incorporated in Los Angeles County during the 1950s and 1960s in order to keep control of local development in the hands of narrowly construed middle-class residents. Under the "Lakewood plan," small cities could contract for services from the county while zoning out the poor. Town boundaries usually marked dividing lines between cheaper and more expensive housing. Some communities carried their resistance to social heterogeneity even further. Wealthy and WASPish San Marino decided to close its parks on weekends to exclude Hispanic and Asian families from nearby towns. Mike Davis has summarized the spread of "nimbyism" (the "not in my backyard" syndrome) in the San Fernando Valley:

> The big, unitary issues of the late 1970s (taxes, busing and density) were supplanted in the late 1980s by an exotic welter of "nimby" protests: against traffic congestion, mini-mall development, airport expansion, school siting, the demolition of the Tail O'Clock restaurant, the erection of a mosque, an arts park, subdivision and apartment construction, road widening, the shaving of a hillside, 'diamond' lanes, trailers for the homeless, the disappearance of horse stables, and the construction of a tortilla factory.[20]

The desire for social distance also has its architectural dimension. As they do in the suburbs of the Northeast, many of the most affluent of the new subdivisions of Texas, Arizona, and California hide behind walls and gates. Names like Hidden Hills and Rancho Mirage are apt descriptors. Downtown architecture follows the same script. Many of the new towers of downtown Dallas are linked by a network of underground passages that allow their middle-class tenants to avoid any direct contact with the street and its people. On redeveloped Bunker Hill on the northwest edge of downtown Los Angeles, skybridges knit great high-rises into a fortified citadel that turns blank walls to the sidewalks and turns streets into tunnels.

Despite these dystopian aspects of southern California and Texas cityscapes, the political adjustment to the polycentric metropolis may well be more effective in many parts of the West and South than in the Northeast or Midwest. The region's institutional openness has allowed Western cities to better adapt their political structures and organizational responses to the new realities of social and economic geography. On the average, the suburban West is served by stronger comprehensive governments (that is, governments that provide a full range of public services) than are the suburbs of the East. Moreover, the realities of political influence in Western metropolitan areas clearly reflect the outward shift of economic power and the rise of functionally independent suburban realms.

General descriptions of government organization in American metropolitan areas commonly stress the fragmentation of their suburban rings
among scores or hundreds of cities, towns, special districts, and other taxing
units. The small suburban governments protect specific land uses (both
residential communities and industrial enclaves) and defend distinct lifestyles by controlling social access. Although small suburban governments
have developed a wide range of techniques for protecting community identity and status, they have limited capacity for public entrepreneurship. They
lack the interest and ability to play an active role in promoting economic
growth or to develop major public facilities. Indeed, there is a positive
association between metropolitan fragmentation and the economic decline
of central cities.

On closer review, however, it appears that many Western cities have
avoided the greatest extremes of government fragmentation. Nine of the
twelve metropolitan cities with the most successful annexation efforts in the
1950s were located in Texas, Oklahoma, Arizona, and California. El Paso,
for example, added twenty-eight square miles of land on its north side in
1954 and forty-four square miles to the south in 1955, allowing the central
city to gain the economic benefit from new subdivisions and shopping centers. The same four states claimed seven of the top twelve most successful
annexation programs for the 1960s. Phoenix, Oklahoma City, and Houston
made the list in both decades; indeed, territory administered from Houston's city hall has grown sevenfold since 1948. Although the pace of annexation slowed in the 1970s, a number of cities have continued to expand
their boundaries. Portland annexed more than 70,000 new residents during
the 1980s. Colorado Springs added more than fifty square miles between
1986 and 1989.

The relative openness of political ecology that has encouraged annexation has also allowed the emergence of supersuburbs—municipalities other
than a metropolitan core city that have populations of 100,000 or more. In
1990, thirty-five of the forty-six such communities in the United States were
located in the greater Southwest of California, Arizona, Colorado, and
Texas. One measure of the overall importance of large suburbs is the proportion of each metropolitan area's population in suburban cities of 50,000 or
more. In 1990, Mesa, Tempe, Glendale, and Scottsdale together accounted
for 32 percent of the population of the entire Phoenix metropolitan area.
Five large suburbs together accounted for 36 percent of all Denver-area
residents. Even in reputedly disorganized Orange County, California, nearly
half of the population lived in six large municipalities with populations
greater than 100,000. Parceling of the suburban ring among supersuburbs

offers a superficial contrast with annexation, but the results in terms of strong, comprehensive government for suburban residents are fundamentally the same. A variety of studies have placed the threshold size for efficient full-service municipal government at between 50,000 and 100,000 residents. A community of this size can employ a diversified professional staff, maintain sophisticated support services, and realize economies of scale in service delivery.[21]

The frequent occurrence of large-scale, comprehensive government in the suburban rings of Western metropolitan areas has helped to tilt the balance of political power toward the same suburban areas. During the first two decades after World War II, downtown-based and central-city-oriented elites controlled local decisions in most Western cities. During the 1970s and 1980s, however, outer cities were able to push their own development agendas in direct competition with central cities.

Aurora, Colorado, is a case in point. Since the early 1970s, Aurora has dealt with Denver as an equal. It invested heavily in infrastructure for economic growth, including a joint water-supply system with Colorado Springs that frees Aurora from dependence on the transmountain pipelines of the Denver Water Board. The city has marketed itself as an office and industrial location and has annexed aggressively at the same time that state law largely locked Denver within its boundaries. Arvada and Lakewood, on the opposite side of the Denver metropolitan area, developed their own plans for territorial expansion and employment growth. In California, Long Beach is another supersuburb that views itself as a peer of its metropolis, with the terminus of a new commuter rail line and the largest port on the West Coast.

In metropolitan Phoenix in the late 1960s, G. Wesley Johnson points out, "Los Angeles–like urban sprawl resulted in the creation of multiple power centers throughout the Salt River Valley."[22] Peripheral development created new, localized sets of business and investment interests different from those of the postwar civic leadership. New centers with their own groups of economic and civic leaders included the independent suburbs of Scottsdale, Glendale, and Mesa-Tempe-Chandler and the growing northwest and Camelback-Biltmore districts. As Bradford Luckingham has described the situation, Mesa boosters energetically pursued both industrial and residential growth. The city bought up water rights, promoted its downtown, and sought new businesses. Glendale offered a $20,000 bonus to the first person who could bring a 100,000-square-foot factory to town in 1984 and hired a marketing director in 1987. Business and civic groups such as the East Valley Partnership, the West Valley Partnership, and Phoenix Together gave

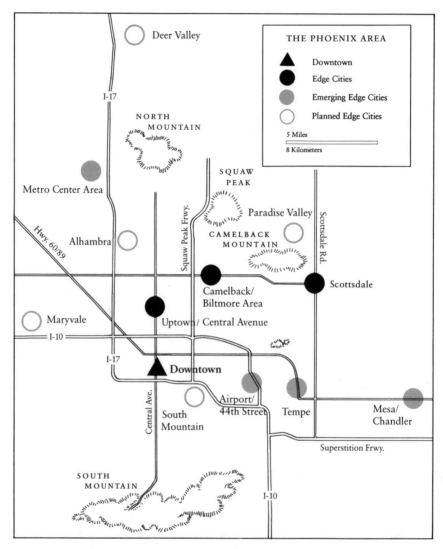

The "edge cities" of Phoenix. With large "suburbs" like Tempe, Mesa, Scottsdale, and Glendale, the retirement town of Sun City, and a city plan that acknowledged the triumph of outlying employment centers, Phoenix is a prototype of the multi-centered metropolis. (From *Edge City* by Joel Garreau. Copyright 1991 by Joel Garreau. Used by permission of Doubleday, a division of Bantam Doubleday Dell Publishing Group, Inc.)

lip service to regional cooperation but "competed for everything from sports facilities to educational institutions in order to offer unique advantages to residents and businesses. For the most part, metropolitan pluralism prevailed in the Valley of the Sun."[23]

There has been the same sort of tension within the 350 square miles of Phoenix proper. The city's Concept 2000 plan of 1979 called for the enhancement of "urban villages" centered on major shopping centers and uptown office clusters. Originating with a citizens' committee in 1975, the plan generated considerable enthusiasm, for it seemed to guide the growth of the city while ratifying the polycentric trend. The General Plan of 1985 incorporated the Concept 2000 idea. Each village, it said, would be "relatively self-sufficient in providing living, working, and recreational opportunities," with the city encouraging concentration of employment and services in each village core. The discussion left the role of downtown unresolved, however. Was it to be one of nine co-equal villages or, in the worlds of Mayor Terry Goddard, "everybody's neighborhood"? The slow coalescing of the central business district and the Uptown Business District (a high-rise cluster along Central Avenue dating from the 1960s) into a single supercore suggests some limits to multicentrism even in a dispersed city like Phoenix.

San Jose has displayed similar tensions between center and periphery. During the 1950s aggressive annexation by city of San Jose disrupted efforts to plan for controlled growth in Santa Clara County. By the 1970s, in contrast, the growth of Silicon Valley's sprawling electronics industry challenged the primacy of the central city and its downtown business interests. Represented by the Santa Clara Manufacturing Group, the newly rich diluted the remaining influence of the downtown elite. In the rebalanced political system, downtown San Jose was not a serious concern for the major corporate interests who built their low-rise headquarters in nearby cities like Mountain View, Sunnyvale, Santa Clara, and Palo Alto. In the 1980s, however, a new generation of *city* leaders pushed a downtown comeback involving more than $1 billion in public and private investment in a sixty-block core. New hotels, office buildings, a convention center, an arena, and two museums aim at creating a single focal point for the south bay.

The competing agendas of downtown development and suburban imperialism were both counterbalanced in the 1970s and 1980s by a growing interest in metropolitan growth management. Often spurred by the specter of suburban gridlock and other threats to the quality of daily life, the growth management impulse has drawn on neighborhood activists and quality-of-life liberals. It amounts to lifestyle politics on the suburban frontier rather than in the gentrifying neighborhoods. Pacesetting programs in the trend included Hawaii's adoption of a state-managed land-use plan for Honolulu and the rest of Oahu and Oregon's adoption of a statewide land planning system in 1973 to fend off what Governor Tom McCall termed "the unfettered despoiling of the land" through "sagebrush subdivisions, coastal condomania, and the ravenous rampage of suburbia in the Willamette Valley."[24] Interestingly, the East Coast states of Maine, New Jersey, Georgia, and Florida followed the West Coast lead in the 1980s with the adoption of "second generation" state planning programs.

A new round of Western growth management politics began in the mid-1980s. San Franciscans in 1986 passed Proposition M after rejecting five similar measures that dated as far back as 1971. This Accountable Planning Initiative imposed a permanent annual limit on office construction and tied the approval of development projects to neighborhood preservation, affordable housing, and tolerable traffic. Limitations on downtown high-rises were explicitly justified by the problems of congestion and skyrocketing rents. Supporters of Prop M included substantial numbers of minority and lower-income voters who joined middle-class renters in a "community versus capital" alignment. Los Angeles voters simultaneously passed their own controlled growth initiative that cut in half the size of new buildings permitted on about 70 percent of the city's commercially zoned land.

Three years later, Seattle voters responded to many of the same concerns as San Franciscans by approving a Citizens Alternative Plan (CAP) that limited new construction in the downtown core through the 1990s. Anyone who has paid a visit to Seattle recently could see the problem. For most of the century, builders and architects respected and complemented the natural landscape that rises from Elliott Bay. In the 1980s, however, an army of ill-conceived high-rises marched in to obliterate the old city and create California-style traffic congestion. Like San Francisco, Seattle spent several years crafting a downtown plan that was supposed to blend the best of both worlds—intense core development with amenities. In fact, the plan's bonusing system allowed one 30-story building to mushroom into a 55-story behemoth in return for plazas, retail space, day-care facilities and similar add-ons. At the same time, many residents of close-in neighborhoods felt that city hall had abandoned the neighborhood conservation programs of the 1970s in favor of inflating residential as well as commercial land values.

Self-defense by suburban homeowners has been a parallel issue in the Bay Area and southern California. Although county-wide growth-control measures failed in 1988 in Orange, San Diego, and Riverside counties, growth limitations have been implemented or strenuously debated in localities from Walnut Creek to Pasadena and San Diego. The mixed record has reflected the uncertain political balance when local control and use values are matched against growth coalitions and their arguments for economic development. A housing construction boom in San Diego in 1985 and 1986, for example, put intolerable pressures on sewers, freeways, and other public facilities. It forced a multilateral debate, which was still in progress in the early 1990s, in which citizen groups offer stringent growth-control proposals, the development industry counters with token proposals, and the city council waffles somewhere in between. The debate in Orange County effectively pitted the Industrial League of Orange County against local community activists. Since 1970 the Industrial League has represented such Orange County giants as Rockwell International, Northrop, and the Fluor Corporation. Its local agenda has been to preserve the ability of its members to expand when and where they wanted. One response in the 1980s was grassroots activism by ad hoc organizations that battled for managed growth and the preservation of local control over the pace of land development. Measure A, or the Citizens Sensible Growth and Traffic Control Initiative, went down to defeat in 1988 but substantially defined the central issue of local politics.

Growth management has even come to Houston, a city that rejected land-use zoning in 1948 and 1962 as a plot against American capitalism. As the last major city to leave land-use patterns to private agreement and the marketplace, Houston found itself politically divided in the late 1980s. Business leaders, the real estate industry, and Mayor Kathy Whitmire all favored continued reliance on restrictive covenants and a market free-for-all. The collapse of housing prices with the energy bust, however, left increasing numbers of professional and managerial families locked financially into unprotected neighborhoods, unable to move up and out at the first sign of problems. They made themselves heard through many of the city's powerful neighborhood associations. Other voices from the business and professional sectors pointed out Houston's need to compete with other cities in its quality of life. A year of bitter debate ended in January 1991, when the City Council directed a reconstituted Planning and Zoning Commission to prepare a comprehensive ordinance for "Houston-style zoning" in 1992.

The suggestion that Americans look to Lubbock and Las Colinas for an image of the typical city is therefore more than a rhetorical device that plays on our national prejudice about things Texan. It is also a concealed argument for a major redirection of our approach to American urban development. For more than a century and a half, Americans have been accustomed to studying the nation's Northeastern cities in detail while glancing only hazily and occasionally to the south and west. If we stand in the clear air of the West, however, it is easy to see that Westerners have taken advantage of new technologies and wide horizons to build metropolitan regions that are leading the United States in new directions. To understand the cities of the American West, it is necessary to think simultaneously in national and regional terms. Basic trends of metropolitan deconcentration are shared nationwide. Major patterns of economic growth and political response are shared by cities throughout a Sunbelt that curves from the southern Atlantic Coast to the Southwest and the Pacific. Western cities share their characteristic "metroscapes," however, largely with themselves. A number of critics have invited our attention to particular aspects of this built environment—to freeways, to commercial strips, to California suburbia. If we put the pieces together, we have a different environment—a different look for Western cities that shapes the responses of locals and outsiders alike.

7

CITIES AND COUNTRY

Condon, Oregon, is a century-old farm town in the heart of the winter wheat country of the Columbia Plateau. First staked out in 1884 and named immodestly for its founder, Condon became a county seat when the state split Gilliam County from Wasco County the following year. With the arrival of a Union Pacific spur line and the dry farming boom of the early 1900s, it grew into a substantial community of more than a thousand residents. By 1990, however, the town had contracted to 635 residents, one main street, a four-block business district, and a long view southward toward Squaw Butte and the Umatilla National Forest.

In 1986, Condonites took time out from raising wheat and cattle, sipping coffee in the Roundup Cafe, swapping stories inside the beige cinder-block walls of the Elks lodge, and cheering for the highly successful Condon High School Blue Devils to take out an advertisement in the *Los Angeles Times*. The phone company manager, the newspaper editor, the realtor, and the district attorney came up with $114 to boast of Condon's advantages: friendliness, thrifty living, and freedom from crime. The targets were harried urban Californians. Overstressed families and disgruntled retirees were invited to purchase undervalued Condon houses and live life in the slow lane. The town got its sixty seconds on the network news and several dozen new residents from as far away as Louisiana and Florida. A few of the newcomers ended up in the even smaller town of Fossil, twenty miles farther from Interstate 84.

Seventy-five miles southwest of Condon across the canyon of the John Day River is the site of the failed utopia of Rajneeshpuram. There may be

Condon, Oregon. Shown is Condon's main drag (Oregon Route 19) on a slow September morning. Residents can now choose espresso as an alternative to a regular cup of coffee at the Roundup Cafe. (Photograph by the author)

Oregon locations that are more isolated from the centers of population—towns like Wagontire and Remote—but Rajneeshpuram is hard enough to reach. The drive from Portland covers 175 miles. The hundred square miles of Rajneesh property spanned two counties. The offices of Jefferson County were seventy miles away in Madras, population 2,235. The offices of Wasco County were ninety miles distant in The Dalles, population 10,265. Between 1981 and 1985, followers of Bhagwan Shree Rajneesh built a substantial utopia in this sagebrush solitude, reaching perhaps 3,000 year-round residents augmented by visitors, students of Rajneeshism, and street people participating in a short-lived Share-a-Home program.

By their own claim, the Rajneeshees placed themselves in the tradition of frontier utopians who sought out locations in the empty West so that they could be alone. According to the city's prime minister, Ma Anand Sheela, they were seeking "a desert sort of land, away from the people so people's neuroses did not have to bother Bhagwan's vision of work, . . . [a] place which was our own."[1] Nevertheless, Rajneeshpuram was fully engaged in the urban system of the American West. It depended on Portland for its land-use attorneys, urban planners, airline connections, and money-making hotel and restaurant businesses. It depended on European, Eastern, and California cities for recruits and contributors. The city's managers financed much of its development by supplying Rajneeshee information and education to an international market of believers and curiosity seekers who came for annual World Celebrations and quarterly festivals, and to attend the International Meditation University.

The fate of Rajneeshpuram was decided by judges and bureaucrats in the county seat of The Dalles and the state capital at Salem. The new city may have *looked* like it was in the middle of nowhere, hours from courtrooms and county planning offices, but it was actually embedded in the dense system of laws and regulations that pervade the United States in the late twentieth century. Opponents of the community mobilized land-use requirements, building codes, state school inspections, election laws, and interpretations of tax laws to create a shrinking box of regulations. When the community collapsed in 1985 after a series of criminal indictments, its future had already been shaped from Salem and Portland.

The brief notoriety of Condon and Rajneeshpuram's well-reported rise and precipitous fall carry the same message: Much of the open West looks as though it has escaped the influence of the big city, but in fact urban growth over the last half-century has not only reshaped cities and suburban zones but also set the terms of life for virtually all of the nonmetropolitan West.

The wide-open spaces of the high plains, the Great Basin, the Southwestern desert, and the Pacific coastal forests are parceled out among nine major metropolitan hinterlands centered on Seattle–Tacoma, Portland, San Francisco–Oakland, Los Angeles, Denver, Dallas–Fort Worth, Houston, Kansas City, and Minneapolis–St. Paul. Metropolitan banks, newspapers, public relations firms, retail chains, and medical schools stand at the center of economic and social networks that structure everyday life in the multistate hinterlands. At the same time, each metropolis connects its region to the larger world.[2]

There has been remarkable stability in the division of the West among the nine regional centers. Between 1845 and 1920, they were the capitals of the

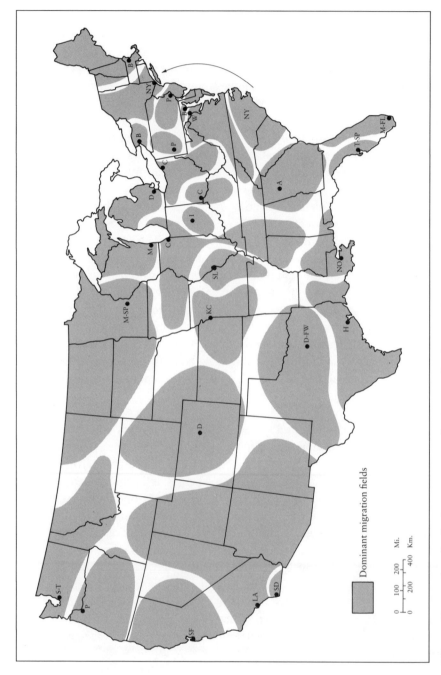

Metropolitan regions in the West. Patterns of migration for the period 1955–60 show the range of influence of the West's dominant regional cities. (From John Borchert, *America's Northern Heartland* [Minneapolis: University of Minnesota Press, 1989], 110)

Western urban frontier—the ports, railroad centers, and "jumping off" points through which Americans settled and developed the plains and mountains. In 1914 the committee that selected locations for the newly created Federal Reserve banks based the choices largely on established importance as private banking centers. The nine regional centers plus Omaha constituted the top ten cities west of the 93d meridian as measured by banking capital and surplus. San Francisco, Dallas, Kansas City, and Minneapolis gained main Federal Reserve banks, and the other five were among the dozen Western cities designated to have Federal Reserve branches.

Using data from 1948, 1950, and 1955, sociologist Otis D. Duncan looked for cities with high per capita levels of wholesaling, business service receipts, nonlocal commercial loans, and bank demand deposits. He defined Los Angeles as a national metropolis, seven of the other eight as regional metropolises, and Houston as a slightly less important regional capital. In addition to its financial dominance, each regional metropolis generated large numbers of airline passengers relative to its population. Economists Thomas Stanback and Thierry Noyelle updated earlier studies to similar effect after 1970. In their classification, San Francisco and Los Angeles were rated as nationally important as "diversified advanced service centers," a phrase that referred particularly to their wide range of financial, business, and professional services. The other seven were classed as "regional diversified service centers."

Readjustments among the set of national and regional centers have been keyed to the basic structural changes in the economy of the postwar West. Most important is what can be called the challenge from the corners. In the nineteenth and early twentieth centuries, when Western urbanization was tied almost exclusively to the development of agriculture and mining, cities gained an advantage from central locations and easy access to the interior. Boosters spoke a language of imperialism in which a favored city like Denver presided over a "Rocky Mountain Empire." Portland and Seattle competed for an "Inland Empire" of wheat and wool. The "Empire Builder" of St. Paul's Great Northern Railway connected the Twin Cities with Fargo, Great Falls, and the western shore.

The changing dynamics of the postwar economy have reduced the importance of regional centrality compared with long-range connections to national and international networks. As discussed earlier, one result has been the growth of Los Angeles relative to San Francisco, Seattle relative to Portland, and Houston relative to Dallas. Geographer John Borchert examined financial and migration data for the period 1955 to 1967 to update the Duncan study. Linkages among banks, which reflect long-established economic relationships, showed relatively large spheres of influence for Dallas, Portland, and San Francisco. Average citizens, however, were far more fickle and footloose than bankers. Upstart Los Angeles in the 1950s and 1960s was the most popular destination for people leaving substantial portions of San Francisco's banking territory. Houston and Seattle similarly stretched their "migration sheds" considerably beyond the influence of the First City Bank and the Rainier National Bank.

Metropolitan influence is transmitted from the regional centers through a nested hierarchy of smaller cities and towns. Most of the large regions are subdivided and shared with one or more second-level cities. Salt Lake City is a junior partner with Denver, Wichita with Kansas City. Spokane and Anchorage are junior partners with Seattle, Stockton and Fresno with San Francisco. Omaha serves a wedge of the Missouri Valley between the larger spheres of Minneapolis and Kansas City. Phoenix and El Paso have carved out secondary territories between Dallas and Los Angeles; and Oklahoma City, between Dallas and Kansas City. In some cases, closely paired cities have divided metropolitan specializations. Forty miles west of Dallas, Fort Worth's promoters have long declared it the city "Where the West Begins." In fact, Fort Worth has specialized in serving the West Texas cattle industry, while Dallas has remained the comprehensive trading and financial center for a larger hinterland that embraces the trading zone of Fort Worth. After Tacoma lost the competition for commercial leadership on Puget Sound to Seattle in the 1890s, it specialized as an industrial city that complemented Seattle bankers and wholesalers. A century later, Tacoma used its abundant and affordable waterfront land to lure away Seattle's most important container lines, starting with Sealand in 1984.

Smaller cities and towns look to the second-tier cities for specialized goods and to the top of the hierarchy for sophisticated business services. Wyoming 220, U.S. 26, and U.S. 87 may lead to Casper from Douglas and Buffalo, but the main-traveled highway *from* Casper is Interstate 25 to Denver. During the first two generations of the automobile era—from the 1920s through the 1960s—the terms of trade between city and country tended to centralize business and other activities in larger and larger cities. As early as the 1920s, the proliferation of Model Ts and farm trucks and the designation of certain roads as state and federal highways boosted the fortunes of county seats at the expense of hamlets and crossroads stores. The new transcontinental highways not only facilitated the great migrations of the mid-1930s and early 1940s but also supported the economies of towns strung at a two-hour spacing of 80 to 100 miles along the red lines of the federal highway system. The travelers who followed the 1946 advice of songwriter Bobby Troup to "get your kicks on Route 66" could ignore the railroad towns at ten-mile intervals but needed the clusters of service stations, restaurants, motels, and stores at Elk City, Oklahoma; Amarillo, Texas; Tucumcari, New Mexico; and Winslow, Arizona.

Construction of the interstate highway system in the 1960s accelerated the process of centralization, often at the expense of the same towns that had benefited during the previous generation. Authorized by Congress in 1956, half of the interstate system's 42,000 miles were finished by 1965 and three-quarters by 1970. The final large gaps in Texas, California, Colorado, Utah, and Montana were graded and paved in the 1970s. Main Street began to wither when the residents of smaller towns could use an interstate to reach the regional mall on the outskirts of the metropolis. This transportation-driven centralization is a national pattern, but it is especially important for the West, where automobiles and high-speed highways have cut the obstacle of vast distances by nearly half.

In the northern plains states of Montana, Nebraska, South Dakota, and North Dakota, for example, business activity between 1960 and 1990 tended to concentrate in the major metropolitan areas such as Omaha and in the regional centers such as Lincoln, Bismarck, and Billings. These are the cities that average at least a thousand businesses in the fields of retailing, wholesaling, transportation, manufacturing, construction, and services. As Carey McWilliams pointed out four decades ago, these cities may be relatively small in population, but they are "big in relation to the territories they serve, big in relation to total state population, big in relation to the functions which they discharge."[3] At the same time, the hamlets and small towns that pepper the countryside have struggled to hold their own while retailing and agricultural service businesses are consolidating in the larger centers. The trend has been accelerated by the rising national importance of service businesses, whose "products" can often be distributed by the Postal Service or the telephone company.

In a series of novels starting with *The Last Picture Show* (1966), novelist Larry McMurtry has traced the ways in which Thalia, Texas, has met the larger world. Thalia is a stand-in for Archer City (population 1,901 in 1950) and similar towns of the Red River Valley of North Texas. The first books chronicled the decline of Thalia businesses in the late 1950s and early 1960s. As the local movie theater went broke, increasingly mobile Thalians found their family entertainment, their models of sophistication, and their thrills in Wichita Falls. Twenty-five years later, the middle-aged Thalians of *Texasville* (1987) readily drove 140 miles to Dallas for a half-hour business appointment or professional consultation. Their daughters sped across two states

Missoula, Montana. Cities like Missoula, Walla Walla, and Grand Junction would be lost along the northeastern or southwestern coasts of the United States. In the heart of the Rangebelt, however, they are major centers. Higgins Avenue developed as the connection between the Northern Pacific station at one end of the downtown (the terminus of the street in this 1952 photo) and the Milwaukee Road station at the other. The elevator hotel at far left is typical of cities aspiring to regional importance. (Courtesy of the Montana Historical Society)

to disco and cruise the bars. "Shoot," said twenty-year-old T. R. in *Some Can Whistle*, "me and Dew went up to Oklahoma City two nights ago looking. We didn't find a thing up there, so we came back and looked in Fort Worth, but the pickings were so slim we still got home just after breakfast. These towns are tame up this way. Too many cowboys."[4]

Urban growth after 1940 did more than boost the "metroplex" at the expense of Thalia. It also split the entire region along a northwest–southeast diagonal from Puget Sound to the Sabine River of East Texas. In the Southwest, the central Rockies, and the Pacific Coast, the fast-growing cities of the Sunbelt West have concentrated population and wealth on a regional scale. The booming Sunbelt contrasts with an uncomfortably changing "Rangebelt" in the northern Rockies and northern Great Plains. Like scores of towns and small cities, the Rangebelt has found itself overshadowed and sometimes overwhelmed by the demands of Sunbelt cities.

Observers began to describe an emerging "amenities belt" in the 1950s, arguing that the attractions of life in the Southwest were outweighing the added costs of doing business from isolated locations such as Phoenix. As late as 1960, however, the most important analysis of the postwar economy treated the booming states of Florida, Texas, and California as distinct phenomena. Kevin Phillips was the first popular writer to use the terms Sunbelt and Sun Country to characterize the entire southern tier of the United States in *The Emerging Republican Majority* (1969). The city of Austin pioneered the promotional use of the Sunbelt idea in a series of advertisements in 1973. National journalists and politicians turned the coinage into a cliché in 1975 and 1976 in response to the economic recession of the mid-1970s. By the end of the decade it had become a convenient shorthand for contrasting the troubled industrial Northeast with the more prosperous South and Southwest.

The popular understanding of the Sunbelt involves the eastward projection of the West's traditional image as a land of prosperity and new beginnings. Using the new terminology allowed Southern cities and states to leapfrog over much of their history and earlier reputation. Having long been defined in negative terms as a land of poverty and premodern values, the South found a sort of rescue from its past by riding the coattails of the Western Sunbelt. In contrast, Westerners beyond the border states of Oklahoma and Texas have been less likely than Southerners explicitly to identify their communities with the Sunbelt. Although Colorado politician Richard Lamm has defined the Sunbelt as "the West and Southwest," the region's chambers of commerce have made sparing use of the term in their promotional literature. Arguing that the term applied more accurately to the West than the Southeast, geographers Clyde Browning and Wil Gesler have commented that the West in the 1970s showed "more characteristics associated with the Sunbelt than the Sunbelt itself."[5] Urban Westerners have tended to agree that they knew they lived in a favored land before it needed the recognition of a special name.

The rise of the Sunbelt West, or the "growth belt," is fundamentally an economic phenomenon. Even leaving aside the historic distinctiveness of the Southeast, efforts to define the western portion of the Sunbelt as an emerging cultural region falter on the vast differences in community values and public styles between Las Vegas and Provo, Santa Barbara and Midland, or Santa Fe and Houston. Nor is the western Sunbelt a coherent political region. States shift from liberal to conservative or mix the persuasions on the basis of complex details of local politics. Residents of the Sunbelt West have backed "emerging Republicans" such as Nixon, Reagan, and Bush in presidential elections, but they have chosen men like Henry Cisneros, Federico Peña, Terry Goddard, and Tom Bradley to preside over their large cities. California is the state of Jerry Brown as well as Ronald Reagan. Arizonans have liked Morris Udall and Bruce Babbitt as well as Barry Goldwater and Evan Mecham.

As a way of understanding the past and present character of the American West, the Sunbelt West is best defined in terms of areas of consistently rapid metropolitan growth and participation in the driving forces of the postwar economy. These forces have included locational decisions made in response to regional amenities, the spatial concentration of "sunrise industries," and the tilt of American trade and immigration toward Latin America and Asia. The standard definition sets the upper edge of the Sunbelt along the conveniently aligned northern borders of Oklahoma, New Mexico, and Arizona, and continues the line westward until it plunges into Monterey Bay. In fact, a consistent economic definition adds the major cities of Colorado, Utah, Nevada, and all five Pacific states. It has often been suggested that the Sunbelt cities are characterized by rapid growth based on federal spending, a favorable business climate, and an attractive quality of life. These criteria fit Denver, Salt Lake City, Reno, San Francisco, Seattle, Anchorage, and Honolulu as much as they do San Diego and Dallas. The Sunbelt-West therefore embraces the cities of both the older Southwest of Texas and Oklahoma and the New Southwest of New Mexico, Arizona, the central Rocky Mountains, and the Pacific Slope.

The spread of Sunbelt as a new regional terminology is mirrored in the definition of Silicon Valley and the proliferation of its Western clones. As previously described, electronics firms began to cluster near Stanford University in the 1950s and 1960s with the help of university engineers and defense contracts. Don Hoefler, the editor of *Microelectronics News,* coined the term "Silicon Valley" for the corridor from Palo Alto to San Jose in 1971. At approximately the same time, the large companies with headquarters in Santa Clara County began to disperse their research-related manufacturing and assembly plants to other Western cities within a three-hour plane ride. In the 1980s, most of the spinoff cities identified themselves with the parent

Silicon Valley by adopting promotional language that imitated the home base. The locations of the Silicon Prairie (Austin and Dallas), the Silicon Desert (Phoenix), Silicon Mountain (Colorado Springs), Biotech Valley (Salt Lake City), and Silicon Forest (Portland) roughly trace the extent of the Sunbelt West.

The differentiation of the Sunbelt from the rest of the West can also be viewed in terms of the expansion and intensification of the metropolitan-regional influence of California and Texas. The big four of San Francisco, Los Angeles, Houston, and Dallas–Fort Worth have acted as dynamic organizing forces for greater California and greater Texas. In broad terms, the supermetropolitan influence of Texas and California may have slowly reoriented the West's regional grain. The transcontinental railroads and economic dependence of the nineteenth-century West on Eastern markets and suppliers established a basic pattern of east–west hinterlands and connections, with Dallas and Albuquerque linked to St. Louis, Denver to Chicago, and Seattle to Minneapolis. Except along the northern tier, recent patterns of travel, migration, and financial control are creating a substantial north–south orientation that cuts across the old grain and draws the West away from the old national core.

On the western edge of the West, Nevada's historic status as a California colony has been well documented from the exploitation of the Comstock Lode to the rise of Reno and Las Vegas as weekend suburbs of coastal cities. Arizona, Hawaii, and Oregon have a similar dependence on the money and markets of California's supercities. Patterns of recreational travel, seasonal migration, and permanent relocation run predominantly north–south, bringing Oregonians to vacation in Anaheim, Honolulu, and Reno, farm workers from southern California to the Willamette and Yakima valleys, and California retirees to Oregon or Arizona. In the second half of the 1980s, California sent 58,000 migrants aged sixty or older to the four states of Arizona, Oregon, Washington, and Nevada.

"Imperial Texas" as an economic region has long included the grazing country of New Mexico and the oil country of Oklahoma, with many key decisions made in Dallas banks and Houston boardrooms. The same area is linked by high volumes of highway traffic and constitutes the core of a "Southern–Western" culture region defined by speech, religion, and musical taste. San Antonio and El Paso have been the staging points for most of the Hispanic migrant workers employed in the Rocky Mountain and plains states. Even more obvious has been the extension of the Houston-Dallas influence into Western oil districts. The development of the northern plains oil fields of the Williston Basin after World War II brought hundreds of

Greater Texas and Greater California. Except for the northern tier and the Mormon country of the Great Basin, economic and social patterns in the West are dominated by the metropolitan complexes of Texas and California. (Redrawn from Gerald Nash and Richard Etulain, eds., *The Twentieth Century West* [Albuquerque: University of New Mexico Press, 1989], 81)

Texans to small cities like Dickinson in North Dakota and Billings in Montana. North Dakotans were suspicious when cars bearing Texas license plates crisscrossed the rural backroads in the summer of 1951 to lock up oil leases, but the bankers and newspaper publishers of Minot and Dickinson were glad to welcome Texans as emissaries of industrial progress. As far as Eugene Hollon could see a decade later, Billings was indistinguishable from Odessa or Amarillo.

Denverites also became accustomed to the influence of oil cities in the 1950s. Dallas oilman Clint Murchison revolutionized the downtown real estate market by constructing the Denver Club Building for the whopping sum of $7 million in 1954 and the First National Bank Building for $10 million in 1957. Other Texas and Oklahoma oil millionaires put up the money for the Petroleum Club and Continental Oil buildings. Houston tycoon Hugh Roy Cullen used his wealth to defeat a Colorado oil severance tax in 1952 and intervened in elections throughout the Rocky Mountain states. When geologists found commercially viable oil fields in the Rocky Mountain overthrust belt in the 1970s and when oil embargoes turned renewed attention to western Colorado oil shale, Denver was the logical base of operations. A building boom in the late 1970s transformed the Denver skyline with new office towers for the energy viceroys.

In the backcountry, Greater Texas and Greater California shared outposts like Grand Junction, Colorado, Evanston, Wyoming, and even Fairbanks, Alaska. In the production centers of the Rockies, the home office was Denver and the standard of success was Dallas or Oklahoma City. Chilton Williamson, Jr., however, observed that, for the wives of the pipeliners, equipment operators, and roughnecks, "Kemmerer [Wyoming] was a sour mirage in the American High Plains to which they had been dragged . . . from comfortable surroundings in lovely lush suburban towns near Oklahoma City, Albuquerque, or Bakersfield."[6] During the height of the Alaska pipeline construction boom of 1974–76, the Alyeska Pipeline Service Company drew many of its 30,000 managers and skilled workers from the oil states of Texas, Oklahoma, and California. Old-timers in Fairbanks fought back by devising "Texan jokes" to put the outsiders in their place.

Seven states of the central and northern plains and the northern Rockies lie outside the world of the Sunbelt West. Kansas, Nebraska, South Dakota, North Dakota, Wyoming, Montana, and Idaho have had an inconsistent record of growth over the past fifty years. Their cities have interspersed prosperity with contraction and recession. North and east of the great diagonal, the older West of the Rangebelt has struggled to survive in the world of Greater California and Greater Texas. The entire area continues to depend on resource industries and the direct use of Bureau of Land Management and Forest Service lands for grazing and lumbering.

No Rangebelt city matches the size of one of the regional capitals. The seven states contain all or the central portion of fifteen metropolitan areas. The largest in 1990 were Omaha (with a population of 618,000) and Wichita (485,000). Next in line were Lincoln and Boise, which just topped 200,000, followed by Topeka and Fargo. Travelers at the end of the nineteenth century tended to visit the West in a loop that connected Chicago,

Seattle, San Francisco, and Denver. Travelers at the end of the twentieth century are likely to choose a southern loop and to examine the shape of the future in Anaheim, Phoenix, Dallas, and Houston. A striking comparison pits the cities of the Union Pacific and Northern Pacific railroads in the interior Northwest against those of the Santa Fe and Southern Pacific railroads in the interior Southwest. Between 1950 and 1990, Bismarck, Butte, Billings, and Boise taken together grew by 94 percent, from 225,000 to 437,000 people. El Paso, Albuquerque, Phoenix, and Tucson grew by 374 percent, from 814,000 to 3,862,000.

Parts of the Rangebelt also overlap into Sunbelt states whose rapid aggregate growth has been driven by a handful of major cities. Policymakers in Salem worry about the "other Oregon" east of the Cascades. Officials in Denver see the crest of the Rockies as an economic divide between the prosperous and failing halves of Colorado. As urban planner Frank Popper has pointed out, 144 Western counties reported fewer than two residents per square mile in 1980—a continuing frontier in anyone's definition. Another 250 counties had fewer than six residents per square mile. The total population of these 400 empty counties was only 2.2 million—fewer than the number of people *added* to metropolitan Los Angeles in the single decade of the 1980s. Much of this persistent frontier is marked by problems indistinguishable from those of inner-city ghettos. Educational achievement is relatively low. Access to health care is limited. The rate of violent death among young white males in Idaho, Montana, Wyoming, Nevada, Arizona, and New Mexico has run consistently above the national average, and in rural counties it matches or exceeds that for young urban blacks.

For many Rangebelt communities, the 1970s and 1980s brought deep economic and social crises. Mining cities have been at the mercy of fluctuating world markets. Timber towns have faced increasing scarcities of cheap trees and competition from the American South and foreign countries. Following the dictates of economic theory, larger resource-based corporations have substituted capital for labor, producing more coal or timber with fewer workers. In many resource towns, young men find it impossible to follow in their father's footsteps to the mine or mill. The shift toward a service and tourism economy can also create a social upheaval that relies for a family's primary income on women working at low wages rather than men in unionized jobs. For men over forty-five, a layoff notice is often the equivalent of forced retirement interrupted by short-term jobs. Harold Walton, a resident of the lumber mill city of Coos Bay, Oregon, described the effect of mill closures: "Losing their cars, losing their homes. People with their homes almost paid for. No way to finish it. Trying to sell out cheap to get to move somewhere to go to work. . . . Forcing the older people into early retirement, taking a reduced pension. Trying to survive."[7]

At the same time, a number of Rangebelt cities have had the opportunity to benefit from a selective rebalancing within the Western urban system. During the 1980s an economic reaction to the cost of metropolitan concentration and congestion caused big city businesses to seek cheaper land, cheaper labor, and low living costs in smaller interior cities. Examples are the revitalization of regional trading centers like Spokane and Sioux Falls. As a business and professional service center for the upper Columbia River Valley, Spokane boomed in the 1970s and suffered in the 1980s with the rise and decline of farm, timber, and metals prices. In the mid-1980s, however, it began to attract spillover business from congested Seattle. The businesses it attracted included a Boeing component plant, a credit card processing office for Seafirst National Bank, and back-office operations for Seattle-based Safeco Insurance. In addition, a handful of small software and high-tech companies have come from more expensive coastal cities. The Guardian Life Insurance Company made the far longer move of back-office functions from New York City to Spokane in 1986. In this respect it was following the lead of Citicorp, which moved its international credit card division to Sioux Falls at the start of the 1980s, creating 2,500 new jobs in "depository institutions." The newcomers did not turn Spokane and Sioux Falls into boom towns like Sacramento, but they substantially widened the cities' range of direct contacts outside their regional hinterlands. Long-distance phone lines have joined the Burlington Northern and Chicago and Northwestern tracks as the symbol of the cities' economies.

The same process could be seen in Rocky Mountain resource cities that actively worked toward more diversified economies. The factory city of Pueblo had suffered a gradual erosion of industrial jobs in the 1970s and careened toward economic disaster when Colorado Fuel and Iron (CF&I) laid off 4,200 of its 6,000 steel workers in 1984. Unemployment neared 20 percent and the *Wall Street Journal* described the city as having an air of "sooty gloom."[8] Over the next half decade, however, Pueblo built on its strengths of low costs and a stable, home-owning, and hungry labor force. Although CF&I remained the largest single employer, Pueblo's diversification strategy lured companies from more expensive settings as close at hand as Colorado Springs. Unisys picked Pueblo for a new manufacturing facility because it offered the lowest cost of living for any city of its size. Other new manufacturing facilities that included an air conditioner plant, a facility for manufacturing aircraft brakes, and a rocket plant pushed unemployment below 8 percent.

Grand Junction has attempted a similar shift from primary production and processing to manufacturers of high-value products. Always the wholesale, service, and medical center for the irrigated farms and orchards of the Gunnison and Colorado river valleys, Grand Junction experienced an explosive boom in 1979–80 because of oil shale development and exploration for natural gas and petroleum. Peaking in May 1982, the boom collapsed as fast as it had built, leaving a devastated real estate sector but an upgraded infrastructure of city services, roads, and an airport. The city's development strategy targeted retirees and mid-tech manufacturing companies like Sundstrand, which rejected Colorado Springs as too large and Fort Collins for its unionized wage rates.

Butte is another city that grew for three generations on the basis of mining and the primary metals industry. The shutdown of the Anaconda smelter in 1980 played the same role as the CF&I layoffs, forcing a radical rethinking of the city's economic prospects. Although mineral industries still provide substantial employment, the future also lies in the direction of the Magnetohydrodynamics Research Center, funded jointly by the Department of Energy and the Mountain State Energy Company. Butte has begun to attract small high-tech firms from more congested and expensive cities such as Seattle. The city has expanded its service sector with a popular mining museum and the pure network activity of the U.S. High Altitude Sports Center for training and competition in speed skating.

The West has shown a limited ability to cope with the internal tensions between city and hinterland, between Sunbelt and Rangebelt, and between growing information cities and declining resource communities. One reason is the failure of the regional imagination to incorporate or understand urban roles. Americans have a powerful desire to disjoin the Western past and future, defining the real West as the empty West. Fifty years after the urban takeoff of World War II, much of the popular and professional understanding of the West remains tied to the resource industries that fueled its nineteenth century growth. There is little place for the strongly centralizing forces of the last half century in consciously regional rhetoric. Since the days of Frederick Jackson Turner, Western historians have found it difficult to factor cities into their interpretations. With a few exceptions, urban growth drops out soon after the disbanding of the San Francisco vigilance committees. Robert Athearn's "authentic West" excludes the Pacific states and has little place for organizing centers such as Denver and Salt Lake City. Donald Worster's "true West" is the land of little rain whose settlers huddled in oasis cities out of necessity rather than choice. Richard Bartlett recently asked whether the cities are not "the least West of the West," with their own versions of Eastern problems. "If there is still a West in this last decade of the twentieth century," Bartlett writes, "perhaps it is in the small towns, the ranches and farms and mines. One might hazard that only there is to be found the western mystique. . . . Perhaps the essence of the West lies on the main street of Douglas, Wyoming . . . rather than in a Los Angeles or Salt Lake City suburb."[9]

Students of Western literature have much the same attitude. South Dakotan John Milton, one of the leading specialists on the Western American novel, has no doubt whatsoever: "The West is not cities. It is small towns, ranches, Indian reservations, Spanish villages, most of them quietly unknown. More importantly, it is space. Unpeopled space." Milton's West stops at the Sierra Nevada, for California "long ago abdicated from the West and became a distorted version of the East." Ensconced among Silicon Valley executives in Los Altos, Wallace Stegner was very much aware that the West "*is* urban; it's an oasis civilization."[10] At the same time, he found the distances between the nodes far more interesting and noted that the predominant Western impression is one of empty space.

The critics are correct that much of the self-consciously *regional* literature of the West deals with life in the open spaces. Essayists chronicle the work of geologists and naturalists as the modern equivalents of miners and mountain men. They write about wolves and wildfire, coyotes, bears, and bison. Serious regional novelists choose their contemporary protagonists from ranchers, farmers, loggers, rodeo riders, and river rafters. Their topics are Native Americans, nature, and life in the land of wind and storm. Cities are not yet incorporated into this regional rhetoric in the same way that New Orleans figures in Southern literature or Chicago and Detroit in the literature of the Middle West. Imaginative writing about *cities* in the West is usually treated as something other than Western literature. Dashiel Hammett and Raymond Chandler were genre crime novelists. Maxine Hong Kingston and John Okada are treated as ethnic novelists. The nationally acceptable depictions of Los Angeles are novels of anomie like Alison Lurie's *Nowhere City* and Joan Didion's *Play It As It Lays*. Critics pan the "Western" writer who sets his stories in present-day Houston and Las Vegas but pile on the prizes when he turns to a nineteenth century trail drive.

The contrast is similarly clear in the public response to two painters who came to the Southwest as outsiders and remained to be captivated by the clarity of Southwestern light. Englishman David Hockney's reaction to Los Angeles in the 1960s was a series of stunning depictions of the lawn sprinklers, high-rise buildings, houses, and swimming pools of Santa

Monica, Hollywood, and Beverly Hills. The surfaces glare and stare back at the viewer in the "technicolor daylight" of California. The clear light of New Mexico similarly drew Easterner Georgia O'Keefe to paint and repaint the sun-bleached skulls of cattle. The international art world has recognized and applauded Hockney's urban and suburban imagery, but the highbrow public has adopted O'Keefe's traditionally regional subject matter as a national icon. As with history and literature, Americans prefer to neglect the urban West and to admire what they know to be comfortably "Western."

Ironically, Western cities have been the support points for distinctive regional cultures. The efflorescence of literary activity in Montana in the 1980s and the production of the massive and valuable state anthology with the backward-looking title *The Last Best Place* depended on the concentration of talent in Missoula. Much of the energy for the Montana Renaissance came from Richard Hugo, who taught at the University of Montana from 1965 to 1982 but whose best poems drew on his early years in working-class Seattle. More than a few Western writers are graduates of the creative writing programs that flourished during the 1960s and 1970s at San Francisco State University and Stanford University with instructors like Wallace Stegner, Ivor Winters, Walter Van Tilburg Clark, and Mark Harris. Greater San Francisco has been an artistic marketplace and nurturer of talent since the nineteenth century heyday of the *Overland Monthly* and the meteoric careers of Frank Norris and Jack London. After World War II, San Francisco brought together a remarkable set of poets and novelists to learn from each other, argue with each other, and address national audiences. The mix included academically based writers from Berkeley, alumni of the wartime conscientious objector work camp in Waldport, Oregon, East Coasters drawn into the California tilt, and a handful of Bay Area natives. Continuity came from Kenneth Rexroth, Lawrence Ferlinghetti, William Everson, and Josephine Miles. Creative and personal sparks came from Muriel Rukeyser, Kenneth Patchen, Gary Snyder, Allen Ginsberg, Jack Kerouac, and Ken Kesey. Some eventually found their way to Cascade mountain tops and Oregon valleys, but their road ran through the city as an intellectual springboard.

Western cities have also played key roles in defining and preserving regional cultures that include the arts within much broader cultural systems. Salt Lake City and Provo house the interconnecting institutions that support and disseminate Mormon culture—universities, scholarly research, religious gatherings and outreach, and genealogical archives. The presence of the University of Texas has helped to make Austin the center for exploring, explicating, celebrating, and complaining about the Texas character.

Walter Prescott Webb and J. Frank Dobie dominated the scene in the 1940s and 1950s, giving partial place in the 1960s to the feisty liberal perspectives of the *Texas Observer*.

Much of the West's explicitly *regional* political analysis has been as uninterested as its literature in the transformative effect of regional urbanization. Much of the analysis has been phrased in terms of Western subordination to the East. The idea that the West has been an exploited economic colony was a strong theme from the 1930s into the 1950s. Utah native Bernard DeVoto enunciated the idea in the famous *Harper's* magazine article "The Plundered Province" in 1934. Walter Prescott Webb developed the idea of the West as an economic colony in *Divided We Stand: The Crisis of a Frontierless Democracy* (1937). In 1943, Joseph Kinsey Howard described Montana as an toy of Wall Street and a victim of the plutocrats.

The prosperity of World War II prompted a partial restatement in which spokesmen for long-depressed farming and mining states argued that there was now a chance to declare independence of the region's quasi-colonial status. Wendell Berge in 1946 called for *Economic Freedom for the West* through industrialization based on the new war industries. Coloradoan Morris Garnsey described the mountain West as *America's New Frontier*. He hoped for a new regional liberalism based on economic development and resource conservation to displace the invidious pressure of outside interests.

Ignored during the prosperity of the 1960s and 1970s, the idea of a plundered province reappeared in the 1980s. The crash of the world petroleum market and the general decline of commodity prices demonstrated to analysts like historian William Robbins that the West remained a peripheral region at the mercy of uncontrollable trends in world capitalism. The precarious status of the rural Western economy was not so much the doing of individual malefactors in New York and Boston as the impersonal product of a system that exploited resource regions worldwide. In *The Angry West* (1982), Colorado Governor Richard Lamm made a similar although less theoretical argument. Robert Gottlieb and Peter Wiley described the Southwest as a set of *Empires in the Sun* (1982), but they described a "hub of the interior," such as Denver, as essentially a conduit for Eastern corporate control.

The political complaint about the colonial status of the West also resurfaced in very different form as the Sagebrush Rebellion. As critics of a "colonial" government rather than exploitive corporations, the Sagebrush Rebels focused their demands on the vast tracts of federally held land in the interior West. In 1979 the legislature of Nevada demanded that the 49 million federally held acres that constituted 86 percent of its territory be deeded over to the state. The goal was presumably to encourage locally controlled development by rapidly selling off the transferred lands to private buyers. In effect, the participants hoped that the solution to the growing weakness of the resource economy was more of the same. The movement gathered support in states such as New Mexico, Wyoming, and Utah and gained an endorsement from presidential candidate Ronald Reagan. In areas like southern Utah, the same sentiments led to bitter confrontations between local politicians and business promoters on the one hand and federal land management officials and environmental advocates on the other. In the view of one county commissioner in southern Utah, the national government was little more than a foreign power trying to alter a way of life that it failed to understand. The Sagebrush Rebellion as an active political effort simmered down after the early 1980s, but the willingness remained in many rural communities to identify the federal government as the colonial oppressor.

In fact, the real opponents for the Sagebrush Rebels are not Easterners but the overwhelming majority of urban Westerners. The rebellion itself has been much more a "civil war" than a "war for independence," because most tensions over resource policy are the product of the long reach of the urban West. In many ways the 1970s and 1980s brought the extension of quality-of-life politics to questions of regional resource use. The Endangered Species Act, the Federal Land Policy and Management Act of 1976, which required evenhanded management of natural resources by the Bureau of Land Management, and similar legislative mandates that have fractured the close relationship between ranchers, miners, loggers, and the federal land agencies, represent the thinking of Western city people as much as Easterners. Samuel Hays has identified the cities of California, Colorado, Washington, Oregon, and Montana as the seedbeds for the Western environmental movement. Along with Alaska, Wyoming, and New Mexico, these are the states that ranked in the top third nationally in the early 1980s in the proportion of residents who held memberships in ten environmental organizations ranging from the National Audubon Society to the Wilderness Society. The effects of urbanization on public policy can also be seen in the Montana Constitution of 1971. In the analysis of Harry Fritz, the new document was "an environmentally conscious monument to a modern, urban, self-confident state."[11] The narrow margin for ratification came from eight of the state's ten largest cities.

It is possible to predict many of the arenas of local conflict by defining the expanding commuting zones and recreation sheds of the metropolitan centers. What sociologist Janet Abu-Lughod calls "saturation urbanization" can leave low-density landscapes between population clusters, but much of this superficially rural West has been centralized into the daily and weekly economic orbits of the major cities. Richard White has examined the "urban shadow" that Seattle vacationers and real estate developers began to cast on Whidbey Island in Puget Sound even before World War II. In Island County, Washington, and dozens of equivalents around the West, dollars earned in cities have kept the stores open in the small towns, employed the country lawyers on land deals, turned schoolteachers into real estate agents, and made underemployed farmers and miners into instant construction contractors.

A systematic study of commuting to metropolitan cities in 1960 and 1970 showed that a majority of the wide-open spaces of California, Texas, Arizona, Washington, and Oklahoma have been incorporated into commuting zones. During the same decade in which the majority of interstate highway mileage was completed, the commuting zones of Oklahoma City, Salt Lake City, San Jose, Stockton, and Midland-Odessa doubled in size. By 1970, the typical city in the Southwest was drawing its labor force from a seventy-mile radius, and the typical city of the Rockies and Pacific Coast reached out seventy-five miles. Houston's commuting region embraced Bryan and Beaumont, and Corpus Christi reached to Victoria. Tulsa and Oklahoma City shared portions of a single labor market, as did Fresno and Bakersfield, Austin and San Antonio, and Phoenix and Tucson. Reno and Galveston anchored a single overlapping set of commuting zones that connected via California and the Southwest.

Recreational dwellings can similarly be estimated with 1980 census data on "homes held for occasional use." The category includes most second homes as well as shared-ownership, or time-sharing, condominiums but presumably excludes "seasonal and migratory" houses occupied by migratory workers. The recreation zones of northern California include Nevada, Eldorado, and Tuolumne counties in the Sierra Nevada. The Portland recreation zone includes Deschutes County (Bend) and the Oregon coast from Newport to Astoria. The Denver–Boulder–Fort Collins metropolitan corridor has direct access to concentrations of second homes in Larimer, Gilpin, Grand, Summit, and Park counties. Albuquerque and Santa Fe are ringed by second-home concentrations in Colfax, San Miguel, Valencia, and McKinley counties. Arizona's recreation zones lie along the Colorado River in Mohave County (Lake Havasu City) and north from Phoenix to Flagstaff in Yavapai and Coconino counties.

The expanding metropolitan commuting and recreation zones bring the world into the heart of the West, continuing the process of incorporating

Rangebelt towns and rural communities into city-centered flows of people, goods, and ideas. The nonurban image grows harder and harder to maintain as urban connections and occupations displace miners and ranchers. In the recent novels of Thomas McGuane, the grazing lands of Montana are inextricably linked to the world of the 1980s. The land in *Keep the Change* (1989) may be special in itself, but it is also a commodity, a launching pad for a career in Minnesota, and an opportunity for an exotic vacation from worldly Florida. In the Western world of *Something To Be Desired* (1985), anything can happen in a "land of Japanese horseshoes, Taiwanese cowboy shirts, and Korean bits."[12]

The transformation of Aspen, Colorado, epitomizes the changes. It was one of dozens of dying Rocky Mountain mining towns in the 1940s. A generation later it is a prime example of efforts to create a modern version of the "middle landscape" sought by nineteenth century Americans. The catalyst was Chicago industrialist Walter Paepcke, chair of the Container Corporation of America. Paepcke established the Aspen Institute for Humanistic Studies in 1949 and assembled an all-star cast for a Goethe Bicentennial Convocation and Music Festival in June and July of the same year. Speakers and performers in a "tent" designed by Eero Saarinen included Thomas Mann, Arthur Rubinstein, José Ortega y Gasset, and Albert Schweitzer, who gave his only public address in the United States. Wintertime skiers and summer visitors to the Aspen Institute and the music festival that became a regular event after 1950 could patronize the same tourist businesses. The condominium boom of the 1960s and the opening of new ski areas like Snowmass completed Aspen's transformation into an annex of urban America, symbolized by the arrival of the spaced-out journalist Hunter Thompson and his campaign for sheriff of Pitkin County in 1970.

The "resettling" of the high country in the 1970s and 1980s followed the Aspen example, in which tourists coexist with artists, writers, consultants, and other dealers in national information markets. The silver town of Telluride, Colorado, was best known in 1970 for its history of bitter strikes by the Western Federation of Miners and for its spectacular setting at the head of a high valley cut into the heart of the San Juan Mountains. But development on a ski resort began in 1972, and summer jazz, chamber music, and film festivals followed to fill up the winter condominiums with summer visitors. In addition, information prophet John Naisbett's Telluride Foundation and Bellwether Institute offered seminars on the hot trends of the year.

Dozens of other Western communities house information workers and jet-setters next door to men and women who try to continue to gain a living from resource industries. There are mellow drop-outs from the 1970s, plugged-in drop-ins from the 1980s equipped with modem and fax, and men who've never taken off their hard hat. These hinterland communities have become the entry points for economic and social change and for incorporation into urbanized information networks on the model of Condon and Rajneeshpuram. The population of St. George, Utah, doubled during the 1980s with an influx of Californians attracted by its high, dry air. The small town of Joseph, in the Wallowa Mountains of Oregon, attracted an entrepreneurial community of writers, craftspeople, and visual artists who work on commissions from around the country and who share the single main street with loggers, ranchers, and summer tourists. Sandpoint, Idaho, was once the market center for a grazing and logging region at the northern tip of the Idaho panhandle. To this economic base have been added retirees, simplicity seekers from Seattle and San Francisco, high-tech post-hippies, and jet-setting entrepreneurs in software, computer components, and medical technology who sell to national markets but who enjoy their refuge among the trees.

The resettling of the frontier in urban guise is more positive than not. The long-term decline in world commodity prices and the reduction of federal expenditures on dams, irrigation canals, and alternative fuels in the 1980s pulled the remaining props from under many resource communities. Much of the replacement economy is supported by the modern equivalent of remittance men—in this case retirees living on pensions and the public transfer payments of social security and Medicare, students paying tuition and rent with dollars earned elsewhere, and professors supported by National Science Foundation grants. Retirees may be explicit about their desire to escape urban problems and prices, but most of them bring values and expectations formed in cities, where communication is quick and quality medical care is readily available. Their net impact will further the incorporation of selected Rangebelt communities into metropolitan networks.

Because of the income sources, many of the small cities and towns that have grown steadily have been university and retirement communities. A recent listing of the "best" small cities in the United States included Corvallis, Pullman, Port Angeles, Wenatchee, San Luis Obispo, Fairbanks, and Carson City. When Bernard Malamud put in a stint in the Oregon State University English department in the 1950s, he found the inspiration for the deeply provincial society that he fictionalized in *A New Life* (1961). The people of Cascadia College hunted, fished, loafed, and preferred the practicalities of English grammar to the nebulous realms of literature. By the 1980s, Corvallis was still small but scarcely provincial, supporting not only a university but also an Intel plant and the headquarters of the international engineering firm CH2M-Hill. In the thirty years since Malamud's "S. Levin" returned to his old life in New York, the town, too, has found a new life.

8

CITIES AND NATION

The continuing urban frontier of the United States is easiest to find in the western half of the nation. Like the people of the historical resource frontier, residents of the postwar West were in constant motion within and among their cities. During the late 1950s, nearly a quarter of the residents of Phoenix had arrived within the previous two years. Sixty percent of all Westerners changed their residence between 1955 and 1960, compared with 50 percent nationwide. Every year during the 1960s, San Jose counted twenty-one arrivals and seventeen departures for every hundred residents.

The thriving Western metropolis has been a focal point for American energies and creativity for the last half century. To borrow from the 1937 report of the National Resources Committee, *Our Cities: Their Role in the National Economy,* their virtues and their faults have been the product of "exuberant vitality crowding its way forward under tremendous pressure—the flood rather than the drought."[1] Thomas Pynchon captured something of this vitality in a whirling description of nighttime Los Angeles from the freeway. There were, he wrote,

> screaming black motorcades that could have carried any of several office seekers, cruisers heading for treed and more gently roaring boulevards, huge double and triple trailer rigs that loved to find Volkswagens laboring up grades and go sashaying around them gracefully and at gnat's-ass tolerances, plus flirters, deserters, wimps and pimps, speeding like bullets, grinning like chimps, above the heads of the TV watchers, lovers under the overpasses, movies at the mall letting out, bright gas-station oases in pure fluorescent spill, . . . the adobe air, the smell of distant fireworks, the spilled, the broken world.[2]

A spilled and broken world may have little connection with traditional forms of community, but it is also ready to be picked up and reassembled according to new and native plans and specifications. As sociologist Nathan Glazer noted in 1959, the cities of the postwar West were consciously chosen environments that matched many of the preferences of their residents. In the judgment of Los Angeles architect Richard Neutra, new metropolitan residents of southern California were open to new forms of culture because they had deliberately left behind the traditional communities of the East.

The design and decoration of Western cities expresses a vernacular exuberance that stands in sharp contrast to the classic American model of the tidy New England village. From Tulsa to Fort Worth to Los Angeles, the downtown streets of prewar oil-boom cities are lined with stores and office towers faced with the forward-looking styles of Art Deco, Zig Zag Moderne, and 1930s Streamline. Sunbursts, chevrons, bright colored zig-zags, and sleekly turned corners tied the growing cities to the imagined future. Los Angeles examples ranged from the gemlike Oviatt Building to the Orpheum Theater and the Richfield Old Building. Fort Worth's Aviation Building, Sinclair Building, and Texas and Pacific Terminal all rose in 1930 and 1931.

The heir of prewar streamlined architecture is southern California's "coffee shop moderne." The mobile society of Los Angeles devised atomic-age coffee shops that were open twenty-four hours a day under sweeping cantilevered roofs. They offered open spaces and bold geometric shapes; glittering surfaces of plastic, glass, and chrome that imitated gull-winged Chevrolets and finned DeSotos; and astral decorations of sunbursts, stars, and frozen sparklers. *House and Home* editor Douglas Haskell named it the "Googie" style in 1952 for Googie's coffee shop on Sunset Boulevard. Bowling alleys, supermarkets, and motels tested out the same styles, and Las Vegas made them famous.

Western cities also display the energy of a fantastic and exuberant folk architecture. Some are individual projects like Simon Rodia's famous towers in Watts, a vernacular monument to California exuberance constructed over decades from scrounged materials. Street murals pepper the blank walls of Berkeley, San Francisco, Santa Monica, Compton, and East Los Angeles. The Old Woman of the Freeway began to look out over the Hollywood Freeway in 1974. Visitors to the beachfront community of Venice are reminded of the moral of the Fall of Icarus. A hundred miles down the coast, Chicano Park lies beneath the ramps of the San Diego–Coronado Bridge. On the concrete bridge supports, Mexican-American artists painted immense murals—a thirty-foot Virgin of Guadalupe, tower-ing serpents, the Aztec emperor Cuauhtemoc.

Otherwise conservative organizations have constructed entire fantastic townscapes. Anaheim's Disneyland, said its builder, was the place for Cal-ifornia "to demonstrate its faith in the future."[3] Houston's Astrodome was the brainchild of politician and entrepreneur Roy Hofheinz. Opened in 1965, the Astrodome reflected Houston's flamboyance and its disregard for traditional forms, in which baseball parks nestled within active urban neighborhoods. It became an instant tourist attraction because of its Texas size and its entirely new and high-tech approach to the classic architectural challenge of enclosing large spaces. In another branch of architecture, most instant universities in the United States—from the University of Chicago in the 1890s to Duke University in the 1930s—have sought the hallowed respectability of Gothic quadrangles. The University of California at Irvine, in contrast, now offers its students a set of buildings that illustrate the full range of uninhibited postmodern architecture. Similarly, the multicolored buildings of Oral Roberts University in Tulsa look like a television spaceport set down in the American West. They declare their allegiance to a popular technological future rather than a European past.

In fact, although its students might be surprised to hear it, Oral Roberts University is an unselfconscious introduction to the postmodern approach to urban design. In the language of cultural criticism, Western cities blend aspects of the modern cityscape with the postmodern. The regularity and legibility discussed in chapter 6 are very much in the modern tradition of universally applicable forms and ideas. At the same time, Westerners have valued their vernacular cityscapes over academic architecture and sym-metrical planning. Metropolitan areas like Los Angeles, Orange County, and Phoenix resonate with the theories of postmodernism by rejecting a centralized structure. The playfulness of pop architecture and community art add to the fluidity that postmodernists so admire.

Western cities have taken on another special role in defining the popular culture of postwar America in their role as a generic "televisionland." The replacement of live television with filmed shows and the transfer of most television production from New York to Los Angeles in the 1960s made southern California the preferred setting for any programs that require outside locations. Southwest cities were not only convenient but also famil-iar to the typical television producer, who was a native Californian with a degree from the film program at UCLA or USC. In particular, writers and producers have picked Western settings for high-energy crime and detective series. One of the earliest realistic drama series was Jack Webb's "Dragnet," which drew its scripts from the Los Angeles police files and filmed them on the city's streets and soundstages. "This is the city, Los Angeles, California," proclaimed the voiceover. "What you're about to see is true." Other cop and detective series from "77 Sunset Strip" to "Mannix" to "Columbo" to "The Rockford Files" to "Hill Street Blues" have been shot in Los Angeles or its outliers like San Diego and Honolulu.

The chosen prime-time "locations" for the soap operas of power in the 1980s offered an important contrast with family-based situation comedies. The latter are studio productions that rely on a limited set of interior sets preceded by scene-setters behind the titles that place them in a generic middle America of Atlanta, Brooklyn, Chicago, Cincinnati, Columbus, Milwaukee, or Minneapolis. By definition, comedic story lines are resolved in favor of family stability and social equilibrium. The evening soaps of the 1980s, in contrast, thrived on the continuing disruption of social norms by J. R. Ewing of "Dallas" and his counterparts. The power soaps have been especially at home in the Sunbelt West of Dallas, Denver ("Dynasty"), the San Francisco Bay area ("Falcon Crest" and "Hotel"), and southern California ("Knott's Landing" and "L.A. Law").

The language of television helps to construct the symbolic understanding of Western cities. As a continuing urban frontier, the cities of the West have a far more central and effective role in our national imagination than in our regional imagination. By representing different ways in which Americans try to project their understanding of the national frontier into an uncertain future, they translate the range of possible meanings for the nineteenth-century nation into the twenty-first century. The result is a direct connection in which even the newest of Western cities draw on the three mythic images of the historic West: democracy, opportunity, and individual fulfillment.

Since the enactment of the Northwest Ordinance in 1787, Americans have identified the Western frontier with the opportunity to create a nation of democratic institutions. The Northwest Ordinance itself helped to make the older West into the "valley of democracy" by defining the procedures by which the English-speaking settlers in the territories northwest of the Ohio River could write republican constitutions and gain statehood, with full privileges in the federal union. For a later generation, resistance to the expansion of slavery westward helped to trigger a Civil War. Summarizing and articulating the common understanding, Frederick Jackson Turner argued that American frontier regions "exercised a steady influence toward democracy."[4]

The frontier also held the possibility of promoting republican virtue and community values alongside individual initiative. As the nation developed, Turner wrote in 1903, the watchword of the frontier became "a steady increase of the social tendency" and a growing "magnitude of social achievement."[5] Fifty years later, historians Stanley Elkins and Eric Mc-Kitrick restated the civic impacts of the frontier for individual communities. Essentially, they argued, the challenges of problem solving and community making in new settlements demanded wide participation, cooperation, voluntary association, and support for public institutions and government. Far from undermining the civil community, the frontier balanced individual competition against the needs of the larger group. As Alexis de Tocqueville observed, westward expansion reproduced a pattern of egalitarian and participatory communities across the continent. Indeed, Americans settled the frontier not as isolated individuals but as members of interlocking communities—gateway cities, market towns, and farming districts.

At the end of the twentieth century, the most promising future for the United States as a civil community is found in the middle-sized cities of the West. A pessimist might plausibly argue that America's small towns retain a Tocquevillian consensus but lack the resources to carry out civic agendas or the willingness to accommodate new ideas. Many larger cities are deeply riven by ethnic divisions and chasms between rich and poor that have destroyed their ability to unite around a conception of the common good. The irreducibility of urban problems and the failure of pluralistic competition among classes and ethnic groups has raised the fear of a permanent urban underclass and a permanent state of impoverishment for central cities. An instructive contrast to deeply divided Philadelphia or Chicago is Seattle, described by one enthusiast as "a paragon and an inspiration, testimony to what urban living could be like if cities were, like Seattle, moderately populated, surrounded by water, hemmed in by mountains, favored by a mild climate and watched over by a citizenry that knows how lucky it is."[6] Over the past generation, that watchful citizenry has taxed itself to clean up Lake Washington, to create a regional park system, and to anticipate the impact of rapid growth. Voters have responded passionately, if not always effectively, to preserve a human-scale downtown and to maintain affordable housing. In part because of the civic commitment, metropolitan Seattle earned first place in quality of life among the American cities ranked by Arthur Louis in 1975 and by the *Places Rates Almanac* in 1989. In between, it has placed first, second, fifth, and twelfth in both specialized and comprehensive ratings. An *international* comparison of a hundred large metropolitan areas showed Seattle-Tacoma in a tie with Melbourne and Montreal as the best cities for average residents.

Portland, according to the British news magazine *The Economist,* provides another example of a city "where it works." Its successes have included refurbished older neighborhoods, a revitalized downtown that is designed for casual users as well as office workers, and a commitment to a strong bus and rail transit system. The underlying reason for Portland's success has been a political system that opened itself to citizen participation in the late 1960s and that remained open after federal requirements for citizen participation became dead letters. Portlanders who care about their city find an accessible and accountable government and structured avenues for input, such as recognized neighborhood associations. Portland is less an illustration of a "state of urban grace," as claimed by *The Economist,* as it is an example of justification through good works.[7]

One of the earlier quality-of-life studies published by Ben-Chieh Liu in 1976 remains the most thorough, with more than two hundred indicators grouped to measure economic performance, political behavior, the environment, health and education, and social support. Using 1970 census data, Liu evaluated metropolitan areas as outstanding, excellent, good, adequate, and substandard. All of the Western metropolitan areas outside Texas and Oklahoma were "good" at the least. More than half of the nation's "outstanding" metro areas (but only 18 percent of all cases) were in the same states. Portland topped the list for metropolitan areas with more than 500,000 residents; Eugene led middle-sized metro areas of 200,000 to 500,000; and Fargo came in second among smaller metro areas.

Apart from the obvious advantages of climate, setting, and prosperity, what underlies these high rankings for Western cities is a shared commitment to the public interest. The health, education, and social components of Liu's data tested each city's sense of community responsibility by measuring such items as per capita investment in education and medical facilities, school enrollment, newspaper circulation, ratio of public library books to population, and the proportion of all professionals who are blacks and women. Overall, 56 of the 68 Western metropolitan areas rated at least good in health and education, and 59 of the 68 were rated this with respect to the social component. Fourteen cities were rated outstanding in both areas, from San Francisco, Sacramento, and Seattle through Provo, Billings, and Denver to Wichita, Lincoln, and Sioux Falls.

Specific evaluations of local government performance and openness of community leadership produce similar conclusions. In the 1950s, *Fortune* cited

Philadelphia, Milwaukee, Cincinnati, Detroit, and New York as among the nation's best-run cities. *Financial World Magazine* offered a very different list for 1991 after examining city management in terms of the administrative basics of accounting, budgeting, performance evaluations, and infrastructure controls. Phoenix, Seattle, Portland, San Jose, and Fort Worth ranked first through fifth, with Dallas, Oklahoma City, and San Diego coming in seventh through ninth.[8] Urban-planning specialists placed Portland and San Francisco at the top of urban design and planning among American cities.

For balance, however, we must remember that one of the unarticulated traits of the well-governed cities of the upper West is their small minority populations. Large cities like Portland and Seattle and smaller cities like Provo and Billings have been at the far ends of northward migration tracks from the rural South, the Caribbean, and Latin America. The same is true in Minneapolis-St. Paul. It is relatively easy to generate civic consensus in homogeneous communities, but during the war migrations of the 1940s, these cities were no better than any others at dealing fairly with African-American newcomers or Japanese-American exiles. Since 1980 they have had to face another rapid expansion of Hispanic, Asian, and black populations. It remains to be seen whether official welcomes for increased diversity will avoid the social divisions that threaten to paralyze many cities in all parts of the nation.

A competing idea of the American frontier has emphasized personal success rather than community achievement—the sort of narrowly ambitious individualism that sociologist Robert Bellah and his associates juxtaposed to communities of citizenship and memory in *Habits of the Heart*. The frontier has long been viewed as the true home of the expectant capitalist, the ambitious individual for whom enterprise is a calling to be tirelessly pursued. In 1868, Henry George noted with understatement that "the sharpest sense of Americans—the keen sense of gain . . . does not lose its keenness in our bracing air of California."[9] Historians Richard Hofstadter and Marvin Meyers characterized this American type as the "Jacksonian Man." Motivated by the promise of capitalism and free from the constraints of feudalism, the Jacksonian American was drawn to new opportunities and horizons. The goal was to throw open new opportunities and achieve success within the limits of the American system, to climb to the top without shaking the social and economic underpinnings. Earlier, in "The West and American Ideals," Turner had quoted in a traveler's reactions the essential story of American success:

As we crossed the Cascades on our way to Seattle, one of the passengers was moved to explain his feeling of the excellence of Puget Sound in contrast with the remaining visible Universe. He did it well in spite of irreverent interruptions from those fellow travelers who were unconverted children of the East, and at last he broke forth in passionate challenge, "Why should I not love Seattle! It took me from the slums of the Atlantic Coast, a poor Swedish boy with hardly fifteen dollars in my pocket. It gave me a home by the beautiful sea . . . it brought abundance and a new life to me and my children and I love it, I love it!"[10]

The natural habitat for the independent, self-reliant and self-interested American, Turner realized, was what we can think of as a constantly changing "frontier of production." As William Cronon has noted, Turner gradually expanded his understanding of the economic frontier from unoccupied public land or "free land" to a broader concept of "the unpossessed resources of the nation."[11] The Western frontier and the West as a region have been the source of much of the abundance that David Potter in *People of Plenty* said shaped the American character. The chance to possess and exploit these abundant resources drew Americans to the successive mineral frontiers from upper Michigan and Illinois to the Alaska oil fields and to farming frontiers from Ohio to Hawaii. William Goetzmann has demonstrated that the fur traders and mountain men of the Missouri Valley and Rocky Mountains shared the entrepreneurial outlook. Michael Allen has rescued Ohio and Mississippi rivermen from the myth of Mike Fink and placed them in the same camp.[12]

This alternative "frontier" of America as a business enterprise has been symbolized in popular culture by Houston, Dallas, and the other cities of Greater Texas. These are cities that have grown by supporting basic resource industries like oil and ranching that extract value directly from the land. "Dallas" and *Giant* have offered classic Westerners recast to fit the realities of the urbanized entrepreneurial frontier. Texans, says native son Larry McMurtry, like their "cities as raw as possible, so as to allow free play to what's left of the frontier spirit." "Wheelerdealerism," he continues, "is an extension of the frontier ethos, refined and transplanted to an urban context."[13]

Settled from the Middle West as well as the South and tied economically to St. Louis and Chicago as well as New Orleans, Dallas has often presented itself as the archetypal American city. Transplanting Midwestern boosterism to an expansive "metroplex," the business-based Dallas Partnership says that the spirit of Dallas is "dynamic, optimistic, and action-oriented." The Goals for Dallas program of 1966–77 was "boosterism at its most grandiose," according to historian Martin Melosi. This updated entrepreneurial frontier meets the world as a business town pure and simple—"a dream location for business" in the judgment of *Fortune* magazine in 1989.[14]

Houston emerged as the "shock city" of the 1970s with the explosive growth of the energy business. To many observers it epitomized the optimistic assumptions of a globally dominant United States as it served the world petroleum industry and sent 80 percent of American grain exports to the Soviet Union. It attracted space-age corporations in the 1970s and housed the headquarters or operating base for twenty-four of the twenty-five largest oil companies in the United States. Its free-form growth uninhibited by zoning, its political conservatism, and its business spinoffs from NASA pushed it forward as a new symbol of American prosperity for both the sober academics of the Urban Institute and the journalists from the *New York Times*.

The most common cliché was to identify Houston with the American future. The *Saturday Review* called it "the last word in American cities . . . rushing hell-bent into tomorrow without much thought about the day after." Architecture critic Ada Louise Huxtable wrote that "Houston is the place that scholars flock to for the purpose of seeing what modern civilization has wrought. . . . Houston is *the* city of the second half of the 20th century." Travel writer Jan Morris identified its energetic growth with the future, writing that "the world converges upon Houston. . . . Hour by hour, the freeways get fuller, the downtown towers taller, the River Oaks residents richer, the suburbs gnaw their way deeper into the countryside, and what was just a blob on the map a couple of decades ago becomes more than just a city but an idea, a vision, the Future Here and Now!"[15]

Houston's energy is released through individuals rather than community action. "Houston is a city of newcomers," Willie Morris commented in 1960, "and the newcomers are on the make." The city's ideology of the free market has favored big business and excused a lack of attention to social needs. It also favors the opportunist and the pursuit of the main chance. Until very recently, even its admirers tended to characterize Houston as "bigger" rather than "better." In *Some Can Whistle* Larry McMurtry writes about the city's "sweaty power . . . its funkiness and energy."[16]

Phoenix is an even newer version of the same dynamic individualism. Reporter Neal Pierce has commented that Phoenix has appropriated much of the Texas image of endless opportunity: "They all view the civilization here as an opening book, full of promise and opportunity." This "Headquarters West of the American free-enterprise ethic," Pierce writes, has been as firmly committed as Houston and Dallas to the ideology of private initiative.

At the same time, the "quintessential Sun Belt boomtown" has lacked strong institutions for community decision making and an ethos of public responsibility. As Peter Wiley and Robert Gottlieb put it, Phoenix has been an example of "free enterprise in the saddle, the market as king . . . southwestern capitalism's quest for immortality."[17]

Dallas, Houston, and "super-American" Phoenix are places where Americans can be "American" in following the dictates of a business culture. California cities, in contrast, have represented the frontier as a land of self-expression. In the American myth, pioneers like Daniel Boone and the frontiersmen of James Fenimore Cooper's novels are self-reliant men constantly in search of new beginnings. Again in Turner's words, "the frontier is productive of individualism. . . . It produces antipathy to control." The margins of settlement have been the place for new beginnings, freedom of individual expression, escape from social constraints. Turner characterizes the frontier as the source of buoyancy and exuberance, of "restless, nervous energy," and of "dominant individualism."[18]

The Western frontier has also offered freedom to groups outside the mainstream of national values. Frontier and rural locations have always attracted social experiments and utopian communities because the absence of close neighbors has presumably meant freedom from social constraints and intolerance. A detailed analysis by Philip Porter and Fred Luckerman found a majority of nineteenth-century utopias located within a hundred miles of the standard frontier line of six persons per square mile. The Mormon settlement of Utah is the most famous and successful of the isolated Western utopias, but Colorado, California, and Puget Sound drew their own clusters of intentional communities. More recently, the Rocky Mountains and the Pacific Northwest have attracted a disproportionate share of ecotopians and counterculture communes. For Americans who retain a belief in the civic community, the negative side of the same impulse has been the proliferation of survivalist enclaves and the appearance in the 1980s of white supremacist communities like the Aryan Nation of northern Idaho.

Twentieth-century Americans who have wanted personal freedom without the commitment of an intentional community have headed in particular to California and its coastal cities. For every utopian colonist, there have been a thousand new San Franciscans or Angelenos who see *urban* California as a practical compromise between individual opportunity and freedom of expression. In the tradition of urban specialization, Greater Los Angeles has represented personal freedom as facilitated by the opportunities of consumption, while the Bay Area has represented the range of American freedom in the choice of individual behavior.

Many social critics since the 1920s have traveled to Los Angeles with a chip on their shoulder. The East Coast image of southern California has been of a combination of craziness and unseemly consumption, depicting a metropolis plunged into a sort of perpetual carnival in which people may be able to have too much fun for their own good. Among cultists and eccentrics, Los Angeles emerged in the 1930s and 1940s as a city of alienation and excess. Similarly, an articulate set of new residents associated with the movie industry developed a strongly colored depiction of Los Angeles as an extravaganza of inappropriate entertainment. Evelyn Waugh took a bemused look at Forest Lawn Memorial Park in *The Loved One* (1948). Aldous Huxley offered a darker satire in *After Many a Summer Dies the Swan* (1939). Carey McWilliams came to believe that he had "a ringside seat at a year-round circus" and profiled the city's religious extremists in *Southern California: An Island on the Land* (1946). Suspicious of too much freedom of expression, other visitors after World War II proclaimed that southern Californians were detached from the larger community. Dependence on individual automobiles and backyard swimming pools rather than crowded subways and public parks marked them as social isolates. Freedom from tradition and community was seen as breeding the anomie of Joan Didion's Maria Wyeth, whose simultaneous alienation and attachment to the world of consumption is symbolized as encapsulation within a pricey automobile in *Play It As It Lays*.

In a more positive evaluation, late-twentieth-century Los Angeles has supplanted late-nineteenth-century Paris as the world capital of consumption. The city's boom coincided with the postwar wave of consumer demand. In the popular media, Beverly Hills and Rodeo Drive came to rival New York and Fifth Avenue as homes of unlimited charge accounts. In the 1950s or even the 1960s, the young person from the provinces might long for breakfast at Tiffany's. In the 1980s, success was much more likely to mean making it in L.A. Academic evaluations from both sides of the political spectrum also stressed the liberating effects of Californian abundance. Conservative political scientists were impressed by the ability of residents to pick and choose among different packages of public services in the region's scores of small cities. Sam B. Warner, Jr., argued that "the land use and transportation structure of Los Angeles gives glimpses of a more humane environment than we have yet enjoyed," based on the "ease and scope of movement of the overwhelming proportion of its citizens." Los Angeles county supervisor John Anson Ford was saying much the same thing when he asserted that "it must not be a second congested London or New York, . . . but a population center with many new characteristics adjusted to the outdoor life of the region and to the era of greater leisure, greater mobility, and a wider distribution of the skills and culture of modern society."[19]

The specialized recreational environments of Disneyland and the week-end suburb of Las Vegas epitomized consumer society as well as innovations in urban design. The Las Vegas casinos and Strip were attracting ten million tourists a year by 1960 and twenty million by 1990. Las Vegas was an entire city that defined its public face in terms of its facilitation of consumption. In fact, as John Findlay suggests, the city offers a future in which consumption and pleasure take place within acceptable social boundaries. The gamblers who fill the city's 74,000 hotel and motel rooms are neither suckers nor escapists from an intolerably conformist America. Instead, they are looking for carefully circumscribed liberation and a careful sampling from what Tom Wolfe called "the super-hyper-version" of an emerging way of life.[20] A modern version of Jacksonian-as-consumer, the visitors to Las Vegas have learned to want adventure and cultural challenge within forms that build on a stable social structure.

Disneyland is Las Vegas for the whole family. Borrowing the skills and values of the movie industry, Walt Disney wanted to create a walk-through fantasy that would outdo Cinerama and Cinemascope as a "real" experience. The Anaheim amusement park that opened in 1956 has given the American vernacular the term *Disneyland,* a generic noun that is as ubiquitous as *kleenex.* The park not only transformed much of Orange County but also identified greater Los Angeles with carefully controlled entertainment. It was advertised in conjunction with Knott's Berry Farm and Forest Lawn as part of southern California's tourist scene, while Disney's television series brought the park to the attention of the entire nation. As is also true in Las Vegas, Disneyland's projection of a future of socially acceptable consumption contains little to challenge the status quo.

Disneyland also helped to make Orange County into the latest version of the highly mobile community of consumption. This new "showplace of America's future" and "ideal landscape for middle-class Americans" coalesced around Disneyland, which made Anaheim into a big-league city and a national convention center. Paul Goldberger has noted that high land prices have forced a surprising density on much of the housing, leading to urban densities amidst suburban lifestyles. The freeway grid allows decentralized consumption organized around shopping malls like South Coast Plaza, which rings up more sales than downtown San Francisco. Orange County by 1990 offered a full range of auto-access culture, with a performing arts center in Costa Mesa, an art museum in Newport Beach, and a commuter university in Irvine.

Whereas postwar Los Angeles represents freedom to enjoy yourself, postwar San Francisco represents the freedom to be yourself. If there ever was (or is) a "greening" of America, it is because the hue seeped outward from the communities around San Francisco Bay. Prewar San Francisco and Oakland were in many ways the most "Eastern" of Western cities, with strong labor movements, large European immigrant communities, substantial industrial sectors, and a heritage of machine politics. Within a decade after the war, however, San Francisco and its satellite cities were laying the groundwork for a "culture of civility" that tolerated efforts to define a wide range of self-conscious "communities" in older neighborhoods around the bay. It has been a testing ground whose residents have actually tried out new values and behaviors as stand-ins for the larger American society.

The Bay Area was very *urban* in its ability to nurture subcultures and to bring together otherwise detached individuals. Poet Gary Snyder has commented that "San Francisco taught me what a city could be, and saved me from having to go to Europe." Groups that resist inclusion in a broad "national culture" can create their own territories within the framework of large central cities. Postwar San Francisco has cycled new lifestyle communities through old buildings in a lifestyle-centered version of immigrant neighborhood succession. "San Francisco," wrote one journalist in 1984, "has far more driving pertinence for the country as a whole than most people, booster or critic, resident or merely observer, might imagine, for in the variety and complexity of its ethnic, social, and economic issues, it seems to speak to the country as a whole."[21]

The cultural mystique of San Francisco in the 1960s and 1970s was grounded in some very specific changes in local politics. William Issel has argued that labor unions, business owners, and social reformers came together in the late 1930s to construct a liberal political regime. The origins of the liberal coalition lay in management's recognition of unions in the wake of the general strike of 1934, in the strength of the new International Longshoremen's and Warehousemen's Union (ILWU), and in labor-management cooperation to implement a competitive growth strategy during World War II. Black migration for war jobs, embarrassment over the treatment of Japanese-Americans, and the public values of antifascism supported postwar attention to a civil rights agenda through a new policy network. The same business leaders, unions, and social-service liberals also supported housing construction, economic development programs, and enhanced social services. By the 1960s the liberal coalition had seized the middle ground in San Francisco politics and had opened the door to more radical experiments in politics and social relations.

For one example, the strength of the liberal coalition helped the Bay Area to emerge as a trendsetter in medical care. The Kaiser Permanente Health Care Program originated as a medical plan for Henry Kaiser's construction workers at Grand Coulee Dam. Its combination of prepayment, group practice, and internally controlled facilities served Kaiser's West Coast steel and shipyard workers during World War II and emerged from the war most firmly grounded in the strong union communities of San Francisco and Oakland. Its twentyfold expansion from 1945 to 1956 drew on the active support of Bay Area labor (including the ILWU and other CIO unions), the tacit backing of San Francisco's liberal regime, and Kaiser's belief in the natural alliance of labor and management. With 1.5 million members in the Pacific states by 1965, Kaiser Permanente became the prototype for the health maintenance organizations that now enroll more than 25 million Americans.

In relatively liberal San Francisco, a small group of political radicals continued to voice demands and protests throughout the Eisenhower years. The movement was based on the labor movement of the 1930s and the continuing radicalism of the ILWU under the leadership of Harry Bridges. Despite a university loyalty oath, the open microphones of radio station KPFA (founded in 1949) made Berkeley one of the few communities that regularly heard the ideas of the radical left. When the House Un-American Activities Committee arrived in San Francisco for hearings in May 1960, it found scores of student protesters in addition to its carefully preselected claque. Sit-down protests at City Hall led to the arrest of sixty-four demonstrators, including thirty-one Berkeley students. An angry HUAC edited television news film into *Operation Abolition,* an antiprotest film that ironically helped to identify the Bay Area as the home of a Left that was alive and kicking.

The coalescence of the Beats in San Francisco's North Beach neighborhood paralleled the survival of the political left. At the center was Lawrence Ferlinghetti's City Lights bookstore, the most famous of a cluster of cafes, bars, bookstores, and other gathering places. Disaffected writers, poets, artists, and musicians drifted in and out of San Francisco and Berkeley.[22] Common themes were a rejection of materialist culture, a longing for community, and a celebration of both straight and gay sexuality. The Bay Area's heritage of cultural and political radicalism was very much on the minds of the new generation of cultural rebels. The district attracted national attention in the years after Allen Ginsberg first recited *Howl* at the Six Gallery in 1955. The poem survived an obscenity challenge that reached the Supreme Court and ended up as a twentieth-century best seller with its call for freedom from stifling social constraints.

The explosion of political protest and social experiment in Berkeley and San Francisco in the 1960s built on the earlier political and cultural critiques. The metropolis was fertile ground, with its unrooted populations and clashing ideas. Berkeley's radical reputation and open atmosphere began to attract leftists from around the country. As William Rorabaugh has noted, "Max Scheer, the founder of the *Berkeley Barb,* came from Baltimore; Jerry Rubin, a deeply alienated young newspaper reporter, from Cincinnati; and Mario Savio, the Catholic leftist, from New York. The migration had begun in the fifties but grew after 1960, when the HUAC protests drew attention to the Left in the Bay Area."[23]

Political protest that began with the Free Speech Movement evolved into antiwar activism. The FSM was a logical extension of the urban/suburban liberalism that had already mobilized around the cause of civil rights for blacks. Mario Savio was one of several Berkeley students who returned in September 1964 from a summer of civil rights work in Mississippi to find new rules limiting political dialogue on campus. The goal of the FSM was to end the customary regulation of political activity on university property. Its protests climaxed with a December sit-in that led to 773 arrests. By the time the protracted FSM trials were over the next summer, the escalation of the American war in Vietnam in the spring of 1965 had diverted campus attention to a new issue. Berkeley's Vietnam Day Committee started with teach-ins and moved on to mass protests and efforts to block munitions trains. Whereas Mario Savio had talked about a "community of protest," old radicals in the antiwar movement hoped to use demonstrations and police repression to teach lessons about the inevitable divisions between the economic system and its future workers.

Radical black protest in Berkeley and Oakland developed simultaneously with the FSM and the Vietnam Day Committee. The Oakland-based Black Panthers drew on the wartime generation of Bay Area blacks born to war workers during the 1940s. Bobby Seale was born in 1936 in North Texas but grew up in Berkeley's Codornices Village housing project—one of the segregated legacies of the World War II boom. Huey Newton was born in 1942 in Louisiana but grew up in Oakland. They developed an ideology of community empowerment on the basis of Franz Fanon's anticolonial Marxism, Seale's work in the North Oakland Anti-Poverty Center, and personal experiences on the streets of Oakland. Newton and Seale created the Black

Panthers in 1966, began to carry firearms, and recruited a visible and articulate ex-convict named Eldridge Cleaver. The Panthers confronted what they saw as biased police. They also tried with limited success to reorganize individual behavior around an agenda of social change, such as a free-breakfast program, and ran candidates for local state legislative and congressional seats. In contrast to the rioters in Watts, the Panthers had a political program, if not the necessary resources to carry it through. The movement was shaken by Newton's 1968 manslaughter conviction after the death of a white police officer and Cleaver's flight to Algeria after the revocation of his parole. Nevertheless, the Panthers survived as a political party, registering black voters and running Bobby Seale as a strong candidate for mayor of Oakland before supporting Lionel Wilson in 1977.

The cultural critique and advocacy of personal freedom transmogrified into the hippies of San Francisco's Haight-Ashbury district in 1966 and 1967. The previously middle-class neighborhood of Haight-Ashbury had filtered down to a working-class population during the 1930s, 1940s, and 1950s. At the start of the 1960s, its increasingly cheap apartments housed African-Americans, San Francisco State University students, and nascent beatnik and homosexual communities run out of North Beach by police harassment. Local activists had already given the Haight a progressive style in local politics and the Haight-Ashbury Neighborhood Council took a leading role in San Francisco's freeway revolt, which blocked completion of a freeway network that would have blighted the city's waterfront and neighborhoods.

The combination of cheap, run-down apartments, a convenient location, and an atmosphere of cultural and political radicalism attracted a sudden influx of students and college dropouts during 1966. One of the attractions was the proximity of the Fillmore Auditorium, where Bill Graham produced rock concerts that dealt openly with the growing drug culture. January 1967 brought a Human Be-In in Golden Gate Park, where political radicals like Jerry Rubin and established poets like Gary Snyder and Allen Ginsberg shared the stage with Jefferson Airplane and The Grateful Dead. In 1967's "summer of love," the Haight was home to perhaps 7,000 permanent hippies and 70,000 short-term visitors. Haight-Ashbury's career as a hippie neighborhood was short. Self-consciously political groups like the Diggers got plenty of takers for their free food, but few of them were adherents of philosophical anarchism. Drugs and violence took over the streets in 1968, psychedelic businesses and counterculture institutions shut down, and a hip but respectable middle class began to buy up the cheap real estate in the early 1970s. The northern California coast, with its favorable climate for growing marijuana, attracted some of the former residents. Others moved to Berkeley, diluting its political ambiance with newcomers more interested in free food and free expression than in political philosophy. The upshot was rioting in 1969 over the creation of People's Park on Telegraph Avenue, an episode in which both sides were more interested in asserting power than in promoting clear political positions.

The rise and fall of free expression in Haight-Ashbury had the additional effect of paving the way for the public emergence of San Francisco's gay community in the 1970s. The city had had a strong homosexual community since World War II, when most gays purged from the armed forces in the Pacific theater were processed out through San Francisco. Openly gay poets such as Allen Ginsberg were prominent among the beats, and many North Beach bars were gay and lesbian as well as bohemian. Gathering places began to arise in other parts of the city at about the same time that *Life* magazine proclaimed San Francisco the country's "gay capital" in 1964. The city's gay population may have peaked around 1980. Certainly the number of business and social gathering places identified as gay and lesbian increased steadily in 1970s to a peak of more than 300 in 1982, and then gradually declined to 223 in 1988. The same period saw the Castro district go through the stages of a gay bohemian influx in the late 1960s and early 1970s, a gay middle-class transition in the mid-1970s, and a "bourgeois consolidation" in the 1980s.[24] The assassination of Mayor George Moscone and City Council member Harvey Milk in 1979 and the crisis of AIDS dampened the growth of the gay community, but San Francisco as an exemplar of personal freedom helped to open other cities to the free expansion of gay communities.

The Beat poets, the labor radicals, the Free Speechers, the Black Panthers, the war protesters, and the San Francisco gays had disparate backgrounds and goals, but they shared a sense of being nascent communities in opposition to mainstream values. Communities of protest gave freedom of expression to individuals by offering social and intellectual support. In the organized society of the mid twentieth century, the frontier of individualism could find effective expression in the environment of pluralism that the Bay Area nurtured so successfully.

In the broadest perspective, Western cities not only recapitulate the varying meaning of Turner's frontier, they also translate Alexis de Tocqueville's interpretation of the American experience from the early nineteenth century to the later twentieth. The Americans that Tocqueville observed in 1831 and wrote about in *Democracy in America* were being pulled between

an impulse toward fierce individualism and one toward enthusiastic association in the pursuit of common interests. Western cities in the past generation have promoted the complementary individualisms of economic success, consumption, and self-expression. They have also pioneered in
developing many community solutions to the problems generated by metropolitan growth. Like Tocqueville's Cincinnatians of 1831, the Denverites
and San Franciscans of the 1990s are caught in the permanent tension
about how best to be American.

AFTERWORD

To find nineteen of the nation's twenty-five fastest-growing metropolitan areas, Americans in the 1940s had to look to the western half of the nation. The same Western states counted sixteen of the twenty-five fastest growing metropolitan areas during the 1950s, thirteen during the 1960s, sixteen for the 1970s, and thirteen for the 1980s. Urban growth was felt at all levels of the urban system. Between 1940 and 1990, Phoenix moved from ninety-first place to twentieth among American metropolitan areas. San Diego moved from fiftieth to fifteenth, Dallas from thirty-first to ninth, Houston from nineteenth to tenth, and Los Angeles became the country's "second city." The dozen largest Western metropolitan areas alone accounted for 28 percent of *all* of the population increase in the United States between 1940 and 1990, and for 36 percent during the 1980s. At the same time, the number of Western cities designated as metropolitan areas by the federal government grew from 32 in 1940 to 68 in 1970 and 101 in 1989 as more and more small cities added to their economic base, population, and regional influence.

The Western metropolitan frontier has connected the old resource West to the world of the late twentieth century. The Burlington Northern railroad still sends its trains rumbling along the edge of downtown Billings on a line that first operated in 1882. Quiet neighborhoods still climb from the Yellowstone River to the base of the rimrock. When local business people fill downtown restaurants to put away a breakfast and talk land, insurance, and hunting, it could still be 1940. Look a little more deeply, however, and Billings owes its new airport, its rehabbed hotels, and its mid-rise office buildings to its role in the world energy business. Employment in Yellow-

The railroad city of Billings. Billings gives a quick nod to the Yellowstone River, but the city's commercial district grew parallel to the Northern Pacific railroad tracks. As the metropolis of the northern Great Plains, Billings has been a focal point for decisions affecting the rural West. The tallest building in this view, for example, is the Northern Hotel in the center, where in 1944 the Army Corps of Engineers and Bureau of Reclamation hammered out the Pick-Sloan agreement that set federal policy for development of the Missouri River. (Courtesy of the Montana Historical Society)

stone County in 1988 included more than a thousand workers in oil and gas extraction and refining and another thousand in engineering and management services. When residents turn out by the thousands at Cobb Field to watch the Billings Mustangs of the Pioneer League, they're not cheering for local heroes but for Georgians, Ohioans, and Dominicans. The visiting teams from Pocatello and Butte, as well as Medicine Hat in Alberta, have their own share of Venezuelans and Californians hoping for a shot at the big leagues.

The metropolitan frontier has also helped to connect the United States to the world outside its borders. There is another meaning for the American frontier that has received less attention than the frontier as a source of opportunity, individualism, or democracy. As the Watts riot, the Black Panthers, and lawsuits under the Voting Rights Act all remind us, Western cities also represent the national future as environments for a new multiethnic culture. Los Angeles, Honolulu, San Antonio, San Diego, and Seattle represent the multiethnic, international future of the American West. Eastern cities from the 1840s to the 1940s struggled with adapting the narrow culture of North Sea Protestantism to the full range of European languages, religions, and national loyalties. They forged various forms of American identity from the 1850s to the 1950s. Newer cities in the Southwest and West now have to incorporate a much wider range of racial and cultural types—European-American, African-American, Mexican-American, Asian-American, and Native American.

In taking on this task, they are also continuing one of the hidden themes of the American frontier. The West has always been the region of contact between native North Americans, westward-moving European-Americans and African-Americans, northward-moving Latin Americans, and eastward-moving immigrants from the Pacific islands and Asia. In the 1850s or the 1890s, Anglo-Americans, Mexicans, Chinese, and others met everywhere across the landscape—in railroad construction crews, in mining camps, in the agricultural valleys of California, Colorado, and Oregon. A century later, they mix primarily in the West's growing cities. World War II added Western cities as the destination of African-Americans fleeing the impoverished South. The war and federal policies of the 1950s pushed Native Americans into Phoenix, Los Angeles, Seattle, Denver, and other cities. The renewed northward and eastward migrations after 1965 also targeted Western cities. In a very real way, communities like Houston, Seattle, and Oakland are the testing grounds for the multicultural America of the next century. As we have seen, the record to date is promising but far from perfect.

One way to summarize the challenge to the urban West is by revisiting downtown Los Angeles. To walk from Main Street to the Harbor Freeway is to cross a series of social and economic divides that tell us a great deal about the past and future of Western cities. The retail and entertainment core of the 1920s and 1930s along Broadway and Spring streets has now become the downtown for Hispanic East Los Angeles. The marquees of the old movie palaces announce films made in Mexico rather than Hollywood. The sidewalks at five in the afternoon are crowded with Latino and Asian immigrants waiting for southbound and eastbound buses. Many of these new Americans earn their living in the garment district east of Main Street, whose shops and factories have survived the 1980s and beyond by employing the cheap labor of legal and illegal immigrants. This old downtown was built with domestic capital to serve southern California consumers, farmers, and oilmen as a sort of Billings writ large. As its loft buildings and Art Deco towers have been refurbished by a new generation of entrepreneurs and immigrants from Asia and Latin America, it also reminds us that Los Angeles has grown from a regional metropolis to a labor market and cultural center for *two* North American nations and a funnel for transferring goods and people between western North America and the western Pacific.

Six blocks farther west, the new upscale city of "L.A. Law" broadcasts the same message in more stylish dress. The sleek towers and self-satisfied complexes of retail stores and offices that cluster along the Harbor Freeway sport the names of overseas banks and global accounting firms. Rather than waiting for buses, their attorneys and bankers can swing out of subsurface parking garages and chase the setting sun on westbound freeways. Much of this new downtown is owned by overseas investors and serves the trading needs of the industrialized Pacific Rim. It encapsulates (and physically insulates) Los Angeles as "the New York of the Pacific Rim," a world city standing just a notch below London or Tokyo in the global urban hierarchy. San Francisco, Houston, Dallas, Denver, Seattle, Honolulu, and San Diego are not far behind.

In the second half of the twentieth century, Western cities have become leaders as much as followers, setting their own styles and creating their own problems. Changes in the sources of population, capital, and commerce have lessened their real and perceived dependence on the country's old industrial capitals. For younger Californians, as Joan Didion recently pointed out, New York is now a trip "out" to the East rather than "back" East. Although historians venture predictions at their peril, it is likely that reductions in military spending during the 1990s will compound the effect by reducing the relative importance of decisions made in Pentagon offices.

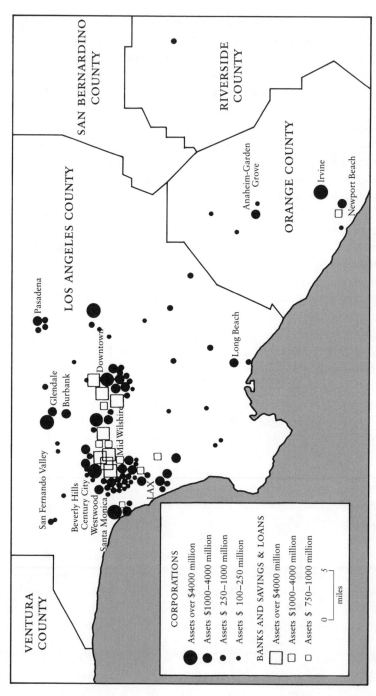

The corporate archipelago in Los Angeles. The location of corporate and banking headquarters in Los Angeles at the start of the 1980s showed the continued importance of the old downtown but also the development of new office concentrations. Such construction was being drawn to the west, north, and southwest by the city's highways and airport. (From Edward Soja et al., "Urban Restructuring: An Analysis of Social and Spatial Change in Los Angeles," *Economic Geography* 59 [April 1983]: 223; used by permission of *Economic Geography*)

In many ways, cities embody the best of American life: economic vitality, individual freedom, an opportunity for people of widely differing backgrounds to advance. In the same way, the cities of the Great Plains, the Western mountains, and the Pacific Coast have been communities designed to accommodate growth. During the period of this study, the accumulation of social inequities and physical problems resulting from headlong growth in the 1940s and 1950s led to a significant broadening of the urban political base in the 1960s and 1970s and efforts to meet the needs of this broad-edged constituency with an economic growth strategy in the 1980s. It appears at the start of the 1990s that another surge of metropolitan expansion has again brought the Western cities face to face with problems reminiscent of the 1960s. The challenge to the present generation of Western city-dwellers is to begin the new century with another era of creative change.

REFERENCE MATERIAL

NOTES

INTRODUCTION

1. William Thayer, *Marvels of the New West* (Norwich, Conn.: Henry Bill Publishing Co., 1891), 404.

2. Thayer, *Marvels,* 404.

3. William Stafford, "Texas," in *Stories That Could Be True: New and Collected Poems* (New York: Harper and Row, 1977), 173.

4. See, for example, David James Duncan, *The River Why* (San Francisco: Sierra Club Books, 1983); Norman Maclean, *A River Runs Through It* (Chicago: University of Chicago Press, 1983); Richard Brautigan, *Trout Fishing in America* (San Francisco: Four Seasons Foundation, 1967).

5. Edward Abbey, *Desert Solitaire* (New York: McGraw-Hill, 1968), 267.

6. James Bryce, *The American Commonwealth* (New York: Macmillan, 1912), 891–901; Charles Dudley Warner, "Studies of the Great West: A Far and Fair Country," *Harper's New Monthly Magazine* 76 (March 1888): 556–69.

7. Gunther Barth, *Instant Cities: Urbanization and the Rise of San Francisco and Denver* (New York: Oxford University Press, 1975).

CHAPTER 1. WAR AND THE WESTWARD TILT

1. Roger Lotchin, "The City and the Sword: San Francisco and the Rise of the Metropolitan Military Complex," *Journal of American History* 65 (March 1979): 1013.

2. Bradford Luckingham, *Phoenix: The History of a Southwestern Metropolis* (Tucson: University of Arizona Press, 1989), 137.

3. Gilbert Guinn, "A Different Frontier: Aviation, the Army Air Force, and the Evolution of the Sunshine Belt," *Aerospace Historian* 29 (March 1982): 42.

4. "Seattle: A Boom Comes Back," *Business Week,* June 20, 1942, p. 26.

5. Catherine Bauer, "War-Time Housing in Defense Areas," *Architect and Engineer* 151 (Oct. 1942): 33.

6. Phillip Funigiello, *The Challenge to Urban Liberalism: Federal-City Relations During World War II and Reconversion* (Knoxville: University of Tennessee Press, 1978), 34.

7. Beth Bailey and David Farber, *The First Strange Place: The Alchemy of Race and Sex in World War II Hawaii* (New York: Free Press, 1992), 95–96.

8. Amy Kesselman, *Fleeting Opportunities: Women Shipyard Workers in Portland and Vancouver During World War II* (Albany, N.Y.: SUNY Press, 1990), 29, 44.

9. Chester Himes, *The Quality of Hurt: The Autobiography of Chester Himes* (Garden City, N.Y.: Doubleday, 1972), 75.

10. *Oregon Journal,* May 12, 1944.

11. James Gregory, *American Exodus: The Dust Bowl Migration* (New York: Oxford University Press, 1989), 191.

12. Laura Fermi, *Atoms in the Family* (Chicago: University of Chicago Press, 1954), 230.

13. Paul Loeb, *Nuclear Culture: Living and Working in the World's Largest Atomic Complex* (New York: Coward McCann and Geoghegan, 1982), 42.

14. George Bates, quoted in Charles Wollenberg, *Marinship at War: Shipbuilding and Social Change in Wartime Sausalito* (Oakland, Calif.: Western Heritage Press, 1990).

15. Carey McWilliams, "Look What's Happened to California," *Harper's Magazine,* Oct. 1949, 21.

16. McWilliams, "What's Happened to California," 24.

CHAPTER 2. THE POLITICS OF GROWTH

1. Max Brooks, interview transcript, Oral History of Colorado Project, Colorado Historical Society.

2. John Gunther, *Inside USA* (New York: Harper and Brothers, 1947), 224. Charles A. Graham and Robert Perkin, "Denver: Reluctant Capital," in *Rocky Mountain Cities,* ed. Ray B. West (New York: W. W. Norton, 1949), 288.

3. Neil Morgan, *Westward Tilt: The American West Today* (New York: Random House, 1963), 279.

4. Constance McLaughlin Green, *American Cities in the Growth of the Nation* (New York: Harper and Row, 1965), 191.

5. Dee Linford, "Cheyenne: Cowman's Capital," in West, *Rocky Mountain Cities,* 112.

6. Mel Scott, *The San Francisco Bay Area: A Metropolis in Perspective* (Berkeley: University of California Press, 1959), 261.

7. Philip Trounstine and Terry Christensen, *Movers and Shakers: The Study of Community Power* (New York: St. Martins Press, 1982), 87.

8. Trounstine and Christensen, *Movers and Shakers,* 89.

9. Robert Lineberry, *Equality and Urban Policy: The Distribution of Municipal Services* (Beverly Hills, Calif.: Sage Publications, 1977), 55–56.

10. Louise Erdrich, *Love Medicine: A Novel* (New York: Holt, Rinehart and Winston, 1984), 132; U. Utah Phillips, "Larimer Street Lament," in Industrial Workers of the World, *Songs of the Workers* (1973).

11. Larry McMurtry, *In a Narrow Grave: Essays on Texas* (Albuquerque: University of New Mexico Press, 1986), 83.

CHAPTER 3. FROM REGIONAL CITIES TO NATIONAL CITIES

1. Murray Morgan, *Puget's Sound: A Narrative of Early Tacoma and the Southern Sound* (Seattle: University of Washington Press, 1979), 301.

2. The list was headed by Boise Cascade (forest products), Albertson's (supermarkets), Morrison Knudsen (construction and engineering), J. R. Simplot (food processing), and Ore-Ida (food processing). Alan Pred, *City-Systems in Advanced Economies* (New York: John Wiley & Sons, 1977), 128–57, 203–6.

3. In 1992, the Strategic Air Command was pared down to a much smaller Strategic Command with planning and coordinating but not operational responsibilities.

4. Roger Lotchin, "The City and the Sword Through the Ages and the Era of the Cold War," in *Essays on Sunbelt Cities and Recent Urban America,* ed. Robert Fairbanks and Kathleen Underwood (College Station, Tex.: Texas A & M University Press, 1990), 95.

5. Frances FitzGerald, *Cities on a Hill* (New York: Simon and Schuster, 1986), 212.

6. Eugene Moehring, *Resort City in the Sunbelt: Las Vegas, 1930–1970* (Reno: University of Nevada Press, 1989), 49.

7. Walter Van Tilburg Clark, "Reno: The State City," in West, *Rocky Mountain Cities,* 33.

8. Duncan Aikman, "El Paso: Big Mountain Town," in West, *Rocky Mountain Cities,* 90–91.

9. Quoted in Edward W. Soja, "Inside Exopolis: Scenes from Orange County," in Michael Sorkin, ed., *Variations on a Theme Park: The New American City and the End of Public Space* (New York: Hill & Wang, 1992), p. 110.

CHAPTER 4. GATEWAYS TO THE WORLD

1. W. H. Timmons, *El Paso: A Borderlands History* (El Paso: Texas Western Press, 1990), 307; Donald W. Meinig, *Southwest: Three Peoples in Geographical Change, 1600–1970* (New York: Oxford University Press, 1971), 109.

2. Won Moo Hurh and Kwang Chung Kim, *Korean Immigrants in America* (Rutherford, N.J.: Farleigh Dickinson University Press, 1984), 63.

3. U.S. Department of Commerce, Office of Area Development, *Future Development of the San Francisco Bay Area, 1960–2020* (San Francisco, 1959), 34.

4. Francine du Plessix Gray, *Hawaii: The Sugar-Coated Fortress* (New York: Random House, 1972), 98.

CHAPTER 5. THE POLITICS OF DIVERSITY

1. Reagan is quoted in Robert Fogelson, *Violence as Protest* (Garden City, N.Y.: Doubleday, 1971), 27; Parker is quoted in Henry F. Bedford, *Trouble Downtown: The Local Context of Twentieth-Century America* (New York: Harcourt Brace Jovanovich, 1978), 183.

2. Political scientist Amy Bridges has identified the same sort of political periodization for Southwestern cities, and historian Richard Bernard for Sunbelt cities. Drawing examples nationwide, political scientists Norman Fainstein and Susan Fainstein have distinguished among "directive regimes," dominant from 1945 to 1964; "concessionary regimes," dominant from 1965 to 1974; and "conserving regimes," dominant after 1975. The Fainstein typology is explicitly based on the interrelations among the local government, local capital, and the working class. Directive regimes served the interests of local capital while ignoring working-class interests. Concessionary regimes responded to grassroots mobilization with new programs outside the realm of development policy. Conserving regimes did a better job of serving lower-income needs than the governments of the 1950s but again clearly responded to the interests of capital. In this model, minority and working-class groups were incorporated into the plans of conserving regimes only for the purposes of buying them off and co-opting them.

3. Trounstine and Christensen, *Movers and Shakers*, 182.

4. Rufus P. Browning, Dale Rogers Marshall, and David H. Tabb, *Protest Is Not Enough: The Struggle of Blacks and Hispanics for Equality in Urban Politics* (Berkeley: University of California Press, 1984), 217.

5. The place system requires candidates to run for specific slots (such as City Council Position No. 2) but allows at-large voting for each seat, or place. In an open at-large election for multiple seats, all candidates run against each other. If three seats are up for election, each voter can vote for up to three candidates, and those with the highest totals are the winners. A block of voters can try to push a favored candidate ahead of the pack by casting single votes only, thus reducing the totals for the competition.

6. Section 5 applied to states and other political jurisdictions that employed a literacy test for voter registration on Nov. 1, 1964, Nov. 1, 1968, or Nov. 1, 1972, and whose voter registration or turnout for any of the 1964, 1968, or 1972 presidential elections was less than 50 percent of voting-age population. Originally aimed at the Deep South, the law was amended in 1974 to add Texas and other Southwestern states. In the 1980s, the measure applied to nine states and parts of thirteen others.

7. *Denver Post*, September 25, 1972.

8. Browning, Marshall, and Tabb, *Protest Is Not Enough*, 159.

9. Frances FitzGerald, "The Castro," *New Yorker* 62 (July 28, 1986): 48; Neil Pierce, "San Francisco Face-Lift More Than Skin Deep," Portland *Oregonian*, June 17, 1984.

10. Marc Simmons, *Albuquerque: A Narrative History* (Albuquerque: University of New Mexico Press, 1982), 378.

11. There were similarities between Houston and Dallas, where Annette Strauss in 1987 was described as her city's "first true coalition mayor of the modern age," with minority and liberal support. Her own opinion was that "a businessman had almost always done a wonderful job of leading this city, and I want to continue that." A product of affluent North Dallas and sister-in-law of Democratic party power-broker Robert Strauss, she might best be understood as a Dallas millionaire with a sense of social obligation. See Dan Hulbert, "Shaking Things Up in Dallas," *Washington Post*, May 4, 1987.

12. Suzanne Weiss, "Denver Nuggets," *Planning* 56 (April 1990): 8; and "Distinguished Leadership: Federico Pena," *Planning* 57 (March 1991): 16.

13. See chapter 6.

CHAPTER 6. MULTICENTERED CITIES

1. Cyra McFadden, *The Serial: A Year in the Life of Marin County* (New York: A. A. Knopf, 1977), 8.

2. Thomas Pynchon, *The Crying of Lot 49*, (Philadelphia: Lippincott, 1966) 24.

3. "Man, Time and Space in Southern California," special issue of the *Annals of the Association of American Geographers* 49 (Sept. 1959); Neil Morgan, *Westward Tilt: The American West Today* (New York: Random House, 1963), 136–37; Richard Austin Smith, "Los Angeles: Prototype of Supercity," *Fortune* 71 (March 1965): 99–100; Richard Elman, *Ill-At-Ease in Compton* (New York: Pantheon, 1967), 4.

4. Daniel Boorstin, *The Americans: The Democratic Experience* (New York: Random House, 1973), 269; "The Far West," *Better Homes and Gardens* 54 (Nov. 1976): 201; *New York Times*, Dec. 18, 1955, Feb. 2, 1957; Andrew Kopkind, "Modern Times in Phoenix," *New Republic* 153 (Nov. 6, 1964): 14–16; Larry King, "Bright Lights, Big Cities," *Atlantic* 235 (March 1975): 84.

5. Robert Riley, "Urban Myths and the New Cities of the Southwest," *Landscape* 17 (Autumn 1967): 23.

6. James Vance, *Geography and Urban Evolution in the San Francisco Bay Area* (Berkeley: Institute for Government Studies, University of California, 1964); Melvin Webber, "The Urban Place and the Nonplace Urban Realm," in Melvin Webber et al., *Explorations into Urban Structure* (Philadelphia: University of Pennsylvania Press, 1964), 79–153.

7. Sam Bass Warner, Jr., *The Urban Wilderness* (New York: Harper and Row, 1972), 134; Dolores Hayden, "The Meaning of Place in Art and Architecture," *Design Quarterly* 122 (Spring 1983): 20.

8. Reyner Banham, *Los Angeles: The Architecture of Four Ecologies* (New York: Harper and Row, 1971), 37.

9. John B. Jackson, "The Vernacular City," *Center: A Journal for Architecture in America* 1 (1985): 27.

10. John Gregory Dunne, "Eureka! A Celebration of California," in *Unknown California,* ed. Jonathan Eisen and David Fine (New York: Macmillan, 1985), 25.

11. *New York Times,* March 14, 1974; Brendan Gill, "Reflections: Los Angeles Architecture," *New Yorker,* Sept. 15, 1980, 109.

12. Alison Lurie, *The Nowhere City* (New York: Coward-McCann, 1965), 25.

13. Clifford E. Clark, Jr., *The American Family Home, 1800–1960* (Chapel Hill: University of North Carolina Press, 1986), 185.

14. Bungalows similar in style to the Denver version also spread to Midwestern cities like Chicago.

15. Elman, *Compton,* 34–35.

16. Lurie, *Nowhere City,* 4, 14.

17. Christopher Rand, *Los Angeles: The Ultimate City* (New York: Oxford University Press, 1967), 95.

18. Jean-Paul Sartre,"American Cities," in *Literary and Philosophical Essays* (London: Rider and Co., 1955), 116; Richard Burton, *The City of the Saints, and Across the Rocky Mountains to California,* ed. Fawn Brodie (New York: A. A. Knopf, 1963), 218; Duncan Aikman, "El Paso: Big Mountain Town," in West, *Rocky Mountain Cities,* 82.

19. Walter Van Tilburg Clark, *The City of Trembling Leaves* (New York: Random House, 1945), 3, 5, 7, 10.

20. Mike Davis, *City of Quartz: Excavating the Future in Los Angeles* (New York: Vintage, 1992), 204.

21. Southern cities as well as Western have frequently been able to unite central cities and suburban rings under single governments. Annexation has been relatively successful in the Deep South; several supersuburbs are found in Florida and Virginia; and city-county consolidation has been most popular in the South. In many of these cases, one motivation for bringing metropolitan residents under a single municipal government has been to dilute black city votes with white suburban votes, a thought that certainly occurred as well to Texans and Oklahomans.

22. G. Wesley Johnson, "Generations of Elites and Social Change in Phoenix," in *Community Development in the American West,* ed. Jessie Embry and Howard Christy (Provo, Utah: Charles Redd Center for Western Studies, Brigham Young University, 1985), 99.

23. Luckingham, *Phoenix,* 267.

24. Tom McCall and Steve Neal, *Tom McCall: Maverick* (Portland: Binford and Mort, 1977), 196.

CHAPTER 7. CITIES AND COUNTRY

1. *The Oregonian,* July 6, 1985.

2. Among the top twelve cities identified in chapter 3, this list omits Phoenix, Sacramento, Salt Lake City, San Antonio, and San Diego. In each of these cases, regional commercial and service functions are carried on within the sphere of one of

the comprehensive metropolitan centers. At the same time, the list of metropolitan centers includes Kansas City and Minneapolis–St. Paul, both of which are "eastern" by my working definition of the West. However, the hinterlands of both cities follow railroad lines and interstate highways deep into the states of the Great Plains.

3. Carey McWilliams, Introduction to West, *Rocky Mountain Cities*, 9.

4. Larry McMurtry, *Some Can Whistle* (New York: Simon and Schuster, 1989), 213.

5. Clyde Browning and Wil Gesler, "The Sun Belt–Snow Belt: A Case of Sloppy Regionalizing," *Professional Geographer* 31 (Feb. 1979): 73.

6. Chilton Williamson, Jr., *Roughnecking It; Or, Life in the Overthrust* (New York: Simon and Schuster, 1982), 13.

7. Harold Walton, quoted in William G. Robbins, *Hard Times in Paradise: Coos Bay, Oregon, 1850–1986* (Seattle: University of Washington Press, 1988), 162.

8. Quoted in Mark Clayton, "Economic Alchemy That Transformed a Town," *Christian Science Monitor,* Nov. 14, 1988.

9. Richard Bartlett, review of Nash and Etulain, eds., *The Twentieth-Century West,* in *Western Historical Quarterly* 21 (August 1990): 351–52.

10. John R. Milton, *The Novel of the American West* (Lincoln: University of Nebraska Press, 1980), 62; Richard Etulain, ed., *Conversations with Wallace Stegner,* rev. ed. (Salt Lake City: University of Utah Press, 1990), 148–49.

11. Harry W. Fritz, "The Origins of Twenty-First Century Montana," *Montana* 42 (Winter 1992): 78.

12. Thomas McGuane, *Something To Be Desired* (New York: Vintage Books, 1985), 51.

CHAPTER 8. CITIES AND NATION

1. Urbanism Committee of the National Resources Committee, *Our Cities: Their Role in the National Economy* (Washington, D.C.: Government Printing Office, 1937), vii.

2. Thomas Pynchon, *Vineland* (Boston: Little, Brown, 1990), 266–67.

3. Walt Disney, quoted in John Findlay, *Magic Lands: Western Cityscapes and American Culture after 1940* (Berkeley: University of California Press, 1992), 67.

4. Frederick Jackson Turner, "Contributions of the West to American Democracy," in *Frontier and Section: Selected Essays of Frederick Jackson Turner,* ed. Ray A. Billington (Englewood Cliffs, N.J.: Prentice-Hall, 1961), 80.

5. Turner, "Contributions of the West," 89.

6. Sarah Pileggi, "Seattle: City Life at its Best," *Sports Illustrated,* July 19, 1982, p. 58.

7. "Town Planning: Where It Works," *The Economist* 316 (Sept. 1, 1990): 24–25.

8. In a slightly different ranking of "fiscally sound" cities in 1991, *City and State Magazine* similarly included Phoenix, San Diego, Portland, and Dallas in the top ten nationally, along with Tucson, Denver, Houston, and Long Beach.

9. Henry George, "What the Railroad Will Bring Us," *Overland Monthly* 1 (Oct. 1868).

10. Frederick Jackson Turner, "The West and American Ideals," in Turner, *Frontier and Section*, 105.

11. Frederick Jackson Turner, "Social Forces in American History," *American Historical Review* 16 (Jan. 1911): 217; William Cronon, "Revisiting the Vanishing Frontier: The Legacy of Frederick Jackson Turner," *Western Historical Quarterly* 18 (April 1987): 171.

12. William Goetzmann, "The Mountain Man as Jacksonian Man," *American Quarterly* 15 (Fall 1963): 402–15; Michael Allen, *Western Rivermen, 1763–1861* (Baton Rouge: Louisiana State University Press, 1990).

13. McMurtry, *In a Narrow Grave*, 119.

14. Martin V. Melosi, "Dallas–Fort Worth: Marketing the Metroplex," in *Sunbelt Cities: Politics and Growth Since World War II*, ed. Richard Bernard and Bradley Rice (Austin: University of Texas Press, 1983), 173; Kenneth Labich, "The Best Cities for Business," *Fortune*, Oct. 23, 1989, p. 79.

15. Lynn Ashby, "The Supercities: Houston," *Saturday Review*, new ser., Sept. 4, 1976, 16–19; Ada Louise Huxtable, "Deep in the heart of Nowhere," *New York Times*, Feb. 15, 1976; Jan Morris, *Among the Cities* (New York: Oxford University Press, 1985), 169.

16. Willie Morris, "Houston's Superpatriots," *Harper's Magazine*, Oct. 1961, p. 48; McMurtry, *Some Can Whistle*, 73.

17. *A Vision for the Future: Highlights of the Neal Pierce Study Commissioned by* The Arizona Republic *and* The Phoenix Gazette (Phoenix: Phoenix Newspapers, Inc., 1988), 3; Peter Wiley and Robert Gottlieb, *Empires in the Sun* (Tucson: University of Arizona Press, 1985), 189–90.

18. Frederick Jackson Turner, "The Significance of the Frontier in American History," in *Frontier and Section*, 56, 61.

19. Sam B. Warner, Jr., *The Urban Wilderness* (New York: Harper and Row, 1972), 136; John Anson Ford, *Thirty Explosive Years in Los Angeles County* (San Marino, Calif.: Huntington Library, 1961), 58.

20. John M. Findlay, "Suckers and Escapists: Interpreting Las Vegas and Post-War America," *Nevada Historical Society Quarterly* 33 (Spring 1990): 1–15; Tom Wolfe, *The Kandy-Kolored Tangerine-Flake Streamline Baby* (New York: Farrar, Straus and Giroux, 1966), xvi.

21. Gary Snyder is quoted in Dennis McNally, "Prophets on the Burning Shore: Jack Kerouac, Gary Snyder, and San Francisco," in *A Literary History of the American West*, ed. J. Golden Taylor (Fort Worth: Texas Christian University Press, 1987), 483; Lacey Fosburgh, "San Francisco: Unconventional City for the Democratic Convention," *New York Times Magazine*, July 1, 1984.

22. Venice, California, on the coast of Los Angeles, was another center for the counterculture of the 1950s, nourishing local representatives of the Beat Generation.

23. William Rorabaugh, *Berkeley at War: The 1960s* (New York: Oxford University Press, 1989), 90.

24. Brian J. Godfrey, *Neighborhoods in Transition: the Making of San Francisco's Ethnic and Nonconformist Communities* (Berkeley: University of California Press, 1988), 121–22.

BIBLIOGRAPHICAL ESSAY

This extended essay on the recent history of Western cities would not have been possible when I first began to explore the history of Denver in 1971. It would have been extremely difficult even a decade ago, for it draws on what seems to be an exponentially growing body of scholarship on the development of cities in the twentieth-century West. The *Western Historical Quarterly* and the *Pacific Historical Review* published three articles on twentieth-century Western cities from 1971 to 1975, seven from 1976 to 1980, seven from 1981 to 1985, and fourteen from 1986 to 1991. Six of the seven articles with a focus on the years since 1940 appeared after 1985.

No one can be equally familiar with the stories of several dozen cities. My own primary research has centered on Portland, Seattle, Denver, San Antonio, and Grand Junction. To supplement this somewhat arbitrary sample, I have drawn on five types of scholarly and analytical literature in developing and illustrating my sense of the broad patterns in recent Western urban development.

For the first two decades after World War II, Ray B. West's edited volume *Rocky Mountain Cities* (1949) stood alone as a source of information on the recent history of middle-sized Western cities. In the mid-1960s, Earl Pomeroy added a chapter on postwar urbanization in *The Pacific Slope* (New York: Alfred A. Knopf, 1965), 302–15; W. Eugene Hollon wrote "Desert Cities on the March," for *The Great American Desert* (New York: Oxford University Press, 1966), 217–37; and Leonard Goodall edited original essays on politics in eleven "Southwestern" cities from Wichita to Phoenix in *Urban Politics in the Southwest* (Tempe: Arizona State University Institute of Public Administration, 1967).

Although these earlier efforts remain valuable sources of information and ideas, my most important debt is to a small group of historians who have undertaken comprehensive and comparative analyses of aspects of Western urbanization in the last two decades. In 1973, Gerald Nash introduced the idea that the West was a set of urban oases in *The American West in the Twentieth Century* and explored the impact of World War II in *The American West Transformed: The Impact of the Second World War* (Bloomington: Indiana University Press, 1985), and *World War II and the West: Reshaping the Economy* (Lincoln: University of Nebraska Press, 1990). Roger Lotchin has examined the relationship between urban growth and the military in a series of articles since 1979, culminating in *Fortress California: From Warfare to Welfare* (New York: Oxford University Press, 1992). John Findlay has looked to Western cities for expressions of twentieth-century American culture in *Magic Lands: Western Cityscapes and American Culture After 1940* (Berkeley: University of California Press, 1992). My discussions of specialized landscapes such as Disneyland, Las Vegas, and Sun City draw on his interpretations.

A growing number of historians have studied and profiled individual cities in comprehensive urban biographies or narrative analyses of political development and socioeconomic change. These studies are the necessary references for any effort to draw patterns from the experiences of dozens of Western cities and tens of millions of Western city dwellers. Including both published and unpublished studies, the list includes Robert Fairbanks and Patricia Hill on Dallas; Howard Rabinowitz and Marc Simmons on Albuquerque; Bradford Luckingham on Phoenix; Spencer Olin on Orange County; W. H. Timmons on El Paso; James Allen and Thomas Alexander on Salt Lake City; William Rorabaugh on Berkeley; Lyle Dorsett, Thomas Noel, and Stephen Leonard on Denver; Roger Sale and Norbert McDonald on Seattle; E. K. MacColl on Portland; David McComb on Houston and Galveston; Eugene Moehring and Perry Kaufman on Las Vegas; Anthony Orum on Austin; A. Theodore Brown on Omaha; and Robert Cherny and William Issel on San Francisco.

An even larger number of historians have focused on specific issues—country-to-city migration; the definition and use of public space; the role of neighborhoods; city planning; public housing; and women as workers and leaders. Relevant books and articles are cited below for each chapter.

In addition, I have made selective use of the writings of social scientists. In many cases, geographers, economists, political scientists, and sociologists are often most interested in using a Western case like San Francisco or Houston to test or illustrate national trends and theories. In contrast, I have been interested in understanding the particularities of the Western urban experience. Nevertheless, social science studies of everything from neighborhood formation to political power are invaluable sources of information on topics as diverse as postwar suburbanization and late-twentieth-century globalization. Greater Los Angeles, for example, has been especially attractive to students of physical form, economic geography, urban design, and planning. The San Francisco Bay area, in contrast, has generated detailed analyses of the process and politics of decisions about transportation, housing, redevelopment, and similar public responsibilities. Smaller cities have also attracted specialized clusters of studies dealing with issues like the power structure and group interests in San Antonio and ethnic patterns and relationships in Denver.

Finally, I have learned a great deal from essayists, journalists, critics, and novelists, whose writings have tended to reflect the concerns of the decades in which they have written. Carey McWilliams in the 1940s and Francine Gray in the 1960s wrote about human adjustment and social relations. In contrast, Neil Morgan in the 1950s and Robert Gottlieb and Peter Wiley in the 1970s focused their attention on economic growth and its political context. At the start of the 1990s, Mike Davis described continuing inequalities in economic and political power.

Along with social scientists, many journalists and writers have been attracted to the cities of California. They are the locations of the largest universities, the biggest newspaper and broadcast markets, and the greatest number of national tastemakers. Although I may not always have succeeded, I have tried to fend off this westward tilt in my own reading and analysis. My coverage of Billings, El Paso, and Denver may not exactly balance that of San Francisco and Los Angeles in this book, but I have tried to include their stories in the process of analysis and the mix of examples.

CHAPTER 1 WAR AND THE WESTWARD TILT, 1940–1950

San Francisco's Golden Gate International Exposition is briefly discussed in Richard Reinhardt, "The Other Fair," *American Heritage* 40 (May/June 1989): 42–53; and in the essay by Donald G. Larson in *Historical Dictionary of World's Fairs and Expositions, 1851–1988*, ed. John E. Findling (Westport, Conn.: Greenwood Press, 1990), 301–303.

The historical analysis of the impact of World War II on the American West was pioneered by Earl Pomeroy in his essay "The New Fast-Growing West of Mid-Century" in *The Pacific Slope* (New York: A. A. Knopf, 1965). The fullest discussions are found in Gerald D. Nash, *The American West Transformed: The Impact of the Second World War* (Bloomington: Indiana University Press, 1985), and in his *World War II and The West: Reshaping the Economy* (Lincoln: University of Nebraska Press, 1990). Arthur C. Verge examined a variety of wartime developments in one city in "The Impact of the Second World War on Los Angeles, 1939–1945" (Ph.D. diss., University of Southern California, 1988).

The expansion of the West Coast shipbuilding industry is treated in Frederick C. Lane, *Ships for Victory: A History of Shipbuilding Under the U.S. Maritime Commission in World War II* (Baltimore: Johns Hopkins University Press, 1951); Mark Foster, *Henry J. Kaiser: Builder in the Modern American West* (Austin: University of Texas Press, 1989); and Roger W. Lotchin, *Fortress California, 1911–1960: From Warfare to Welfare* (New York: Oxford University Press, 1992). Case studies of the expansion of military facilities include Gilbert Guinn, "A Different Frontier: Aviation, the Army Air Forces, and the Evolution of the Sunshine Belt," *Aerospace Historian* 29 (March 1982): 34–45; Thomas Alexander, "Ogden: A Federal Colony in Utah," *Utah Historical Quar-*

terly 47 (Summer 1979): 291–309; Leonard J. Arrington and Anthony Cuff, *Federally Financed Industrial Plants Constructed in Utah During World War II* (Logan: Utah State University Press, 1969); James Eastman, "Location and Growth of Tinker Air Force Base and Oklahoma City Air Material Area," *Chronicles of Oklahoma* 50 (Autumn 1972): 326–46.

The development of the atomic cities is detailed in Vincent C. Jones, *Manhattan: The Army and the Bomb* (Washington, D.C.: U.S. Army Center for Military History, 1985); James W. Kunetka, *City of Fire: Los Alamos and the Birth of the Atomic Age* (Englewood Cliffs, N.J.: Prentice-Hall, 1978); and Marjorie Chambers, "Technically Sweet Los Alamos: The Development of a Federally Sponsored Scientific Community" (Ph.D. diss., University of New Mexico, 1974).

Early efforts to describe the migrations include the President's Committee for Congested Production Areas, *Final Report* (Washington, D.C., Dec. 1944); Henry Shryock, "Wartime Shifts of the Civilian Population," *Milbank Memorial Fund Quarterly* 25 (July 1947): 269–83; Philip M. Hauser, "Wartime Population Changes and Post-War Prospects," *Journal of Marketing* 8 (Jan. 1944): 238–48. Journalistic accounts of reporters who visited Western cities include Selden Menefee, *Assignment: U.S.A.* (New York: Reynal and Hitchcock, 1943); Agnes Meyer, *Journey Through Chaos* (New York: Harcourt, Brace and Co., 1944); and a series of articles by A. G. Mezerik published as "Journey in America" in *The New Republic* in 1944.

The problems of housing and social adjustment in wartime boom communities are the focus of Marilynn Johnson, *Conscripted Cities: World War II and San Francisco's East Bay* (Berkeley: University of California Press, forthcoming); Charles Wollenberg, *Marinship at War: Shipbuilding and Social Change in Wartime Sausalito* (Oakland, Calif.: Western Heritage Press, 1990); and Carl Abbott, "Portland in the Pacific War: Planning from 1940 to 1945," *Urbanism Past and Present* 11 (Winter/Spring 1980–81): 12–24. Different interpretations of the war housing experiment at Vanport, Oregon, are found in Dolores Hayden, *Redesigning the American Dream: The Future of Housing, Work, and Family Life* (New York: W. W. Norton, 1984); and Manly Maben, *Vanport* (Portland: Oregon Historical Society Press, 1987). Related issues of wartime planning are discussed in Philip Funigiello, *The Challenge to Urban Liberalism: Federal-City Relations During World War II* (Knoxville: University of Tennessee Press, 1978); Martin Schiesl, "City Planning and the Federal Government in World War II: The Los Angeles Experience," *California History* 58 (April 1979): 127–43; and Carl Abbott, "Planning for the Home Front in Seattle and Portland, 1940–45," in *The Martial Metropolis,* ed. Roger W. Lotchin (New York: Praeger, 1984), 163–89.

Opportunities and problems of women as war workers are detailed in Amy Kesselman, *Fleeting Opportunities: Women Shipyard Workers in Portland and Vancouver During World War II and Reconversion* (Albany, N.Y.: SUNY Press, 1990); Sherna Berger Gluck, *Rosie the Riveter Revisited: Women, the War, and Social Change* (Boston: Twayne, 1987); and Karen Anderson, *Wartime Women: Sex Roles, Family Relations, and the Status of Women During World War II* (Westport, Conn.: Greenwood Press, 1981).

Aspects of black migration are treated in Ira De A. Reid, "Special Problems of Negro Migration During the War," *Milbank Memorial Fund Quarterly* 25 (July 1947): 284–92. Specific studies of African-American experiences are Howard Droker, "Seattle Race Relations During the Second World War," *Pacific Northwest Quarterly* 67 (Oct. 1967): 163–74; Charles S. Johnson, *The Negro Worker in San Francisco* (San Francisco, 1944); and Alonzo N. Smith, "Blacks and the Los Angeles Municipal Transit System, 1941–45," *Urbanism Past and Present* 11 (Winter/Spring 1980–81): 25–31. Novelist Chester Himes drew on his own experiences in wartime Los Angeles to write *If He Hollers Let Him Go* (1945) and *Lonely Crusade* (1947).

Other studies that examine the wartime experiences of ethnic minorities are Carey McWilliams, *North from Mexico* (New York: J. B. Lippincott, 1948); John Modell, *The Economics and Politics of Racial Accommodation: The Japanese of Los Angeles, 1900–1942* (Urbana: University of Illinois Press, 1977); Barron Beshoar, "Report from the Mountain States," *Common Ground* 4 (Spring 1943): 23–30. Particularly interesting is Beth Bailey and David Farber, *The First Strange Place: The Alchemy of Race and Sex in World War II Hawaii* (New York: Free Press, 1992).

The extensive literature on long cycles in economic growth is conveniently summarized in Peter Hall and Paschal Preston, *The Carrier Wave* (London: Unwin Hyman, 1988).

CHAPTER 2 THE POLITICS OF GROWTH

A good starting place for the political history of postwar cities is a group of volumes that include chapters on individual cities. Among the most useful are Harold A. Stone, Don K. Price, and Kathryn H. Stone, *City Manager Government in Nine Cities* (Chicago: Public Administration Service, 1940); Ray B. West, ed., *Rocky Mountain Cities* (New York: W. W. Norton, 1949); Edward Banfield, *Big City Politics* (New York: Random House, 1965); Lorin Peterson, *The Day of the Mugwump* (New York: Random House, 1961); Leonard Goodall, ed., *Urban Politics in the Southwest* (Tempe: Arizona State University Institute of Public Administration, 1967); Richard Bernard and Bradley Rice, eds., *Sunbelt Cities: Politics and Growth Since World War II* (Austin: University of Texas Press, 1983); and Susan Fainstein et al., *Restructuring the City* (New York: Longman, 1984).

Efforts to provide general interpretations of urban politics include Daniel Elazar, *Cities of the Prairie* (New York: Basic Books, 1970); Carl Abbott, *The New Urban America: Growth and Politics in Sunbelt Cities* (Chapel Hill: University of North Carolina Press, 1987); Amy Bridges, "Boss Tweed and V. O. Key in Texas," in *Urban Texas: Politics and Development*, ed. Char Miller and Heywood Saunders (College Station: Texas A&M University Press, 1990), 58–71; and "Politics and Growth in Sunbelt Cities," in *Searching for the Sunbelt*, ed. Raymond Mohl (Knoxville: University of Tennessee Press, 1990), 85–104.

The ways in which rapid metropolitan growth and physical planning needs challenged local political structures are examined in Mel Scott, *The San Francisco Bay*

Area: A Metropolis in Perspective (Berkeley: University of California Press, 1959); Gerald Nash, "Planning for the Postwar City: The Urban West in World War II," *Arizona and the West* 27 (July 1985): 99–112; Howard Rabinowitz, "Growth Trends in the Albuquerque SMSA, 1940–1978," *Journal of the West* 18 (July 1979): 62–74; and Sy Adler, "Why BART But No LART," *Planning Perspectives* 2 (May 1987): 149–74.

Studies with a particular focus on the conservative turn of the 1950s include Don Parson, "The Development of Redevelopment: Public Housing and Urban Renewal in Los Angeles," *International Journal of Urban and Regional Research* 6 (Sept. 1982): 393–413 and "Los Angeles' 'Headline-Happy Public Housing War'" *Southern California Quarterly* 65 (Fall 1983): 251–85; Thomas S. Hines, "Housing, Baseball, and Creeping Socialism: The Battle of Chavez Ravine, Los Angeles, 1949–1959," *Journal of Urban History* 8 (Feb. 1982): 123–43; Don Carleton, "A Crisis of Rapid Change: The Red Scare in Houston, 1949–1955," in *Houston: A Twentieth Century Urban Frontier,* ed. Francisco Rosales and Barry J. Kaplan (Port Washington, N.Y.: Associated Faculty Press, 1983), 139–59; and Willie Morris, "Houston's Superpatriots," *Harper's Magazine,* Oct. 1961, pp. 48–56.

The entrepreneurial impulse is central to much of Anthony Orum's discussion of Austin in *Power, Money and the People* (Austin: Texas Monthly Press, 1987); to Larry Schweikart, "Financing the Urban Frontier: Entrepreneurial Creativity and Western Cities, 1945–1975," *Urban Studies* 26 (February 1989): 177–86; to Lynne Pierson Doti and Larry Schweikart, "Financing the Postwar Housing Boom in Phoenix and Los Angeles, 1945–1960," *Pacific Historical Review* 58 (May 1989): 173–94; and to Robert Gottlieb and Irene Wolt, *Thinking Big: The Story of the* Los Angeles Times (New York: G. P. Putnam's Sons 1977).

Broadly useful on political change are David R. Johnson, John A. Booth, and Richard J. Harris, eds., *The Politics of San Antonio: Community, Progress, and Power* (Lincoln: University of Nebraska Press, 1983); Philip J. Trounstine and Terry Christensen, *Movers and Shakers: The Study of Community Power* (New York: St. Martin's Press, 1982); and Thomas G. Alexander and James B. Allen, *Mormons and Gentiles: A History of Salt Lake City* (Boulder, Colo.: Pruett Publishing Co., 1984).

CHAPTER 3 FROM REGIONAL CITIES TO NATIONAL CITIES, 1950–1990

My comparison of Seattle and Portland in this chapter is based on Carl Abbott, "Regional City and Network City: Portland and Seattle in the Twentieth Century," *Western Historical Quarterly* 23 (Aug. 1992): 293–322; and John M. Findlay, "The Off-center Seattle Center: Downtown Seattle and the 1962 World's Fair," *Pacific Northwest Quarterly* 80 (Jan. 1989): 2–11.

The economic role of military spending is examined at the regional and state level in Roger E. Bolton, *Defense Purchases and Regional Growth* (Washington, D.C.: Brookings Institution, 1966); Maureen McBreen, "Regional Trends in Federal Defense Expenditures, 1950–1976," in Congressional Research Service, *Selected Essays on*

Patterns of Regional Change (Washington, D.C.: Senate Appropriations Committee Print, 1977); Keith McLaughlin, *The Flow of Federal Funds, 1981–1988* (Washington, D.C.: Northeast-Midwest Institute, 1990); and James L. Clayton, "Defense Spending: Key to California's Growth," *Western Political Quarterly* 15 (June 1962): 280–83, and "The Impact of the Cold War on the Economies of California and Utah, 1946–1965," *Pacific Historical Review* 36 (Nov. 1967): 449–73.

The expansion of the metropolitan-military complex is the central topic of Roger W. Lotchin's magisterial study *Fortress California, 1911–1960: From Warfare to Welfare* (New York: Oxford University Press, 1992) and of Ann Markusen, Peter Hall, Scott Campbell, and Sabina Deitrick, *The Rise of the Gunbelt: The Military Remapping of Industrial America* (New York: Oxford University Press, 1991).

The aerospace industry is examined in William Glenn Cunningham, *The Aircraft Industry: A Study in Industrial Location* (Los Angeles: Lorrin L. Morrison, 1950); David L. Clark, "Improbable Los Angeles," in *Sunbelt Cities: Politics and Growth Since World War II*, ed. Richard Bernard and Bradley Rice (Austin: University of Texas Press, 1983), 268–308; Martin Schiesl, "Airplanes to Aerospace: Defense Spending and Economic Growth in the Los Angeles Region, 1945–1960," in *The Martial Metropolis*, ed. Roger W. Lotchin (New York: Praeger, 1984): 135–49; and Stephen Oates, "NASA's Manned Spacecraft Center at Houston, Texas," *Southwestern Historical Quarterly* 67 (Jan. 1964): 350–75. The story is brought through the 1980s in Rosy Nimroody, *Star Wars: The Economic Fallout* (Cambridge, Mass.: Ballinger, 1988).

The definition of high-tech industries is taken from Richard W. Riche, Daniel E. Hecker, and John U. Burgan, "High Technology Today and Tomorrow," *Monthly Labor Review* 106 (Nov. 1983): 50–59. John Findlay treats the development of the Stanford Industrial Park in *Magic Lands* (Berkeley: University of California Press, 1992). The rise of the electronics industry is discussed in Everett M. Rogers and Judith K. Larsen, *Silicon Valley Fever: Growth of High-Technology Culture* (New York: Basic Books, 1984); Peter Hall and Ann Markusen, eds., *Silicon Landscapes* (Boston: Allen and Unwin, 1985); Manuel Castells, ed., *High Technology, Space, and Society* (Beverly Hills, Calif.: Sage Publications, 1985); Ann Markusen, Peter Hall, and Amy Glasmeier, *High Tech America: The What, How, Where and Why of the Sunrise Industries* (Boston: Allen and Unwin, 1986); and Allen J. Scott, *Metropolis: From the Division of Labor to Urban Form* (Berkeley: University of California Press, 1988).

The maturing of the atomic weapons industry is discussed in A. Costandina Titus, *Bombs in the Backyard: Atomic Testing and American Politics* (Reno: University of Nevada Press, 1986); Tad Bartemus and Scott McCartney, *Trinity's Children: Living Along America's Nuclear Highway* (New York: Harcourt Brace Jovanovich, 1991); Necah C. Furman, *Sandia National Laboratories: The Postwar Decade* (Albuquerque: University of New Mexico Press, 1991); Hal Rothman, *On Rims and Ridges: The Los Alamos Area Since 1880* (Lincoln: University of Nebraska Press, 1992); Paul Loeb, *Nuclear Culture: Living and Working in the World's Largest Atomic Complex* (New York: Coward, McCann and Geoghegan, 1982); and Michele S. Gerber, *On the Home Front: The Cold War Legacy of the Hanford Site* (Lincoln: University of Nebraska Press, 1992).

The changing political response to atomic energy in Western cities is examined in Roger Lotchin, *Fortress California,* and Daniel Pope, "'We Can Wait. We Should Wait': Eugene's Nuclear Power Controversy, 1968–1970," *Pacific Historical Review* 59 (Aug. 1990): 349–74.

University research as part of the military-technological economy is treated in Clayton Koppes, *JPL and the American Space Program: A History of the Jet Propulsion Laboratory* (New Haven: Yale University Press, 1982), and in several articles by Edward Malecki, including "Federal R and D Spending in the United States of America: Some Impacts on Metropolitan Economies," *Regional Studies* 16 (Feb. 1982): 19–35; and "High Technology and Local Economic Development," *Journal of the American Planning Association* 50 (Summer 1984): 262–69.

The urban implications of the leisure economy are far less thoroughly explored. Bryan H. Farrell, *Hawaii: The Legend That Sells* (Honolulu: University Press of Hawaii, 1982), places tourism in the context of a general economic analysis. Las Vegas as a leisure city is the subject of Eugene Moehring, *Resort City in the Sunbelt: Las Vegas, 1930–1970* (Reno: University of Nevada Press, 1989), and John M. Findlay, "Suckers and Escapists? Interpreting Las Vegas and Post-War America," *Nevada Historical Society Quarterly* 33 (Spring 1990): 1–15.

Retirement is systematically analyzed in C. Taylor Barnes and Curtis C. Roseman, "The Effect of Military Retirement on Population Redistribution," *Texas Business Review* 55 (May/June 1981): 100–108; Jeanne Biggar, "The Sunning of America: Migration to the Sunbelt," *Population Bulletin* 34 (1979): 3–39; Michael B. Barker, *California Retirement Communities* (Berkeley: Center for Real Estate and Urban Economics, University of California, 1966); and Charles F. Longino, Jr., and William H. Crown, "The Migration of Old Money," *American Demographics* 11 (Oct. 1989): 28–31.

The position of Western cities within the national urban system is described by Otis D. Duncan et al., *Metropolis and Region* (Baltimore: Johns Hopkins University Press, 1960), and John Borchert, "America's Changing Metropolitan Regions," *Annals of the Association of American Geographers* 62 (June 1972): 352–73. Patterns of corporate headquarters location are detailed in John D. Stephens and Brian P. Holly, "City System Behavior and Corporate Influence: The Headquarters Location of U.S. Industrial Firms, 1955–1975," *Urban Studies* 18 (October 1981): 285–300; R. Keith Semple, "Recent Trends in the Spatial Concentration of Corporate Headquarters," *Economic Geography* 49 (Oct. 1973): 309–318; and James O. Wheeler, "The Corporate Role of Large Metropolitan Areas in the United States," *Growth and Change* 19 (Spring 1988): 75–86.

Manuel Castells, *The Informational City: Information Technology, Economic Restructuring, and the Urban-Regional Process* (Oxford: Basil Blackwell, 1989), explores the urban implications of the information economy. An effort to measure the importance of cities as information centers is James O. Wheeler and Ronald L. Mitchelson, "Information Flows Among Major Metropolitan Areas in the United States," *Annals* of the Association of American Geographers 79 (Dec. 1989): 523–43. Data on tall buildings are found in James E. Vance, Jr., *The Continuing City* (Baltimore: Johns Hopkins Press, 1990).

CHAPTER 4 GATEWAYS TO THE WORLD

Starting points for exploring the globalization of Western cities are the focused studies of Houston and Los Angeles, including Joe R. Feagin, *Free Enterprise City: Houston in Political and Economic Perspective* (New Brunswick, N.J.: Rutgers University Press, 1989); Edward Soja, Rebecca Morales, and Goetz Wolff, "Urban Restructuring: An Analysis of Social and Spatial Change in Los Angeles," *Economic Geography* 59 (April 1983): 195–230; Ivan Light, "Los Angeles," in *The Metropolis Era*, vol. 2: *Mega-Cities*, ed. Mattei Dogan and John D. Kasarda (Newbury Park, Calif.: Sage Publications, 1988), 56–96; and Carl Abbott, "International Cities in the Dual System Model: The Transformations of Los Angeles and Washington," *Urban History Yearbook, 1991* (Leicester: Leicester University Press, 1991), 41–59.

A measured evaluation of urban futures in the global era can be found in John R. Logan and Harvey L. Molotch, *Urban Fortunes: The Political Economy of Place* (Berkeley: University of California Press, 1987). In contrast, Joel Kotkin, *The Third Century: America's Resurgence in the Asian Era* (New York: Crown, 1988), is unfailingly upbeat.

The "new immigration" of the 1970s and 1980s is discussed in Alejandro Portes and Ruben G. Rumbaut, *Immigrant America: A Portrait* (Berkeley: University of California Press, 1990); Thomas Muller and Thomas Espenshade, *The Fourth Wave: California's Newest Immigrants* (Washington, D.C.: Urban Institute, 1984); Elliott Barkan, "New Origins, New Homeland, New Region: American Immigration and the Emergence of the Sunbelt, 1955–1985," in *Searching for the Sunbelt*, ed. Raymond Mohl (Knoxville: University of Tennessee Press, 1990), 124–38; James T. Fawcett and Benjamin V. Carino, eds., *Pacific Bridges: The New Immigration from Asia and the Pacific Islands* (New York: Center for Migration Studies, 1987); Robert W. Gardner, Bryant Robey, and Peter C. Smith, "Asian Americans: Growth, Change, and Diversity," *Population Bulletin* 40 (Oct. 1985): 1–51; Nestor P. Rodriguez, "Undocumented Central Americans in Houston: Diverse Populations," *International Migration Review* 21 (Spring 1987): 4–26; James P. Allen, "Recent Immigration from the Philippines and Filipino Communities in the United States," *Geographical Review* 67 (April 1977): 195–208.

The experience of immigrants in West Coast cities is treated in Ivan Light, *Ethnic Enterprise in America: Business and Welfare Among Chinese, Japanese, and Blacks* (Berkeley: University of California Press, 1972); Edna Bonacich and John Modell, *The Economic Basis of Ethnic Solidarity: Small Business in the Japanese-American Community* (Berkeley: University of California Press, 1980); Edna Bonacich, Ivan Light, and Charles Wong, "Koreans in Small Business," *Society* 14 (Sept./Oct. 1977): 54–59;

Donald Teruo Hata, Jr., and Nadine Ishitani Hata, "Asian-Pacific Angelinos: Model Minorities and Indispensable Scapegoats," in *20th Century Los Angeles: Power, Promotion, and Social Conflict*, ed. Norman M. Klein and Martin J. Schiesl (Claremont, Calif.: Regina Books, 1990), 61–100. A good popular survey is Kurt Anderson, "The New Ellis Island," *Time*, June 13, 1983, pp. 18–25.

A starting point for understanding the American-Mexican border region remains Leo Grebler, Joan W. Moore, and Ralph C. Guzman, *The Mexican-American People: The Nation's Second Largest Minority* (New York: Free Press, 1970). The character of the border cities and their economies is discussed in Lawrence A. Herzog, *Where North Meets South: Cities, Space, and Politics on the United States–Mexico Border* (Austin: University of Texas Press, 1990); W. H. Timmons, *El Paso: A Borderlands History* (El Paso: Texas Western Press, 1990); D. W. Meinig, *Southwest: Three Peoples in Geographical Change, 1600–1970* (New York: Oxford University Press, 1971); and Niles Hansen, *The Border Economy: Regional Development in the Southwest* (Austin: University of Texas Press, 1981). A recent summary of the development of maquila industries is Robert B. South, "Transnational 'Maquiladora' Location," *Annals of the Association of American Geographers* 80 (Dec. 1990): 549–70. The idea of a larger Mexican/American cultural region anchored by its metropolitan areas is explored in Raymond Gastil, *Cultural Regions of the United States* (Seattle: University of Washington Press, 1975), and Joel Garreau, *The Nine Nations of North America* (Boston: Houghton Mifflin, 1981).

Differences and similarities among United States and Canadian cities are examined in Norbert McDonald, *Distant Neighbors: A Comparative History of Seattle and Vancouver* (Lincoln: University of Nebraska Press, 1987); Leonard Eaton, *Gateway Cities and Other Essays* (Ames: Iowa State University Press, 1990); and Michael A. Goldberg and John Mercer, *The Myth of the North American City* (Vancouver: University of British Columbia Press, 1986).

The roles of San Francisco, Los Angeles, Houston, and Dallas as international banking and information centers are documented in Ingo Walter, *Global Competition in Financial Services* (Cambridge, Mass.: Ballinger, 1988); Howard Curtis Reed, *The Preeminence of International Financial Centers* (New York: Praeger, 1981); and R. B. Cohen, "The New International Division of Labor, Multinational Corporations, and Urban Hierarchy," in *Urbanization and Urban Planning in Capitalist Society*, ed Michael Dear and Allan J. Scott (New York: Methuen, 1981), 287–315. An effort to develop a comprehensive index of international connectivity is Carl Abbott, "Through Flight to Tokyo: Sunbelt Cities in the New World Economy," in *Urban Policy in Twentieth Century America*, ed. Raymond Mohl and Arnold Hirsch (New Brunswick, N.J.: Rutgers University Press, 1993), 183–212.

CHAPTER 5 THE POLITICS OF DIVERSITY

In addition to the general interpretations of recent political change by Bridges, Abbott, and Bernard cited for chapter 2, also see Norman Fainstein and Susan

Fainstein, "Regime Strategies, Communal Resistance, and Economic Forces," in Susan Fainstein et al., *Restructuring the City* (New York: Longman, 1983), 245–82; H. V. Savitch and John Clayton Thomas, "End of the Millennium in Big City Politics," in *Big City Politics in Transition*, ed. Savitch and Thomas (Newbury Park, Calif.: Sage Publications, 1991), 235–51; and Ronald H. Bayor, "Models of Ethnic and Racial Politics in the Urban Sunbelt South," in *Searching for the Sunbelt*, ed. Raymond Mohl (Knoxville: University of Tennessee Press, 1990), 105–23. The idea of quality-of-life liberalism as echoed in the concept of "postmaterialist" politics is discussed in Ronald Inglehart, *Culture Shift in Advanced Industrial Society* (Princeton, N.J.: Princeton University Press, 1990).

The impact of the Voting Rights Act and shifts in representation structures are evaluated in Chandler Davidson, ed., *Minority Vote Dilution* (Washington, D.C.: Howard University Press, 1984); Rufus P. Browning, Dale Rogers Marshall, and David H. Tabb, *Protest Is Not Enough: The Struggle of Blacks and Hispanics for Equality in Urban Politics* (Berkeley: University of California Press, 1984); Delbert Taebel, "Minority Representation on City Councils: The Impact of Structure on Blacks and Hispanics," *Social Science Quarterly* 59 (June 1978): 142–52; Chandler Davidson and George Korbel, "At Large Elections and Minority Group Representation," *Journal of Politics* 43 (Nov. 1981): 982–1005.

Growth politics and public responses in middle-sized cities can be followed in Janet R. Daly-Bednarek, *The Changing Image of the City: Planning for Downtown Omaha, 1945–1973* (Lincoln: University of Nebraska Press, 1992); Donald L. Stevens, Jr., "Government, Interest Groups, and the People: Urban Renewal in Omaha, 1954–1970," *Nebraska History* 67 (Summer 1986): 134–58; Mark S. Foster, "Colorado's Defeat of the 1976 Winter Olympics," *Colorado Magazine* 53 (Spring 1976): 163–86; and Carl Abbott, *Portland: Planning, Politics, and Growth in a Twentieth Century City* (Lincoln: University of Nebraska Press, 1983).

The dynamics of Houston politics have been probed by Chandler Davidson, *Biracial Politics: Conflict and Coalition in the Metropolitan South* (Baton Rouge: Louisiana State University Press, 1972). Also see Robert D. Bullard, *Invisible Houston: The Black Experience in Boom and Bust* (College Station: Texas A&M University Press, 1987); Arnoldo De Leon, *Ethnicity in the Sunbelt: A History of Mexican Americans in Houston* (Houston: Mexican American Studies Program, University of Houston, 1989); Richard Murray, "Houston: Politics of a Boomtown," *Dissent* 27 (Fall 1980): 500–504; Robert E. Parker and Joe R. Feagin, "Houston: Administration by Economic Elites," in Savitch and Thomas, *Big City Politics*, 169–88; and a discussion of Houston civic clubs in Robert Fisher, *Let the People Decide: Neighborhood Organizing in America* (Boston: Twayne Publishers, 1984).

Race relations in Los Angeles are the focus of Robert Fogelson, *Violence as Protest* (Garden City, N.Y.: Doubleday, 1971); Rodolfo F. Acuna, *A Community Under Siege: A Chronicle of Chicanos East of the Los Angeles River, 1945–75* (Los Angeles: Chicano Studies Center, University of California, Los Angeles, 1984); Francine Rabinowitz and William J. Siembieda, *Minorities in Suburbs: The Los Angeles Experience* (Lexington, Mass.: Lexington Books, 1977); and R. J. Sonenshein, "The Dynamics of Biracial Coalitions: Crossover Politics in Los Angeles," *Western Political Quarterly* 42 (June 1989): 333–53.

The recent politics of Denver and San Antonio must largely be traced through newspaper accounts. However, see Carlos Muñoz, Jr., and Charles Henry, "Rainbow Coalitions in Four Big Cities," *PS* 19 (Summer 1986): 598–609; Carter Whitson and Dennis Judd, "Denver: Boosterism Versus Growth," in Savitch and Thomas, *Big City Politics,* 149–68; Stephen J. Leonard and Thomas J. Noel, *Denver: From Mining Camp to Metropolis* (Boulder: University Press of Colorado, 1990); and David R. Johnson, John A. Booth, and Richard J. Harris, eds., *The Politics of San Antonio* (Lincoln: University of Nebraska Press, 1983).

The politics of San Francisco can be traced in Frederick Wirt, *Power in the City* (Berkeley: University of California Press, 1975); Chester Hartman, *The Transformation of San Francisco* (Totowa, N.J.: Rowman and Allenheld, 1984); John H. Mollenkopf, *The Contested City* (Princeton, N.J.: Princeton University Press, 1983); Susan Fainstein, Norman Fainstein, and P. Jefferson Armistead, "San Francisco: Urban Transformation and the Local State," in Susan Fainstein et al., *Restructuring the City* (New York: Longman, 1984), 202–44; and Richard DeLeon, "San Francisco: Postmaterialist Populism in a Global City," in Savitch and Thomas, *Big City Politics,* 202–15.

The role of women in San Jose politics is described in Janet A. Flammang, "Filling the Party Vacuum: Women at the Grassroots Level in Local Politics," in *Political Women,* ed. Janet A. Flammang (Beverly Hills, Calif.: Sage Publications, 1984), 87–113. Philip J. Trounstine and Terry Christensen, *Movers and Shakers: The Study of Community Power* (New York: St. Martin's Press, 1982), and Anthony Orum, *Power, Money and the People* (Austin: Texas Monthly Press, 1987), show the importance of women as agents of political change.

Spencer Olin introduces new dimensions for political analysis in "Globalization and the Politics of Locality: Orange County, California, in the Cold War Era," *Western Historical Quarterly* 22 (May 1991): 143–62.

CHAPTER 6 MULTICENTERED CITIES

Los Angeles as the prototype for the American metropolis is a theme that runs from the 1950s to the 1990s. The classic statement is Reyner Banham, *Los Angeles: The Architecture of the Four Ecologies* (New York: Harper and Row, 1971). His populist aesthetic is echoed in Robert Venturi, Denise Scott Brown, and Stephen Izenour, *Learning from Las Vegas* (Cambridge, Mass.: MIT Press, 1972); Robert Riley, "Urban Myths and the New Cities of the Southwest," *Landscape* 17 (Autumn 1967): 21–23; and J. B. Jackson, "The Vernacular City," *Center: A Journal for Architecture in America* 1 (1985): 27–43.

Recent discussions of Los Angeles as the city of the future by those on the scene include Dolores Hayden, "The Meaning of Place in Art and Architecture," *Design*

Quarterly no. 122 (Summer 1983): 18–20; Edward Soja and Allen J. Scott, "Los Angeles: Capital of the Late Twentieth Century," *Environment and Planning D: Society and Space* 4 (Sept. 1986): 249–54; Frederick Jameson, "Postmodernism, or the Cultural Logic of Late Capitalism," *New Left Review* no. 146 (July–Aug. 1984): 53–93; David Reid, ed., *Sex, Death, and God in L.A.* (New York: Pantheon, 1992); and Mike Davis, *City of Quartz: Excavating the Future in Los Angeles* (New York: Vintage Books, 1992). Orange County gets the same honored position in Rob Kling, Spencer Olin, and Mark Poster, eds., *Postsuburban California: The Transformation of Orange County Since World War II* (Berkeley: University of California Press, 1991).

The rise of the "outer city" has recently been summarized by Joel Garreau, *Edge City: Life on the New Frontier* (New York: Doubleday, 1991). Also see Christopher Leinberger and Charles Lockwood, "How Business Is Reshaping America," *Atlantic,* Oct. 1986, pp. 43–52; and "Los Angeles Comes of Age," *Atlantic,* Jan. 1988, pp. 31–56. Earlier efforts to understand the changing structure of Western metropolitan areas include John Friedmann, "The Urban Field," *Journal of the American Institute of Planners* 31 (Autumn 1985): 312–19; James E. Vance, Jr., *Geography and Urban Evolution in the San Francisco Bay Area* (Berkeley: Institute of Government, University of California, 1964); and Melvin Webber, "Order in Diversity, Community Without Propinquity," in *Cities and Space,* ed. Lowden Wingo (Baltimore: Johns Hopkins University Press, 1963): 23–54. Compare these views with those of William S. Whyte, Jr., "Urban Sprawl," in *The Exploding Metropolis,* ed. the Editors of *Fortune* (Garden City, N.Y.: Doubleday, 1958), 133–56.

Planned residential environments are discussed in George T. Morgan, Jr., and John O. King, *The Woodlands: New Community Development, 1964–1983* (College Station: Texas A&M University Press, 1987); Martin Schiesl, "Designing the Model Community: The Irvine Company and Suburban Development, 1950–88," in Kling, Olin, and Poster, *Postsuburban California,* 55–91; and John Louv, *America II* (New York: Penguin Books, 1983).

Quantitative data on housing styles are offered in Richard Fusch and Larry Ford, "Architecture and the Geography of the American City," *Geographical Review* 73 (July 1983): 324–40 and Larry Ford, "Multiunit Housing in the American City," *Geographical Review* 76 (Oct. 1986): 390–407. A starting point for understanding stylistic choices is Clifford E. Clark, Jr., *The American Family Home, 1800–1960* (Chapel Hill: University of North Carolina Press, 1986). A general discussion is Carl Abbott, "Southwestern Cityscapes: Approaches to an American Urban Environment," in *Essays on Sunbelt Cities and Recent Urban America,* ed. Robert Fairbanks and Kathleen Underwood (College Station: Texas A&M University Press, 1990), 59–86.

Transportation choices in Western cities are considered in Sy Adler, "The Transformation of the Pacific Electric Railway: Bradford Snell, Roger Rabbit, and the Politics of Transit in Los Angeles," *Urban Affairs Quarterly* 27 (Sept. 1991): 51–86; Scott Bottles, *Los Angeles and the Automobile* (Berkeley: University of California Press, 1987); and Robert Cervero, *Suburban Gridlock* (New Brunswick, N.J.: Center for Urban Policy Research, Rutgers University, 1986).

Bradford Luckingham, *Phoenix: The History of a Southwestern Metropolis* (Tucson: University of Arizona Press, 1989) discusses the problems of planning for a low-density city. Carl Abbott, "The Suburban Sunbelt," *Journal of Urban History* 13 (May 1987): 275–301, examines patterns of suburban governmental structure. A "suburban biography" is Stephen F. Miels, Carol J. Drake, and James E. Fell, Jr., *Aurora: Gateway to the Rockies* (Evergreen, Colo.: Cordillera, 1985).

Growth management is discussed in Fred Bosselman and David Callies, *The Quiet Revolution in Land Use Control* (Washington, D.C.: Council on Environmental Quality, 1972); Roger Caves, *Land Use Planning: The Ballot Box Revolution* (Newbury Park, Calif.: Sage Publications, 1991); Richard DeLeon and Sandra Powell, "Growth Control and Electoral Politics in San Francisco: The Triumph of Urban Populism," *Western Political Quarterly* 42 (June 1989): 307–31; and Mike Davis, "The Homegrown Revolution," in *City of Quartz*.

CHAPTER 7 CITIES AND COUNTRY

The strange story of Rajneeshpuram can be found in Frances FitzGerald, *Cities on a Hill* (New York: Simon and Schuster, 1986), and Carl Abbott, "Utopia and Bureaucracy: The Fall of Rajneeshpuram, Oregon," *Pacific Historical Review* 59 (Feb. 1990): 77–103.

A baseline for studies of city-hinterland relations in the West was set by Mildred Hartsough, *The Twin Cities as a Metropolitan Market*, University of Minnesota Studies in Social Sciences, no. 18 (Minneapolis, 1925); Chauncy D. Harris, *Salt Lake City: A Regional Capital* (Chicago: University of Chicago, Department of Geography, 1940); and Roderick McKenzie, *The Metropolitan Community* (New York: McGraw-Hill, 1933). Hartsough's study is brought up to date by John Borchert, *America's Northern Heartland* (Minneapolis: University of Minnesota Press, 1989). Comprehensive information on the metropolitan division of the West can be found in Richard Bensel, *Sectionalism and American Political Development, 1880–1980* (Madison: University of Wisconsin Press, 1984); Otis D. Duncan et al., *Metropolis and Region* (Baltimore: Johns Hopkins University Press, 1960); John Borchert, "America's Changing Metropolitan Regions," *Annals of the Association of American Geographers* 62 (June 1972): 352–73; and Thomas M. Stanback, Jr., and Thierry J. Noyelle, *The Economic Transformation of American Cities* (Totowa, N.J.: Rowman and Allenheld, 1981).

The idea of "Greater Texas" is adumbrated in D. W. Meinig, *Imperial Texas* (Austin: University of Texas Press, 1969). Supporting data for describing the reach of Texas and California cities can be found in the maps in John F. Rooney, Jr., Wilbur Zelinsky, and Dean R. Louder, *This Remarkable Continent: An Atlas of United States and Canadian Society and Culture* (College Station: Texas A&M University Press, 1982).

The Sunbelt is defined and explained in a variety of incompatible ways in Kirkpatrick Sale, *Power Shift: The Rise of the Southern Rim and Its Challenge to the Eastern Establishment* (New York: Random House, 1975); Clyde E. Browning and Wil Gesler, "Sun Belt—Snow Belt: A Case of Sloppy Regionalizing," *Professional*

Geographer 31 (February 1979): 66–74; Alfred E. Watkins and David Perry, eds., *The Rise of the Sunbelt Cities* (Beverly Hills, Calif.: Sage Publications, 1977); and Bernard L. Weinstein and Robert E. Firestine, *Regional Growth and Decline in the United States* (New York: Praeger, 1978). The origins of the term and its regional applications are critically analyzed in Carl Abbott, "New West, New South, New Region: The Discovery of the Sunbelt," and Bradley R. Rice, "Searching for the Sunbelt," both in *Searching for the Sunbelt: Historical Perspectives on a Region,* ed. Raymond Mohl (Knoxville: University of Tennessee Press, 1990), 7–24, 212–23.

Resource boom (and bust) towns are discussed in W. Eugene Hollon, *The Great American Desert* (New York: Oxford University Press, 1966); Mim Dixon, *What Happened to Fairbanks: The Effects of the Trans-Alaska Oil Pipeline on the Community of Fairbanks, Alaska* (Boulder, Colo.: Westview Press, 1978); Chilton Williamson, *Roughnecking It; or, Life in the Overthrust* (New York: Simon and Schuster, 1982); William G. Robbins, *Hard Times in Paradise: Coos Bay, Oregon, 1850–1986* (Seattle: University of Washington Press, 1988); Andrew Gulliford, *Boomtown Blues: Colorado Oil Shale, 1885–1985* (Boulder: University Press of Colorado, 1989); and Robert Engler, *The Politics of Oil: A Study of Private Power and Democratic Directions* (Chicago: University of Chicago Press, 1967).

The negative aspects of the Rangebelt are discussed in Frank J. Popper, "The Strange Case of the Contemporary American Frontier," *Yale Review* 76 (Dec. 1986): 101–21; and Michael Greenberg, George Carey, and Frank Popper, "Violent Death, Violent States, and American Youth," *The Public Interest,* no. 87 (Spring 1987): 38–48. Ed Marston, ed., *Reopening the Western Frontier* (Washington, D.C.: Island Press, 1989) examines the balance between forces of economic decline and change. Most information on the economic transformation of secondary cities is buried in newspapers and trade journals. An accessible and upbeat account of Boise can be found in David A. Heenan, *The New Corporate Frontier: The Big Move to Small Towns* (New York: McGraw-Hill, 1991). G. Scott Thomas, *The Rating Guide to Life in America's Small Cities* (Buffalo: Prometheus Books, 1990) directs readers to the top "micropolitan" centers. The expansion of commuting zones is detailed in Brian Berry and Quentin Gillard, *The Changing Shape of Metropolitan America* (Cambridge, Mass.: Ballinger, 1977).

The political consequences of the extension of urban influence are discussed in Samuel P. Hays, *Beauty, Health, and Permanence: Environmental Politics in the United States, 1955–1985* (New York: Cambridge University Press, 1987). Data on levels of environmental activism are found in Kathleen Ferguson, "Toward a Geography of Environmentalism in the United States" (M.A. thesis, California State University–Hayward, 1985).

The plundered-province literature is easily approached through Gene M. Gressley, "Colonialism: A Western Complaint," *Pacific Northwest Quarterly* 54 (Jan. 1963): 1–8; and William G. Robbins, "The 'Plundered Province' Thesis and the Recent Historiography of the American West," *Pacific Historical Review* 55 (Nov. 1986): 577–97.

CHAPTER 8 CITIES AND NATION

Western cities as visually innovative environments are discussed in Alan Hess, *Googie: Fifties Coffee Shop Architecture* (San Francisco: Chronicle Books, 1986); Judith Singer Cohen, *Cowtown Moderne: Art Deco Architecture of Fort Worth, Texas* (College Station: Texas A&M University Press, 1989); Joel Garreau, *The Nine Nations of North America* (Boston: Houghton Mifflin, 1981); Keith L. Bryant, Jr., "Roman Temples, Glass Boxes, and Babylonian Deco: Art Museum Architecture and the Cultural Maturation of the Southwest," *Western Historical Quarterly* 22 (Feb. 1991): 45–72; Charles W. Moore, Peter Becker, and Regula Campbell, *The City Observed: Los Angeles, A Guide to Its Architecture and Landscape* (New York: Random House, 1984); Calvin Trillin, "Reporter at Large: I Know I Want To Do Something," *New Yorker*, May 29, 1965, pp. 72–120 describes the Watts Towers.

Turner's essays are collected in *Frontier and Section: Selected Essays of Frederick Jackson Turner*, Ray A. Billington, ed. (Englewood Cliffs, N.J.: Prentice-Hall, 1961). Turner has been interpreted by Stanley Elkins and Eric McKitrick, "A Meaning for Turner's Frontier," *Political Science Quarterly* 59 (Sept., Dec. 1954): 321–53, 565–602; William Cronon, "Revisiting the Vanishing Frontier: The Legacy of Frederick Jackson Turner," *Western Historical Quarterly* 18 (April 1987): 157–76; David Potter, *People of Plenty: Economic Abundance and the American Character* (Chicago: University of Chicago Press, 1954).

The literary culture of the West Coast is explored in Dennis McNally, "Prophets on the Burning Shore: Jack Kerouac, Gary Snyder, and San Francisco," and William Lockwood, "Present Trends in Western Poetry," both in *A Literary History of the American West*, ed. J. Golden Taylor et al. (Fort Worth: Texas Christian University Press, 1987), 482–95, 1202–31; John Arthur Maynard, *Venice West: The Beat Generation in Southern California* (New Brunswick, N.J.: Rutgers University Press, 1991); Michael Davidson, *The San Francisco Renaissance: Poetics and Community at Mid-Century* (New York: Cambridge University Press, 1989); Lawrence Ferlinghetti and Nancy J. Peters, *Literary San Francisco: A Pictorial History* (San Francisco: City Lights Books, 1980); David Fine, ed., *Los Angeles in Fiction* (Albuquerque: University of New Mexico Press, 1984). Contrasting perspectives on the urban and regional character of Western writing are found in William Everson, *Archetype West: The Pacific Coast as a Literary Region* (Berkeley, Calif.: Oyez, 1976,) and William Kittredge and Annick Smith, eds., *The Last Best Place: A Montana Anthology* (Helena: Montana Historical Society Press, 1988).

Because livability and sound urban management are seldom headline stories, the available literature is limited. Daniel Elazar, *American Federalism: The View from the States* (New York: Thomas Y. Crowell, 1972), attributes the political character of northern-tier cities to their "moralistic" political culture. Ben-Chieh Liu, *Quality of Life Indicators in U.S. Metropolitan Areas, 1970* (Washington, D.C.: Environmental Protection Agency, 1975), quantified levels of civic activity, as did Arthur Louis, "The Worst American City," *Harper's Magazine*, Jan. 1975, pp. 67–71; and Richard Boyer and David Savageau, *Places Rated Almanac,* 3d ed. (New York: Prentice-Hall Travel, 1989). Louis found nine of his top ten cities in the West. For a specific case, see "Town Planning: Where It Works," *The Economist,* Sept. 1, 1990, pp. 24–25; and Carl Abbott, "Urban Design in Portland, Oregon, as Policy and Process, 1960–1989," *Planning Perspectives* 6 (Jan. 1991): 1–18.

There are three comprehensive introductions to Houston. David McComb provides a balanced urban biography in *Houston: A History,* rev. ed. (Austin: University of Texas Press, 1981). Joe Feagin argues that Houston has always depended on federal spending in *Free Enterprise City: Houston in Political and Economic Perspective* (New Brunswick, N.J.: Rutgers University Press, 1989). A contemporary profile is Beth Anne Shelton et al., *Houston: Growth and Decline in a Sunbelt Boomtown* (Philadelphia: Temple University Press, 1989).

The political tone of the Dallas–Fort Worth "metroplex" is analyzed in Warren Leslie, *Dallas Public and Private* (New York: Grossman Publishers, 1964); Patricia Hill, "The Origins of Modern Dallas" (Ph.D. diss., University of Texas at Dallas, 1990); Martin Melosi, "Dallas–Fort Worth: Marketing the Metroplex," in *Sunbelt Cities: Politics and Growth Since World War II,* ed. Richard Bernard and Bradley Rice (Austin: University of Texas Press, 1983), 162–95; and Robert Fairbanks, "The Good Government Machine: The Citizens Charter Association and Dallas Politics, 1930–1960," in *Essays on Sunbelt Cities and Recent Urban America,* ed. Robert Fairbanks and Kathleen Underwood (College Station: Texas A&M University Press, 1990), 125–50.

The Texas style is interpreted in Larry McMurtry, *In a Narrow Grave: Essays on Texas* (Albuquerque: University of New Mexico Press, 1986). Peter Wiley and Robert Gottlieb, *Empires in the Sun* (Tucson: University of Arizona Press, 1985) profile Phoenix, Denver, and Las Vegas as other entrepreneurial cities.

The utopian impulse in the American West is discussed in Philip Porter and Fred E. Lukermann, "The Geography of Utopia," in *Geographies of the Mind,* ed. David Lowenthal and Martyn Bowden (New York: Oxford University Press, 1976), 197–223; Dolores Hayden, *Seven American Utopias* (Cambridge, Mass.: MIT Press, 1976); Robert V. Hine, *California's Utopian Colonies* (San Marino, Calif.: Huntington Library, 1953); and Charles LeWarne, *Utopias on Puget Sound, 1885–1915* (Seattle: University of Washington Press, 1975). The recent counter-utopian impulse of white supremacism is treated in James A. Aho, *The Politics of Righteousness: Idaho Christian Patriotism* (Seattle: University of Washington Press, 1990).

Greater Los Angeles as a capital of consumption is a central theme in John Findlay, "Far Western Cityscapes and American Culture Since 1940," *Western Historical Quarterly* 22 (Feb. 1991): 19–43; Norman M. Klein, "The Sunshine Strategy: Buying and Selling the Fantasy of Los Angeles," in *20th Century Los Angeles: Power, Promotion, and Social Conflict,* ed. Norman Klein and Martin Schiesl (Claremont, Calif.: Regina Books, 1990), 1–38; and Paul Goldberger, "Orange County: Tomorrowland—Wall to Wall," *New York Times,* Dec. 11, 1988.

The political culture and political geography of San Francisco–Oakland are discussed in Howard S. Becker, ed., *Culture and Civility in San Francisco* (New Brunswick, N.J.: Transaction Books, 1971); Rickey L. Hendricks, "Liberal Default, Labor Support, and Conservative Neutrality: The Kaiser Permanente Medical Care Program After World War II," *Journal of Policy History* 1 (1989): 156–80; William Rorabaugh, *Berkeley at War: The 1960s* (New York: Oxford University Press, 1989); Brian J. Godfrey, *Neighborhoods in Transition: The Making of San Francisco's Ethnic and Nonconformist Communities* (Berkeley: University of California Press, 1988); and William Issel, "Liberalism and Urban Policy in San Francisco from the 1930s to the 1960s," *Western Historical Quarterly* 22 (Nov. 1991): 431–50.

INDEX

Abilene, Tex., 104–5

Accountable Planning Initiative (San Francisco), 146

AEC. *See* Atomic Energy Commission

Aerospace industry, xiii, 58, 61–62, 64–65

African-Americans, 16, 21, 43, 48, 101, 179, 185, 194; political power of, 99–100, 103, 104, 105, 107, 108, 113; radicalism of, 187–88; segregation of, 19–20, 22, 24, 26

After Many a Summer Dies the Swan (Huxley), 183

Agnos, Art, 120

Aikman, Duncan, 73, 138

Aircraft industry, 9, 11, 16, 28, 57

Airports, 6

Alameda, Calif., 4, 7

Alaska, 53, 59–60, 168. *See also various cities*

Albuquerque, N.M., xiii, 26, 78, 127, 129, 137, 162, 169; downtown development in, 118, 119; economy of, 58, 65, 68, 159; government reform in, 39, 42, 107; as Hispanic, 83–84; politics in, 114, 116

Albuquerque Citizens Committee, 41, 42

Alinsky, Saul, 106

Alioto, Joseph, 104

Aluminum industry, 12

Alyeska Pipeline Service Company, 161

Amarillo, Tex., xxii, 160

American Municipal Association, 36

America's New Frontier (Garnsey), 167

Anaheim, xviii, 159, 162, 175

Anchorage, 59, 60, 91, 118, 154, 158

Angry West, The (Lamm), 167

Annexation, 40, 106, 142, 145

Antigrowth activists, 102–3

Archer City, Tex., 155

Architecture, 78, 141; contemporary, 133–34; folk, 174–75; residential, 132–33; working class, 134–36

Arizona, 6, 19, 89, 120, 123, 134, 141, 142, 158, 159, 162, 169; defense spending in, 60, 61; retirement to, 68, 70. *See also various cities; counties*

Art, 165–66, 174–75, 186

Arts and Architecture, 134

Asia, 3, 79–80, 89, 91, 93, 98, 158

ABOUT THE AUTHOR

Carl Abbott is Professor of Urban Studies and Planning at Portland State University, where he has taught since 1978. He has also taught at the University of Denver and Old Dominion University and has served as Aspinall Professor at Mesa College and Banneker Professor at George Washington University. He holds a bachelor's degree in history from Swarthmore College and master's and doctoral degrees in history from the University of Chicago. Professor Abbott is the author of several books about the history of American cities and the American West, including *The New Urban America: Growth and Politics in Sunbelt Cities* (rev. ed., 1987), *Portland: Planning, Politics, and Growth in a Twentieth Century City* (1983), and *Colorado: A History of the Centennial State* (rev. ed., 1983). He is also a contributor to several edited volumes on the history of the West, including the forthcoming *Oxford History of the American West*. Professor Abbott teaches courses on the history of cities and on urban policy, with special attention to issues of economic development, neighborhood change, and downtown revitalization. His current research centers on styles of city and regional planning in the Pacific Northwest during the twentieth century and on public responses to the globalization of American cities.